'RACE', ETHNICITY AND DIFFERENCE:

Imagining the Inclusive Society

Peter Ratcliffe

Open University Press

Open University Press
McGraw-Hill Education
McGraw-Hill House
Shoppenhangers Road
Maidenhead
Berkshire
England
SL6 2QL

email: enquiries@openup.co.uk
world wide web: www.openup.co.uk

and Two Penn Plaza, New York, NY 10121–2289, USA

First published 2004

Copyright © Peter Ratcliffe 2004

A catalogue record for this book is available from the British Library.

ISBN 0 335 21095 3 (pb) 0 335 21096 1 (hb)

Library of Congress Cataloging-in-Publication Data
CIP data applied for

Typeset by YHT Ltd, London
Printed in Great Britain by Bell & Bain Ltd, Glasgow

'RACE', ETHNICITY AND DIFFERENCE: Imagining the Inclusive Society

To the memory of Valerie Karn and Barry Troyna

Contents

Preface

W. E. B. DuBois, the celebrated American civil rights activist and writer, saw the principal challenge of the twentieth century as that of finding a solution to the problem of the 'color line'. As we move into the twenty-first century, not only is this solution proving elusive, the challenges have grown ever more complex and apparently intractable. The irony is that the key question can still be expressed with remarkable simplicity. Alain Touraine, the French social theorist, did so in his most recent book: he asks 'Can We Live Together?' (Touraine 2000).

Only a few years into the new millennium, the global implications are evident. The events of 11 September 2001, the subsequent war in Afghanistan, the 'war' on terrorism, and the assault on the Saddam Hussein regime in Iraq amply attest to the importance of finding answers to Touraine's question. Closer to home (for those of us based in the UK) there are ongoing concerns about the state of relations between Protestant and Catholic communities in Northern Ireland, and the apparent political void created by the impasse in the Peace Talks.

It is tempting to rush to simplistic diagnoses of these problems. Deep-seated religious enmities represent the prime candidate in these cases. The genocide in Rwanda towards the end of the last century was largely interpreted as a result of conflict between two major ethnic groups, the Hutu and the Tutsi. In the Balkan wars of the late 1980s and early 1990s, the popular view was that these were the result of a desire for separate nation status for such peoples as the Croatians, Slovenians, Bosnians and Kosovans. A key sub-theme was once again religion, in the form of age-old conflict between Muslim and Christian. Roughly the same ingredients were identified in interpretations of the ongoing war in Chechnya.

Whilst there is certainly a kernel of truth in all these hypotheses, none comes close to providing a convincing sociological explanation. It is the primary purpose of this volume to provide the reader with the tools to find better answers to arguably the most pressing questions of global society. In most cases, it will be seen that divisions are rooted in forms of 'difference' conceptualized in terms of 'race', ethnicity, culture, religion and nation; invariably mediated by issues of class, status, power and gender. None of these have a reality independent of history. An appreciation, where relevant, of the impact of colonialism, imperialism and slavery will therefore contextualize the analysis.

In such a short book it would be a great mistake to attempt a summary of the salience of difference in the analysis of global social relations. The result would simply be a sort of 'Cook's Tour' of world conflict, devoid of any real substance. This is especially so given that local factors always play a mediating role between the various social forces which constrain or enable agency. As a result, substantive debates about contemporary issues will mainly focus on Britain and the United States. Most of the conceptual analysis will nevertheless be transferable in the sense of possessing a more general analytical utility. And, of course, it is not possible to discuss historical social relations in Britain and the US independent of more global forces.

There is little room for detailed empirical data of different societies: the text will refer the reader to sources where these are readily available. The principal intention is to provide a conceptual and theoretical analysis that enables us to comprehend contemporary events. This entails a nuanced interpretation of the complex dialectical relationship between structural forces and social agency (usually referred to as the structure–agency dualism). Though not burdening the analysis with overly theoretical debates, we shall nevertheless draw much inspiration from contemporary realist social theory, most notably the work of Archer (1995) and Carter (2000). The intention is to present an accessible account free from sociological jargon, except where this is absolutely unavoidable. In such circumstances, concepts will be subjected to critical analysis rather than being left to speak for themselves. Indeed, it will be necessary at various points to highlight jargon which, if left uncontested, will actually obstruct our analysis.

So, what does the book aim to do? It aims to take a detailed look at the nature and sources of inequality in contemporary societies. As suggested above, the substantive focus will be on social divisions as defined by such factors as 'race', ethnicity, religion, class and gender. But, as suggested by the volume's subtitle, the intention is to go beyond description and explanation of contemporary social relations. The ultimate goal is to look to the future by examining prospects for what might be called the 'inclusive society'.

So as to keep this aim in mind, the book opens with an evaluation of this concept. Like its *alter ego*, social exclusion, the concept will be seen as deeply problematic. The empirical content is nevertheless important, as most modern democratic societies ostensibly espouse the virtues of social stability and cohesion alongside notions of equality and human/citizenship rights. In evaluating these value systems, however, remarkably few sociological accounts address, explicitly at least, the difficulties which contemporary societies face in dealing with the multiplicity of individual and collective aims, aspirations and expectations which are part and parcel of multi-ethnic societies in the twenty-first century.

Having discussed the notion of social inclusivity, the argument is then divided into four sections. The first deals with the issue of difference. As argued by Mason (2000: 2–3), a distinction needs to be drawn between difference and diversity. 'Difference' may arise from the assertion of distinctiveness on the part of putative groups, may be a function of role ascription, or a combination of both. The desire to draw, and maintain, such boundaries often leads to conflict. On the other hand, a society may exhibit immense diversity in terms of people's self-identity and a host of socially relevant characteristics, yet be largely harmonious. This suggests that little or no significance is vested in the ways 'we' are perceived to differ from 'them'.

Chapter 2 examines the historical roots and ontological status of the concept of 'race'. It is important to begin with this aspect of 'difference' since, despite its lack of scientific validity, it retains a pivotal position in contemporary discourse. This, in turn, leads to a continual reification of 'race' and a racialization of social relations. The key point, however, is that it is much more than a discursive tool. If it were merely this, it would be of considerably more interest to philosophers than to sociologists. The latter are compelled to discuss the concept because, through various forms of social agency, it continues to invoke significant material effects.

'Race-thinking' will be seen to have deep roots, embedded in Enlightenment thought and the history of imperialism and colonialism. Despite this, it is somewhat curious that a concept that has been shown to be devoid of scientific value still retains such a stranglehold over popular consciousness. It is reified in the UK, for example, not only through lay and media discourse, but by the passing of successive **Race** Relations Acts and the establishment of the Commission for **Racial** Equality.

Those who rightly question its utility have looked for an alternative way of expressing this form of difference. The obvious candidate is 'ethnic group'. But there is the obvious question of whether this is any more 'real' than 'race'. Not only is ethnicity a very slippery concept, the notion of group also implies an essential collectivity that is in itself questionable. Chapter 3 explores these debates, in particular the implications of resorting to rigid cultural and ethnic essentialisms in explaining the dynamics of difference. It also looks at the implications of following the postmodernist and poststructuralist route, which perceives endless diversity but ultimately little difference.

The core argument of the volume is that various forms of ascribed difference are at the fulcrum of various exclusionary processes. The latter in turn are embedded in systemic mechanisms and/or are a function of individual or collective agency. Whatever the precise forces involved, there are clearly various sites of exclusion. This is the focus of Part II.

As a site of literal exclusion (that is, at a state's borders), immigration and immigration control is an obvious starting point. It is also instructive for quite another reason. Some of the forces behind large-scale transnational migratory movements have their roots in colonial, neocolonial and postcolonial relationships. How states deal with the marshalling of migrant flows can tell us a great deal about the official characterization of 'the other' (Cohen 1994), hence also the implicit definition of who 'we' are. Nowhere is this clearer than in the case of one issue of prime importance at the beginning of the twenty-first century: the treatment of refugees and asylum seekers. Heightened levels of global political instability over the past few decades have resulted in millions of displaced persons, and an unseemly squabble amongst the richer countries as to how to share responsibility for them.

Although some reference will be made to the US and Australia, the focus of Chapter 4 is essentially on immigration policies and practices in post-World War II Britain. This raises important questions about how ever-tighter immigration controls on those from the New Commonwealth (in both policy and practice) can be reconciled with legislation ostensibly geared towards combatting discrimination against those already in the UK. Hostility against refugees and asylum seekers, expressed in 'race', ethnic and cultural terms, has resulted in a swathe of increasingly restrictive legislation since the mid-1990s. This has been supplemented, especially since 9/11, by a radical tightening of anti-terrorism laws. The state's policy on 'race' has therefore become dominated by a dual strategy; namely, to minimize migrant in-flows and monitor 'the enemy within'.

Much of the recent debate about refugees and asylum seekers in Britain has focused on settlement, and in particular the so-called dispersal policy. Real doubts are raised about the underlying rationale for the strategy, in particular whether the lack of sensitivity to migrants' wishes might be the result of a deliberate attempt to undermine their desire to remain (and to act as a deterrent to others planning to come to Britain).

Housing and spatial patterns constitute both a direct link to migration debates and another common site of exclusionary policies and practices. As is all too evident, spatial patterns have also become the locus for genocide and mass population displacements (now labelled, euphemistically, 'ethnic cleansing'). Legally enforced segregation was at the core of apartheid in South Africa and Jim Crow policies in the US. Collectively, these concerns provide the agenda for Chapter 5.

As we know from research around the globe, where one lives tends to have a significant bearing on the chances of acquiring a good standard of education. It seems natural, therefore, to follow debates about spatial exclusion (and 'inclusion') with a consideration of educational opportunity and the prospects of social mobility. Chapter 6, which once again focuses on Britain, explores the ways in which migrants of differing ethnic and cultural origins and from various spatial locations experience the educational system. This takes account both of marked shifts in state policy over the last half century and of the strategies adopted by migrant parents in search of quality education for their children.

Educational success clearly increases the likelihood of accessing employment that matches one's ability and aspirations. The labour market is, however, another key site of exclusionary policies and practices. These issues provide the basis for Chapter 7. It also addresses the potential power of individual agency in exploiting niches in the market; a process which can ultimately lead to significant transformations in the market itself. This provides a simple illustration of a common theme of the book, namely the need to recognize the dialectical relationship between social agency and systemic processes.

Part II concludes with a consideration of the relations between minority ethnic communities and 'whites'/majority society. Research points to a marked increase in the level of racist harassment, both at an individual and an organized, collective level (for example in the form of extremist right-wing activity). In Britain, there has also been a well-documented history of urban unrest over the past two decades. How central government and nationwide police forces respond to the challenges posed by these events provides a further indicator of a commitment towards the social inclusivity they claim to espouse. Thus far, as argued in Chapter 8, they have failed miserably.

Reading Part II, it will become clear that it is not strictly possible to separate debates about sites of exclusion from those addressing the means by which exclusionary processes can be undermined. In deferring the main discussion of the latter to Part III, it is accepted that this is a somewhat artificial device. However, in terms of overall clarity, the advantages of doing so far outweigh the disadvantages. One has simply to be aware of the intrinsic interplay between forces of social regulation and those of social agency, that is of constraining forces and enabling processes.

The principal aim of Part III is to examine the very different ways in which social agency can contribute to the removal of exclusionary forces (for example in the form of racism and discrimination). Rather than following the more conventional textbook approach by addressing first the contribution of state policy and legislation, this volume begins with an evaluation of grass-roots strategies. Chapter 9 explores the efficacy of national civil rights movements, political representation, and more localized community-based activism. A particularly interesting comparative question is why social mobilization in countries such as the US and Britain has been so different in form and approach.

Just as grassroots movements vary from society to society, so do policy and legislative strategies. Chapter 10 focuses principally on the radically different approaches of successive US and UK governments to outlawing discrimination and promoting equitable treatment. Once again investigation of the comparative dimension provides important insights as to why states elsewhere have adopted particular variants of these models (and not others). Two clear conclusions emerge. First, legislation requires the unwavering support of government to have any chance of success. Second, by its very nature it can only deal with discriminatory actions or behaviour *demonstrably* driven by racism (individual or institutional): it cannot deal, directly at least, with belief structures and feelings (of members of both superordinate and subordinate groups).

The volume concludes by reflecting on the prospects of progress towards greater inclusivity. In doing so, it attempts to pull together earlier debates on the ongoing significance of 'difference' to social relations, and the impact of wider forces (such as those somewhat loosely termed 'globalization'). The efficacy of various drivers for change is assessed. Amongst these, crucially, is academia itself. We look at the actual and potential role of sociology and sociologists in promoting equality and social cohesion.

Each chapter concludes with a brief annotated guide to further reading. Where appropriate, this will also include pointers towards available data sources. The volume as a whole aims to provide the reader with the basic theoretical and substantive tools to undertake comparative research involving societies with very different historical trajectories and ethnic profiles.

Hopefully, it might even inspire the reader to explore the scope of sociology (and social science more generally) as both transformatory and emancipatory. The book is dedicated to the memory of two friends and colleagues whose lives were very much guided by this mission: Valerie Karn in the arena of housing and Barry Troyna in that of educational inequalities.

As to those who have also provided inspiration and support at key moments in my working life, and thereby contributed indirectly to my decision to write this particular book, there are far too many to list here. Special mention, however, should go to Sheila Allen, David Gillborn, Rose Gilroy, David Mason, Ceri Peach and Deborah Phillips.

I am extremely grateful to Justin Vaughan, then a publisher at Open University Press, for encouraging me to write the book. My working relationship with the Press has been a delight (from my perspective at least!) in that I have always found staff, not least Mark Barratt, to be extremely helpful and supportive. I then owe an enormous debt of gratitude to Beverley Lockton for insightful comments on early parts of the manuscript and help with the bibliography. There are also the many unsung heroes who are no doubt blissfully unaware that they acted as sounding boards for my ideas and passions; namely successive cohorts of students in the Department of Sociology at the University of Warwick.

To none of these people, of course, can any blame be attributed for the final end product. I can only hope that I have done justice to their various contributions.

1 Introduction: Imagining an Inclusive Society

If there is one concept that dominates European social policy discourse in the early years of the twenty-first century it is 'social exclusion'. This is deemed to be the principal reason why contemporary societies lack cohesion. The solution, it is suggested, lies in policies that actively promote social inclusion. This would be helpful were it not for an eerie silence about both what the term actually means and how the goals are to be achieved.

I have argued elsewhere (Ratcliffe 1999a) that this is no accident. In the political sphere this discourse has invariably been deployed in such a way as to mask the continuation of neo-liberal policies by ostensibly left-leaning, or centre-left, parties. A particularly disturbing feature of the ensuing debates, however, has been the tendency of social scientists to adopt these same concepts uncritically, thereby creating what could be characterized as a soundbite sociology.

Although clearly based on value judgement, there would, I think, be a general consensus that societies should avoid 'excluding' their citizens from certain rights and material goods and, by the same token, that the latter should be 'included' in the general distribution of rights and resources. It is equally clear that, without significant qualification, this does not as yet happen in contemporary nation states, (even) those claiming well-functioning democratic systems. This much was seen in the empirical examples cited in the Preface. The central aim of this first chapter is to challenge current discourse, and to attempt to develop a clear idea of what an inclusive society might look like.

The first point to make is that inclusivity is not synonymous with the negation of social exclusion. In order to justify this assertion we need to explore the meaning of the latter term, and to look at the ways in which it has been deployed theoretically and in policy and practice. The remainder of the chapter is devoted to an analysis of social inclusivity and an assessment of the barriers to its actualization.

What is social exclusion?

In referring to exclusion as an example of a resort to soundbite, the intention was not to deny substantive content to the concept. It was merely to suggest that its use by politicians and policy-makers has tended to conceal more than reveal. As a discursive device, it has come to supplant an array of concepts which were central to socialist, or at least social democratic, agendas. This is important in practice because it has served to blunt our analytical and policy edge by essentially incorporating key notions such as poverty, inequality, racism, sexism, discrimination and so on. As such, it is part of a new politics that seeks to distance itself from the emancipatory, redistributive agendas of the old Left.

The politics of difference has been transformed into the politics of the excluded and, by implication, of those who are not. But how, and in what ways, does it do this?

There are four key problem areas:

1. Universalism

In its most crude incarnation, it may lead the unwary to two conclusions: first, that all minority ethnic or migrant groups (and presumably all members within these groups) suffer exclusion; and second that the latter applies to core aspects of citizenship rights, both political and social (Marshall 1950). Sadly, this is not confined to the sphere of political rhetoric. One of the UK's premier ethnicity research centres made precisely this error in an annual report (CRER 1995), by asserting without qualification that minorities suffer exclusion.

Blanket exclusion of this form is a fallacy because of what we shall define in Chapter 3 as 'difference within difference'. Whilst those from minority groups routinely face affronts to their dignity, sometimes unwittingly on the part of the perpetrator, many, due to their social background, wealth and/or gender (not to mention their abilities and personal qualities), have achieved a marked degree of material success. This will be very evident in later chapters.

This argues for a much more particularistic focus, both with respect to the subject of 'exclusion' and to the good from which the person is being 'excluded', such as education, work, housing, health and welfare services, and so on.

2. Dichotomization

Most accounts of social exclusion appear to suggest that an individual is either excluded, or is not. When one is assessing access to complicated, and differentiated, goods such as democratic rights, education and housing, matters are obviously not so clear-cut. There has to be space in the analysis for a more nuanced understanding of social position.

3. State versus process

The question here is whether exclusion is a process (or set of processes) which afflicts people or whether it is a state in which individuals find themselves. If the latter, is it an end to which they have personally contributed, knowingly or unwittingly?

4. Disempowerment

As a corollary of the last point, there is much to suggest that the social exclusion paradigm represents in certain guises another variant of the tendency to 'blame the victim', that is a form of social pathologization. This stems from the argument that some people, whether out of fecklessness, lack of respect for the normative value system or perhaps even intrinsic personal failings, place themselves outside the cultural mainstream.

The very fact that the concept of exclusion has so many different, and mutually contradictory, interpretations clearly undermines its utility. But this is rather more than simply a fine ontological point, in that they invariably lead to very different substantive propositions and policy conclusions. Confronted with a proposal framed in terms of exclusionary states or processes, we must therefore ask: 'Who, and/or what, is excluding whom from what, and how?'

Theoretically, the social exclusion paradigm as applied to the position of subordinate groups has an affinity with (modern) plural society theory as developed by Leo Kuper and M.G. Smith (1969). Unequal societies, they argued, are often characterized by a system of 'differential political incorporation'. The resulting structural pluralism tends to be associated with a high degree of group concentration and segregation: it also effectively implies a differentiated citizenship. Importantly, this can be *de facto* or *de iure*. In other words, access to certain rights might be controlled by law (as in apartheid South Africa or in the US under Jim Crow – of which more later), or may occur without legal sanction.

In earlier versions of the theory, there tended to be an overriding universalism (in both of the earlier senses). Later versions, for example that outlined in Kuper (1974), present a rather more nuanced approach. Modes of incorporation are seen to have a differential impact on members of putative groups, and in various institutional areas. So, for example, individuals might gain employment appropriate to their abilities and aspirations, but be denied housing and fail to secure a proper education for their children. Furthermore, differentially poor 'incorporation' (or 'exclusion') was no longer seen as a dichotomous entity. There could be varying degrees of incorporation in different spheres, (say) in employment, housing, education, health or political representation.

The inclusive society: key issues

Given the level of confusion over the concept of exclusion, it would be naïve to expect a simple answer to the question: what is an inclusive society? So it proves. Most writers accord pride of place to social stability and cohesion, but there is rather less agreement as to whether or not this implies the redressing of general economic and class-based inequalities (as well as those inequalities which are associated with particular sections of the populace, women, the elderly, or religious and ethnic minorities). But, even if these issues are clarified, many questions remain. For example, might stability and cohesion come at a price? Would it unduly compromise certain freedoms, such as the right to opt out, to be different?

Over the past decade the literature on the inclusive society has grown massively. One of the most influential books is that written by Ruth Levitas (1999). Although very much focusing on European debates, and in particular on UK political economy, it raises some key issues with broader significance. She argues that from a policy perspective there are essentially three principal approaches to inclusion, characterized by the acronyms RED, MUD and SID. These are seen as embedded in three very different discourses of exclusion.

1. RED, the Redistributionist Discourse

This embodies a comprehensive notion of citizenship based ultimately on the work of people like T.H. Marshall (1950). It addresses a wide range of material inequalities grounded in class, gender and ethnic difference. In the UK, this is associated very much with left, and even centre-left, politics prior to the election of the New Labour Government of Tony Blair in 1997. The hegemony of neo-liberalism, represented by Thatcherism and 'Reaganomics', transformed the politics of difference in both the US and UK, not to mention much of Western Europe. New Labour discourse consciously marks a radical departure from anything that might echo elements of the politics of the old Left (for old read old-fashioned). The shift in basic philosophy is justified by the argument that the forces of globalization limit the scope for individual states to reduce inequality.

2. MUD, the Moral Underclass Discourse

This locates the causes of exclusion firmly in the realm of the 'excluded' themselves. There are distinct echoes of the culture of poverty thesis. The argument, seen above in the guise of a philosophy of disempowerment, is that the 'underclass' has placed itself outside mainstream society. It blames them for their impoverished position, and also sees welfare dependency as morally corrosive, on the grounds that individuals come to rely more and more on state handouts. There are clear implications here for debates about 'race' and ethnicity, with US writers such as Charles Murray (1996) linking the moral and cultural characteristics of the 'excluded' to the *intrinsic* qualities of blacks or African Americans.

3. SID, the Social Integrationist Discourse

SID was seen by Levitas as the dominant paradigm in the UK and mainland Europe by the mid-1990s. This places paid work at the centre of the integrationist project. In the process it de-emphasizes inequality and poverty, housing and the built environment, quality of working conditions, and so on. As a fundamentally colour- and gender-blind approach, it is largely silent on broader inequalities grounded in aspects of difference. In terms of UK policy, the only exception lies in the rather grudging acceptance of the need to adopt a 'joined-up' approach to policy formulation and practice. It is difficult to avoid the conclusion that this is essentially a smokescreen, however. True, focus groups assisting the government's Policy Action Teams (PATs) have discussed the implications for successful social integration of such issues as ethnicity, age, gender and disability. But the focal point for social policy formulation and strategy, the Social Exclusion Unit (founded in 1997), still appears to regard 'exclusion' as essentially a white, or at least colour-neutral, issue.

The crucial question to ask at this point is how these approaches relate to social inclusivity. Both RED and SID view the core issue as economic: the former promoting the idea that shifts in the overall distribution of material resources are required; the latter, that access to wage labour alone is the key. MUD, in contrast, places the primary focus on the responsibilities of individuals to meet their duties as citizens. This is in essence merely a more extreme variant of much current thinking on both sides of the Atlantic.

There is considerable debate about the role of stakeholders and the notion of active citizenship: a citizenship, that is, with both rights and responsibilities. Hence, in the UK we have witnessed the emergence of 'Welfare to Work', or in US terms, 'workfare'. Under these systems, access to welfare benefits is no longer an unqualified right: it is only available to those deemed to be making appropriate efforts to support themselves without assistance from the state.

The most notable conclusion to be drawn from this brief, and somewhat simplified, review of policy discourse in Western societies is that it has little bearing on sociological conceptions of inclusivity. There is some purchase on the social integration-disintegration dualism, but this does not take matters far enough. The Parekh Report, based on the deliberations of the Commission on the Future of Multi-Ethnic Britain, brings us much closer to an under-standing of the inclusive society by assessing a number of competing models (Runnymede Trust 2000).

Rather than referring directly to inclusivity, it characterizes the appro-priate criteria for these models of society as 'cohesion, equality and difference' (ibid.: 42). Having considered five possible models, it suggests two which have certain merit:

> **Liberal** – there is a single political culture in the public sphere but substantial diversity in the private lives of individuals and commu-nities.

> **Plural** – there is both unity and diversity in public life; communities and identities overlap and are interdependent, and develop common features.

The first of these is preferred to the 'nationalist' model which the report rejects on the grounds that the unitary nature of the political culture effec-tively imposes second-class citizen status on those who are not members of the hegemonic group. The liberal model has one critical weakness, however, in that it assumes that it makes sense to separate the private and public domains. One example alone is necessary to see that this is highly proble-matic. Islam transcends the public-private divide, being intrinsic to the way a Muslim lives her/his life.

The pluralist vision promoted by the second model is very different from the structural variant discussed earlier, and no longer implies a formal se-paration of the public and private domains. Although the envisaged 'unity and diversity' may lead, for example, to a certain degree of spatial segregation between some communities, this is seen as compatible with material equality and stability/cohesion. In other words, universalism is a core feature of citi-zenship rights (both *de iure* and *de facto*).

The Commission present a rather complex picture of the inclusive so-ciety. It seems essentially to combine the need for a respect for difference (enshrined in their concept of a 'community of communities') with a general state of cultural pluralism entailing equal access to the polity (including equal rights and treatment) by members of the various cultural segments (or 'communities'). So, there is respect for diversity in a spirit of mutual toler-ance, and the acceptance that groups will often want to exercise their right to be different (in both private and public spheres). This is the model of mul-ticulturalism invoked by Parekh (2000). Crucially, it stops short of calling for the promotion of a more general egalitarianism (see Chapter 11).

The inclusive society: challenges and prospects

It is clear from this that the socially inclusive society is not easy to conceptualize. In fact, it could be argued that the concept is as problematic, and just as much a 'soundbite', as social exclusion. Certainly this would be true were it not to be given a clear, unambiguous meaning. It would be wrong to conceive it as simply the negation of social exclusion or, more narrowly, of exclusionary forces. Achieving the latter is clearly a crucial part of the process, and will certainly provide a positive context within which a more inclusive entity can be built. Thus, for example, legislation outlawing certain forms of behaviour does not normally, except by inference, promote a more positive agenda; nor does it spell out the broader picture containing a means-ends schema. Laws, by definition, are limited to proscribing certain actions: they cannot deal directly with attitudes and beliefs. This implies the need for a consensus around the broader aims of the legislation, clearly a much more difficult process, especially in societies with a history and culture infused with vestiges of colonial and imperialist values.

Describing the essence of an inclusive society invites one rather obvious response; namely just how far away from this ideal the vast majority of contemporary societies are. The main aim of the current volume is to sketch out the terrain, pointing out the most obvious challenges and problem areas. It then attempts to assess the prospects for change, including an evaluation of the more promising avenues for progress, bearing in mind the probable need for different approaches in different societal contexts.

At this stage, it is probably helpful to outline the main dimensions of the argument. To reassure those with little prior sociological training, it should be pointed out that substantive debates in later chapters will not be overburdened with unnecessarily complex theoretical argument. Where theoretical issues are invoked, they will broadly follow the familiar sociological terrain of the structure-agency dualism. Structure will be interpreted as encompassing all those features of society which constitute a context for constraint or enablement. Agency is taken to refer to meaningful social action of an individual or collective nature. So, structure may refer to institutions or organizations of various kinds, but may also connote other forces of social regulation such as laws or normative processes arising (say) from custom and practice. Agency will be seen as multi-layered and multi-dimensional. The relations between structure and agency are anything but static. Analyses will constantly remind the reader of the need to see them as mutually reinforcing or transformative.

So, what are the principal factors barring progress towards a greater inclusivity? The first is that there is no consensus even about the desirability of working towards this sort of society. Although the Commission on the Future of Multi-Ethnic Britain rightly rejected the nationalist model as a blueprint for social cohesiveness, it is much in evidence in contemporary Britain and elsewhere. As will be seen in the chapters to follow, there is nothing inclusive about the particular concept of Britishness, or Englishness, adopted by many of its citizens and politicians (Alibhai-Brown 2000). Furthermore, despite its secular nature and the fact that it has been a *de facto* multicultural, or multi-ethnic, society for many centuries (even without the steadily increasing number of citizens with origins beyond its shores), the political culture and public sphere remain essentially 'white' and Christian in ethos.

This is, not surprisingly, how the major political parties see it. New Labour administrations since 1997, like the previous Conservative governments of John Major (though *not* those of Margaret Thatcher) have all espoused the notion of 'One Nation' as an inclusive citizenship. Labour governments have also supported legislation to outlaw discrimination against citizens on the basis of 'race', ethnicity, gender and disability. They have also more recently endorsed a Human Rights Act and a strengthening of the legislation on 'race' (cf. Chapters 10 and 11). Unfortunately, however, this has always been a qualified support. For one thing, the political will (to make the legislation work effectively) has never been there. More tellingly, the same governments have always sent out conflicting messages to migrants and minority ethnic communities. This is because the non-discrimination legislation has been accompanied by a series of Immigration Acts which have made it very clear that people like them are unwelcome (crucially, despite the widely acknowledged demand for labour, especially in the recent past).

In so far as governments (such as those in the UK and Australia) are seen to make judgements about the desirability of potential new citizens on the basis of their ethnic, cultural or 'racial' identity, this negates the 'One Nation' ideal and gives tangible, moral support to those who adhere to exclusivist, nationalist views. Combined with the less than forceful backing given to the non-discrimination legislation, it lessens the momentum for change in the key substantive areas targeted by it. It effectively makes it all the more difficult to tackle exclusionary policies and practices in education, housing, the labour market, and so on, as key actors gain, or retain, the impression that these issues are not core priorities in the government's policy agenda. This is a serious problem because, as we have seen, they are all vital elements in the overall package of social citizenship rights. In Britain, we are essentially talking about *de facto* denial of (full) rights and, in the case of certain groups such as refugees and asylum seekers, this sometimes also applies *de iure*.

The situation has worsened dramatically since the events of 9/11. Following the attacks on New York and the Pentagon, the world has witnessed an overt US-led 'war on terrorism', evidenced first by the (formal) removal of the Taliban leadership in Afghanistan and then the targeting of the Saddam Hussein regime in Iraq. To some it was evidence of a global clash of Muslim and Christian civilizations, an atavistic process harking back to the Holy Wars. But these major conflagrations were only the more visible manifestations of a much wider process of demonization and repression. Whereas ethnic, cultural and especially religious minorities were often seen, at least by liberal thinkers and the liberal establishment, as part of a multicultural mosaic, suddenly almost overnight they once again became 'the enemy within'.

This was certainly true in the case of Muslim communities in Britain. The teachings of Imams in mosques now entered the public sphere: they were no longer regarded as a private matter. Those felt to be guilty of sedition were singled out, especially those suspected either of connections (direct or indirect) with terrorist groups, or of voicing support for Osama Bin Laden. Ways were sought to expel radical Muslim clerics from the country. Fundamental questions were raised as to whether the followers of Islam could live peaceably alongside those of other faiths.

Residential segregation merely exacerbated the sense of social distance: it was regarded as empirical evidence of cultural separateness. Islamophobia, which had already been on the increase through the 1990s (Runnymede Trust 1997), was given a further boost. In the immediate wake of 11 September, there was a steep increase in the number of racist attacks on South Asians in general: anyone who wore a turban, or simply 'looked Asian', was at risk of physical assault or verbal abuse. This also followed a summer that had witnessed widespread unrest in towns and cities in northern England containing large concentrations of Muslims of Bangladeshi and Pakistani origin.

This reminds us once again of Touraine's (2000) question 'can we live together?' Given the evidence, the prospects for an inclusive society appear remote. But there is another, very different, way of looking at these issues. Those who knew little about Islam, or about Muslim communities, were suddenly confronted with the need to engage in debate on the nature of grievances. Although some sections of the media and, obviously, right-wing activists and sympathizers, appear unwilling to concede the possibility of a British-Asian or British-Muslim identity, this is by no means universal.

As will be discussed in some detail later, there is evidence of tentative steps towards constructive dialogue. Indeed, one of the most positive outcomes of a report into the causes of urban violence in the summer of 2001 was a national debate about the problem of different communities living 'parallel lives' (a term used by Ouseley 2001). This, in turn, provoked high-level policy discussions around, among other things, the potential role of secondary schools in helping to engender a more inclusive notion of citizenship and civic culture.

It remains the case that minorities *taken as a whole* suffer relative (material) disadvantage in a number of ways. However, some members of all minorities are experiencing rapid upward social mobility and, through their own efforts, are gaining a much greater degree of acceptance and respect

(Modood et al. 1997). The big question is whether we are witnessing a similar phenomenon to that in the US, namely a bifurcation on class lines (Wilson 1978, 1987; Pinkney 1984; Oliver and Shapiro 1997) accompanied by a continuing racialization of social relations.

This raises in sharp relief the question of accounting for 'difference within difference' (bearing in mind broader interlocking systems which perpetuate certain forms of structural inequality). Though a rather clumsy term, it will be used here in preference to that advocated by the Parekh Report (Runnymede Trust 2000). Their idea of a 'community of communities' complementing a 'community of citizens' is certainly not without appeal. It permits a focus on diversity and on individual rights whilst at the same time recognizing the significance of collective group identities. It has a number of significant flaws, however.

To begin with, there is a point briefly noted by the authors. The notion of community is somewhat problematic, in that it suggests forms of (close) social relations and a level of cohesion that may not conform to empirical reality. As is widely recognized, the term also tends to be used rather loosely to refer simply to collectivities of individuals who have one or more objective characteristics in common: thus the local community, the Sikh community, the scientific community, the mining community, the retired community and so on (ibid.: 47). It is precisely this vagueness that leads to a further problem. At times, it is unclear which of the various meanings of community is being adopted: sometimes the context is ethnicity; on other occasions reference is being made to quite different commonalities.

The final analytical problem emanates from two areas. One relates to the fact that, not only do these various 'communities' intersect at many levels, the term implies convergence between objective label and subjective notions of selfhood and identity. More important, however, is the second problem. In the understandable quest to avoid terms that might appear to make inferior certain putative groups, the Commission has neutralized the key issue of role ascription. In unequal societies, the latter is a reflection of the power of hegemonic groups to cement their (superordinate) position. Those of certain ethnic, cultural or 'racial' origins are rarely seen as simply one community among a community of communities. This is precisely the problem in a non-inclusive society. As will be seen in the next two chapters, oppressive forces attach significance to certain forms of supposed difference which do not necessarily accord with subjective notions of common interest or ethnic identity.

Although the term 'minority' is seen by some (including the Commission) as representing a disempowering discourse, it does at least keep the focus on (actually or potentially) exclusionary processes. Also to deploy the apparently clumsy term 'minority ethnic' makes it clear that 'majority' groups also have an ethnicity. The two key issues are size and power, which are, of course, not necessarily positively correlated: apartheid South Africa being a case in point. To argue, as the Commission does, that the term 'minority' is often statistically inappropriate is to miss the point. True, in the society about which they are writing, there are some areas where the so-called minority constitutes the numerical majority. These areas are, however, both very small and very few in number (Ratcliffe 1996a). More importantly, the treatment to which these groups are subjected stems from their presence nationally at least as much as it does from their local visibility.

The first challenge facing those wishing to build a more inclusive society (in terms of ethnicity, broadly defined) is to transform relations between majorities, that is larger groups with power, and minorities, that is smaller groups with less power. This, as we shall see, is a function of a wide range of agential forces. It is not simply a question of a change in political priorities at the centre, though this is a vital prerequisite. (Even this is unlikely to happen without sustained grassroots pressure of various kinds – see Chapter 10.) Further along the road to morphegenesis the likelihood of ongoing, and fundamental, social change depends on a concerted programme of political action and a radical rethink as to the nature and future of civil society. Intrinsic to the latter is a recognition of the fact that the aims and aspirations of individuals and the many intersecting 'communities' to which they are aligned (or might have aligned themselves) are rarely in concert. This accounts for the elusiveness of social cohesion and stability. Furthermore, as Touraine (2000) and many others remind us, the forces of globalization impact locally in both economic and cultural spheres.

Further selected reading

For those seeking a thought-provoking, if slightly idiosyncratic, theoretical account of the issues covered by this chapter, Alain Touraine's book (2000) is to be recommended. It takes a much broader global perspective than the other suggested reading, focusing on the relation between culture, identity and modernity. He rejects the melting-pot solution to difference and argues that the increasingly differentiated nature of ethnic and cultural formations presents a major problem for contemporary society. Ethnic essentialisms are rejected in the quest for ways of theorizing the relationship between culture, identity and society. He takes as his starting point the notion of the active Subject developing personal life plans. The analysis then explores the relations between the individual so conceptualized and 'the other', who is also a Subject with life plans. The result is an analysis that provides important insights into the internal tensions both within and between contemporary societies.

The books by Ruth Levitas (1999) and David Byrne (1999) are highly readable accounts of the politics of social exclusion. Although largely based on European debates, much of the analysis is of broader utility. Levitas' work develops the points made earlier in the chapter about the economistic interpretation of exclusion. Byrne's book is useful in reviewing theories of social exclusion and relating them to more general debates about political economy. He develops in more detail the argument presented in this chapter that 'the excluded' are often (wrongly) seen as the principal architects of their own demise.

The reader by Askonas and Stewart (2000) provides an excellent up-to-date account of very different perspectives on the inclusive society. A number of chapters discuss the underlying moral and political philosophy behind the idea of inclusion: others focus in detail on the position of groups such as women and minorities.

PART I
THE SOCIAL SIGNIFICANCE OF DIFFERENCE

2 'Race-Thinking', 'Race' and Racism(s): Exploring the Roots of Exclusionary Forces

Ashley Montagu (1974) described the notion of 'race' as 'man's most dangerous myth'. To underline the point that the concept is essentially a social construct, albeit one with significant implications for material reality, it is placed in inverted commas throughout the current volume. There is arguably no other core concept in the social world which, despite being devoid of scientific validity, has nevertheless retained a hegemonic position in public consciousness. This raises a series of obvious questions for the current chapter, namely: what is 'race', how did 'race-thinking' emerge, and why does the term still dominate the way that contemporary society views human difference?

That we need answers to these questions is self-evident. In the context of the current book it is particularly important to explore the social significance of 'race' discourse because perceived differences take a hierarchical form and provide the basis for exclusionary behaviour. Quite simply, 'races' are assumed to be unequal in a variety of respects, and these collective, *intrinsic* ('natural', innate) inequalities are regarded as providing legitimate grounds for differential treatment. In this sense, 'race-thinking' leads to racism(s), which in turn results in acts of a discriminatory nature.

The key to understanding the contemporary significance of 'race' lies in an exploration of its historical roots. This will be seen to explain not only why the idea became so popular in the Western world, but also why it retains its hegemonic status. It is also vital to understand, however, that 'it' has changed. 'Race' is now described in some sections of the literature as a floating signifier (Rattansi and Westwood 1994; Malik 1996a, b), in that it has imported a variety of different meanings far removed from the original formulation, which was grounded unambiguously in notions of biological difference.

Human difference and the origins of 'race-thinking'

At a simple common-sense level it is easy to understand why some form of categorization of the world's peoples might seem reasonable. Looking at this from a contemporary viewpoint, one only has to sit outside a café in a major thoroughfare in any Western city and observe the remarkable variation in physical appearance of the people who pass. Differences in height and weight are obvious criteria, but these will probably be viewed as more or less randomly distributed in various populations across the globe. Gender differences will clearly be seen in this light. People will obviously present themselves in different ways, through dress styles and deportment, but this will normally be seen simply as evidence of ethnic and cultural diversity.

Skin colour and facial features are a different matter, however. Despite a century that has witnessed massive demographic change involving large-scale transnational migration and intermarriage, the average people-watcher is still likely to associate these with fundamental biological difference. It is an indication of the power, and invasiveness, of the ideology of 'race' that each and every one of us has 'learned' to regard these forms of observed difference as significant. But the key point will emerge from a transposition of the café experiment to a time far removed from the contemporary world.

In the fourteenth and fifteenth centuries, geographically defined populations were much less heterogeneous, in terms of physiognomy, than they now are. Tales from missionaries, traders and booty adventurers of apparently strange peoples in other parts of the world would abound (Césaire 1972). Although the term 'race', at least in the modern sense, did not appear until many centuries later, some crucial elements of its substantive content did. Not only was significance attached to skin colour and facial features, these differences (especially the former) were also seen as associated with deterministic, and naturalized, cultural and character traits.

Most important of these forms of essentialized difference was the black-white dualism. As Césaire (1972) points out, black was associated with paganism, savagery, barbarism and evil; white with purity and goodness. Subsequently, these discursive linkages were constantly reinforced and reproduced in the writings of clerics, historians and authors of fiction, not to mention those of early physical anthropologists. By the seventeenth century, these arguments were deployed by many as a means of justifying not only the enslavement of Africans but also colonialism and imperialist expansion.

Whereas the term 'race' had formerly referred, rather narrowly, to familial lineage, it was to acquire a radically new meaning in the mid-eighteenth century. The successes of Newtonian physics, as evidenced by the formulation of laws of the natural world, led many philosophers of the day to believe that they might be able to make sense of the social world using the power of rationalism and the scientific method. They also began to think that the new social laws, or at least regularities, might lead to the better planning of society (though importantly not necessarily a fairer one). The period of history in which these radical intellectual developments took place is popularly known as the Enlightenment.

Stimulated by the belief that they could dispense with speculative theorizing and what they saw as religious dogmatism, the 'taxonomic quest' was born. This was the process characterized by the description of elements of the world prior to the formulation of laws. In terms of the development of 'race-thinking', the key groundwork was undertaken by the Swedish botanist Linnaeus (Carl von Linné). His *magnum opus Systema Naturae* was published in ten volumes between 1735 and 1758. Starting with a taxonomy of the world's flora and fauna, he then undertook an analogous study of the animal kingdom.

The key underlying assumption was that it was possible for scientists to describe, categorize and then formally classify the world's human population. Montagu (1964) identified this as the crucial error in the scientific argument. The process, he said, required (as an assumption) precisely that which was to be proven, that is that separate, distinct sub-groups of the human population (or 'races') exist. If one denies this initial premise the entire edifice collapses.

Montagu's view, endorsed as early as 1775 by the German comparative anatomist Blumenbach, was that the existence of distinct 'races' was purely hypothetical. He was inclined to see the essence of human variation as akin to the process involved in making an omelette. By this he meant that, whilst the balance of the ingredients (in this case, genes) might differ slightly, the result is essentially the same.

This is not how positivists such as Cuvier saw it. In 1805, he suggested confidently that humanity comprised of three 'races'. Crucially, his three categories 'white', 'yellow' and 'black' were placed in a hierarchy with 'white' at the pinnacle and 'black' in the lowest position. This classification roughly conforms to the classic anthropological schema: caucasoid, mongoloid and negroid.

In accord with normal scientific practice, others then sought to 'refine' the system of categorization. Physical anthropologists devised ever more sophisticated ways of measuring and then subdividing the world's peoples. Few, however, ever questioned the underlying logic, even when the data they collected failed to confirm their theory. The idea of 'race' had become a paradigm in the sense in which Thomas Kuhn (1970) used the term. It effectively became a world-view; an uncontestable 'fact' about the way the world was ordered. People 'knew' that 'races' existed, and therefore 'saw' them everywhere they looked. When anthropological data did not fit the model, it was simply assumed that the data (and not the theory) were erroneous. It would therefore clearly require a drastic paradigm shift to dislodge this particular way of slicing social reality. So, to paraphrase Miles (1982) slightly: was 'race' simply a scientific error?

A scientific error it certainly was, but this is not sufficient to explain how it acquired (and still retains) hegemonic status. The answer is to be found in a wider contextualization of the scientific quest. Scientists and philosophers clearly do not work in a social vacuum. Intrinsic to Enlightenment thinking and the subsequent development of positivism was a desire to understand the social (as well as the natural) world so as to be able to influence, even control, its direction and destiny.

Few questioned the desirability of the quest for a definitive map of the world's 'races'. This was because built into the endeavour was a form of Eurocentrism which, by definition, led to an assumption of 'white' superiority. The pre-existing images of 'the other' noted earlier were taken as unambiguous empirical evidence of this superiority. Common-sense constructs of white and black were central to the discourse surrounding the enslavement of Africans and the development of colonialism (Fryer 1984). Whilst in no sense 'explaining' slavery or colonialism they nevertheless provided a convenient way of justifying these forms of exploitation and oppression. As we shall see later, their legacy can also be seen in elements of contemporary racist ideology and discourse (Lawrence 1982a).

'Race' in nineteenth- and twentieth-century thought

There is no space here to present an in-depth account of the development of 'race-thinking' over the last two centuries. This has in any case been done elsewhere (Fryer 1984; Malik 1996a). The present discussion will be confined to those elements of the debate which help us to understand the continued salience of the concept of 'race' and its power as a vehicle for exclusion.

For our purposes, the key figure is the nineteenth-century biologist Charles Darwin. His seminal work *The Origin of Species*, published in 1859, was to have a fundamental influence on the ways in which the relations between the peoples of the world were viewed. He concluded that evolutionary change in the animal kingdom occurred through a process of interaction with the environment, involving competition and conflict over resources. Central to the process of change were the notions of 'inclusive fitness' and 'survival of the fittest'. This led some to suggest that Darwin's theory *naturalized* conflict between human groups and provided both an explanation and a justification for the dominance of the strong over the weak. Those adhering to the theory of 'race' then substituted 'races' for human groups. In subverting Darwin's theory, the Social Darwinists, as they became known, conveniently ignored one key conclusion of his work. This is that all humans have a common genetic inheritance (encapsulated within the theory of monogenesis).

This misreading of Darwin was compounded by the eugenics movement in the late eighteenth century. To the social fact of 'race' they added the social fact of class. If the hegemony of one 'race' over another (or others) could be explained (and, by implication, rationalized/justified) by inclusive fitness then, so the argument went, so could the hegemony of one social class over others (assumed to be intrinsically/naturally inferior). To this could be added gender, health status (for example disability) and a host of other forms of difference. It is not difficult to see that this could form the theoretical rationale for a political agenda based on the imperative for planned 'racial' development, along with interventionist demographic policies on (say) class, disability and gender.

It is clear that many of the early proponents of the decennial Census of Population in Britain (first held in 1801) saw this as an ideal opportunity to measure the characteristics of the population in order to detect 'problem areas'. Besides the obvious concerns of the state to assess the size of the population in relation to food supply, industrial production and potential recruits for the armed services, there was therefore another agenda. In one notable debate a prominent nineteenth-century parliamentarian complained about the 'overbreeding amongst the Irish and other feebler elements of society' (Dale and Marsh 1993: 11).

There was particular concern with regard to increasing levels of miscegenation. This came to light in debates about the causes of rioting in Liverpool in 1919 (May and Cohen 1974). The conflict was triggered by a series of attacks by local whites on members of the black community in the docks area of the city, and subsequent retaliation by the latter. In a reaction eerily similar to that following more recent unrest (see Chapter 4), the focus of debate turned to immigration policy.

The argument was that black males, largely of Caribbean origin, were a particular threat to the stability of the local community because of their allegedly predatory sexual nature. This not only replicated age-old commonsense 'knowledge' about the hyper-sexuality of this 'race', but also generated fears for the 'racial' purity of the population given the increasing number of relationships with local white women. The additional subtext, of course, was that they were stealing 'our women', a position which conveniently ignores the fact that forced miscegenation in the form of the abuse of white male power was integral to the enslavement of Africans (Dadzie 1990).

So, ideas about 'race' in the early decades of twentieth-century Britain were subject to two major influences. One was the pervasive influence of Social Darwinism and eugenics. The other might be characterized as common-sense definitions of otherness implicit in the ideologies surrounding slavery and colonialism (Lawrence 1982a). Migration of colonial citizens to the metropolis, at this time largely as a result of maritime labour, in a sense resulted in both the importation of colonial ideology and a development of a distinctive form of inferiorization driven by political economy. In the case of Liverpool, black sailors were subjected to attack not simply because they were regarded as 'racially' inferior, but because they were occupying jobs which might be done by those, that is whites, who were assumed to be more entitled to them (by virtue of birthright and 'race'). May and Cohen (1974) saw the underlying phenomenon as reflecting the growth of the International Division of Labour.

The real significance of 'race-thinking', or the racialization of relationships (Small 1994), lies in the associated ideology of racism and, in particular, the material effects which derive therefrom. But, what is racism? In truth, this is a term that has been subject to widespread misuse and misinterpretation. The most basic of these is the tendency to conflate ideology with various forms of discourse and disparate forms of social agency associated with the holding of certain ideas. These 'ideas' may also stem from very different interpretations of the underlying concept, that is 'race'.

Pierre van den Berghe (1967: 11) defined racism as:

> ... any set of beliefs that organic, genetically transmitted differences (whether real or imagined) between human groups are intrinsically associated with the presence or the absence of certain socially relevant abilities or characteristics, hence that such differences are a legitimate basis of invidious distinctions between groups socially defined as races.

This clearly locates the concept firmly within the sphere of belief systems. It also sees the basis of alleged difference as fundamentally biological and associated with a deterministic theory of social difference. The term 'races' is clearly interpreted as a social construct. Racism seen in these terms essentializes and naturalizes difference and provides a justification for certain forms of social agency.

In the work of theorists such as John Rex (1983), the biological dimension to alleged difference was replaced by any factor serving the same function. Taguieff (1985) talks about a differentialist racism, where culture replaces biology as the basis of 'race'. In the contemporary literature it is common to see discussions of racisms. This acknowledges both the plurality of interpretations of 'race' and the different discursive forms attaching to putative groups. It is most commonly associated, as will be seen later, with the 'postmodern turn'. The current text resists the temptation to follow this convention. Simply to argue that the substantive content of the ideology takes different forms does not to my mind justify the suggestion that there is a plurality of racisms. To do so may even result in a loss of focus and analytical edge.

As with the concept of 'race', the origins of racism are complex. Césaire (1972) associates these with the 'European disease' of colonialism, but with much of its content stemming from earlier transmitted images of the other (such as the black-white dualism noted earlier). Memmi (1974) sees it as integral to the process of colonialism. He argues persuasively that colonials, even if they are not in any way predisposed to make the other inferior, *ne-*

cessarily come to adopt such a stance. The argument is that colonialism and 'racial' equality are incompatible. For colonialism to 'work', in an economic sense, those in a structurally subordinate social position are compelled to suffer relative deprivation/disadvantage in material terms. But this, Memmi argues, can only hold over time if there is an effective hegemonic ideology to which all those in relatively powerful positions (that is, colonialists) sub-scribe, at least implicitly. To Jean-Paul Sartre, who wrote the introduction to the book, the key point was economic and not psychological. In other words, irrespective of a possible psychological need on the part of colonists to find a means of rationalizing their unjustified superordinate position, the key pro-tagonists were locked into a structurally unequal relationship between the colonial and metropolitan economies.

For our present purposes these broader issues of political economy in historical perspective are vital. In conjunction with what Memmi describes as colonial racism they help to explain the longevity of certain forms of de-terministic theory. Ample testimony to their pervasiveness is provided by the fact that even those aspiring to an objective sociological analysis of coloni-alism are sometimes tainted by them. Maunier (1948), for example, in talking about French colonialism, equates the philosophy behind protectorates to benign guardianship. This is precisely the tendency of which Césaire (1972) warns, when he argues that certain elements within European academe have been deeply implicated in the historical process of inferiorization.

In the twentieth century, there is no clearer example than so-called 'race science'. At its zenith, it led to systematic genocide. Although the 'science' of Nazi Germany in the 1930s bears little resemblance to the theories and methods of most physical anthropologists, the suggestion that there were separate 'races' with distinct phenotypical, as well as genotypical, character-istics provided the basis for Nazi experimentation on Jews and other assumed *Untermensch*.

Vestiges of the eugenics movement could be seen even in the latter half of the century. Sir Keith (later Lord) Joseph, who held a series of senior ca-binet posts in UK Conservative governments in the 1970s and early 1980s (including, significantly, Minister of Education) famously, or rather in-famously, expressed concerns about the implications of relatively high birth rates amongst 'immigrants' and poorer elements of the working class. More significant, at least in terms of material impact, was the linkage between 'race' and one attribute widely regarded as 'socially relevant' (see the above defi-nition of racism), namely IQ.

It was the US psychologist Arthur Jenson (1969) who first provoked a furore by suggesting that blacks were intrinsically less gifted than whites. Shrugging off claims that the intelligence tests on which his conclusions were based were culturally biased (putting the former at an unfair advantage), he claimed that the average IQ score for US blacks was markedly lower than that for whites. Hans Eysenck (1971) subsequently replicated the research in Britain (with similar results), provoking a similar reaction to that which had greeted the publication of Jenson's findings. Although methodological critiques of this research appeared to have discredited their work (Montagu 1999), this did not prevent the publication of *The Bell Curve* by Herrnstein and Murray (1994). The special significance of this work was that it was explicitly linked to the core argument in the social policy agenda promoted by Charles Murray both in the US and UK. This suggested that the 'black underclass' were doomed to their fate (that is, 'social exclusion' in contemporary, and as we have seen, somewhat empty rhetoric) by the lack of intrinsic ability.

The corollary, of course, is that 'racial' inequalities in educational outcomes are to be expected (because they are the result of innate, that is intrinsic, natural abilities, and not – say – the lack of a level playing field). Nature therefore wins over nurture. Improved educational facilities may produce minor improvements in the performance of those with lesser genetic inheritance but, so the argument runs, a significant residual difference will remain. By the same token, occupational inequalities are to be expected. Below-average intelligence is also linked to unemployment and, importantly, to lack of employability.

Add allegations of fecklessness and welfare dependency to the mix, and one arrives at a theory justifying exclusion from mainstream civil society. This is where cultural essentialisms and the sedimentation of historical common-sense knowledge enter the equation (Lawrence 1982a). Laziness and a general 'laid back' attitude to life, so often peddled as generalizable and fixed (for all time) attributes of African-Caribbean peoples are ironically rooted in strategies of resistance to the exploitation inherent in the slave mode of production. Undermining the productivity of the plantation economy could be as effective as more radical measures involving direct action on the part of slaves.

To sum up, we have seen that 'race', while initially conceived as a way of characterizing what were assumed to be distinct biological types, came to import other forms of determinism. The common feature of all of these was a desire on the part of superordinate groups to distinguish sharply between 'we' and 'the other'. The substantive content of assumed difference then influenced the ways in which different segments of 'the other' were treated. In so far as 'race' became a floating signifier importing, for example, elements of biology, culture, religion and nation it became, ironically, ever more difficult to eradicate from the language of everyday discourse (as Ashley Montagu and others had advocated).

It seemed to be an extremely convenient generic concept capturing all the various elements of difference. As with the concepts of inclusion and exclusion, of course, this process also resulted in an empirical content which became ever more vague and elusive (Mason 1990). Accordingly, the term racism came to be associated with quite different ideological forms or, alternatively and misleadingly, with actions resulting from the holding, however obliquely, of such (disparate) beliefs.

Popular images of 'race' in the twenty-first century

So, in the early years of the twenty-first century, we are in a quagmire of ambiguity when it comes to analysing relations between those of differing heritage. The term 'race' is in common everyday usage, and is reified formally by official discursive representations. Successive UK legislation established to redress discrimination and undermine racism (in its social agency guise) are known as **Race** Relations Acts, as will be seen in Chapter 10. The body that has the statutory duty both to police the law and to promote good relations between the various communities is the Commission for **Racial** Equality (CRE). This not only legitimizes use of the term 'race', it also suggests that the fundamental problems to be addressed are those stemming from '**race** relations'. Both tendencies are unfortunate; the latter because relations between groups cannot be divorced from the wider power dynamic which is responsible in large part for such relations.

Confusingly, those protected by the Acts are defined in terms of race, colour or national origins (though, significantly, not religion). In the US, the relevant legislation is enshrined within various Executive Orders (from the President), Civil Rights Acts and Voting Rights Acts. Despite the lack of explicit mention of 'race', the term is in equally common usage in everyday discourse as in the UK. Where there is a radical departure is in the academic sphere. This raises some extremely important comparative questions.

In the UK, and much of Western Europe, social scientists widely acknowledge serious ontological problems with the concept: many place it in inverted commas as we have done. This convention is most definitely not observed in the US, except, that is, by a small number of scholars outside the mainstream. The obvious question is 'why?' To answer this, and to see why 'race' is reserved for some group differences and 'ethnicity' for others, we need to look to historical relations between the contemporary peoples of North America.

The key factor is the enslavement of Africans on US soil, and the resulting virtual caste line dividing white and black segments of society (Davis, Gardner and Gardner 1941). Subsequently, these divisions were reinforced by Jim Crow laws, which provided for legal segregation between the 'races' in most areas of public life (see Chapter 10). Growth in the rates of intermarriage in recent decades appears not to have shaken the conviction, even amongst social scientists, that contemporary African Americans are a different 'race' from whites of European origin. Differences between white Americans and those of other (non-African) heritages are seen in terms of ethnicity, the subject of the next chapter.

In the public mind, in Europe at least, 'race' remains a sort of catch-all term for 'the other'. With the rise in Islamophobia from the 1980s (Runnymede Trust 1997), religion moved to centre stage. In Britain, and especially in the wake of the Salman Rushdie affair, where some prominent Muslim clerics in the UK vowed to enforce the *fatwa* on him declared by the then Iranian regime, followers of Islam were increasingly demonized as the archetypal 'enemy within'. This has, of course, been raised to new heights by the events of 9/11, as was noted in the previous chapter.

This issue will be developed in later chapters, as will the question of how exclusive or inclusive the concept of Britishness is. As to how central 'race-thinking' is in the mind of contemporary Europeans, there is little disagreement: it is absolutely pivotal. Everyday discourse may exhibit certain silences about the issue, not least because some are uneasy about being seen as racist, but euphemisms serve the same purpose. As to what 'race' means to the average person in the street, there are certainly vestiges of the old physical anthropological typologies, principally to do with skin colour. But there is, as suggested earlier, a widespread tendency to 'float' between different images of 'race' as based on colour, nationality (especially in the context of debates about the rights of refugees and asylum seekers), culture and/or religion.

Those on the Right bemoan the fact that (what they regard as) political correctness has reduced the openness with which 'we' talk about 'them'. Central to this is the contention that the former is necessarily (intrinsically) incompatible with the latter. In other words, 'they' cannot become 'we'. This is, in many ways, the crux of the matter. The essence of 'race' is its assumed immutability. What precisely it is that is allegedly immutable (beyond certain obvious physical traits) is less easy to discern.

The fact that the term 'race' is legitimated by national legislation is significant. Those, like Montagu, who press for its replacement by a term without such historical baggage face an uphill struggle. For one thing, there are no ideologically, or methodologically, neutral ways of expressing differences between peoples of differing heritages. The concept ethnic group, to be discussed in the following chapter, is itself problematic. Also, as noted earlier, use of terms like 'minority' is not universally acceptable (as a means of representing subordinated groups).

A much more significant issue is the question of how such a term is erased from public consciousness. The whole point about 'race' is that it acquired paradigmatic status through a long history of slavery, colonialism and imperialism, and is constantly reified in contemporary discourse. To remove it will take more than a decision on the part of social scientists. Even if it were removed, there is every likelihood that another term, such as 'ethnic group', will come to perform the same function. It already acts as a euphemism for 'race' in cases where the latter's use is deemed likely to offend.

The most important criterion for an emancipatory discourse is a transformation in the ways in which difference is perceived. If the social significance attached to difference can be reduced (to the point where superordinate groups see only diversity – see Mason 2000: 2–3), and crude essentialisms are challenged as a matter of routine, progress will have been made. But for this to be possible requires a radical shift in the material relations between superordinate and subordinate groups.

'Race', racism(s) and contemporary sociology: a guide to further reading

The sociological literature on the concept of 'race', and on racism more generally, is absolutely vast. Accordingly, this brief guide focuses simply on some of the more accessible treatments of particular issues. It also focuses as far as possible on relatively recent contributions.

Miles (1982), despite being a little dated, presents a very useful account of the historical and ideological basis of the concept of 'race', and this is complemented by a more recent book in which he reflects on his earlier work (Miles 1993; see also Miles and Brown 2003). Probably the most comprehensive work in this area, however, is Malik (1996a). Whereas Miles adopts a fairly uncompromising neo-Marxian position, Malik also reflects on very different theoretical approaches. Notable amongst these is the recently fashionable tendency to embrace poststructuralism and the postmodern turn. Here, he presents a nicely nuanced account of the ways in which an understandable desire to dispense with crude 'race' (and ethnic) essentialisms can lead to a dangerously nihilistic tendency which undermines attempts to address social divisions and inequalities.

Because of its remit as a brief introduction, the current work has little space to devote to a survey of the many different theoretical approaches to 'race' and racism adopted by sociologists. Although now a little long in the tooth, there is still very little to rival Rex and Mason (1986) as a comprehensive review of the key positions. Whereas many edited collections suffer not only from differences of style and substance but also from the very different perspectives of contributing authors, here this is a major strength. Whether we are reading about pluralism, race-class debates, rational choice theory or sociobiology, we know that the author is both an advocate of her/ his position, and an expert in that field. Two obvious omissions can be explained by the period in which the collection was assembled. The first is postmodernism which, as intimated earlier, was very much a child of the

1990s. The other, very important perspective has as yet few explicit champions.

Bob Carter (2000) makes a strong case for adopting a critical realist perspective. Although much of the earlier part of the volume is fairly theoretical, he then presents some extremely useful empirical examples in defence of his position. Not only does he reiterate many of the debates concerning the ontological status of 'race', he also usefully reminds us of the dangers of its oversimplistic use as an explanatory variable. This is not a difficult point, but an extremely important one nonetheless. When, for example, sociologists link 'race' to a substantive area such as education, housing or labour market position, they should beware of an all too frequent tendency to suggest or infer (even if only implicitly) some form of (direct) causal relationship between them. This provides, if nothing else, a timely warning ahead of the more substantively embedded debates later in the current volume. The same warning applies, of course, to analyses based on ethnicity and 'ethnic group'. It is to these issues we now turn.

3 Ethnicity, Culture and Difference

We have seen that, despite being devoid of scientific validity, the concept of 'race' retains a central position in the contemporary mind. It is still assumed by large swathes of the world's population to represent real, empirically identifiable differences between groups of its peoples. To some, it may be little more than a convenient set of descriptors; to others it represents something considerably more sinister. It is a way of ordering groups hierarchically and deterministically, that is the inferiorization of certain groups is deemed to apply in all places and for all time.

This has led Montagu (1964) and others to propose its replacement by a more neutral-sounding term like 'ethnic group'. The big problem (quite apart from engineering the demise of a centuries-old paradigm) is that, as noted in Chapter 2, it may simply become a euphemism for 'race'; in other words, it may act as simply another way of essentializing and naturalizing difference. But this is only one of a swathe of problems. If ethnicity and ethnic group are truly to be more 'neutral' in the sense of not leading to invidious distinctions between groups, we need to ask some fundamental questions.

- What exactly is ethnicity?
- Is there such a thing as an ethnic group?
- Our analysis thus far has intimated that 'race' divisions have essentially been defined from without: in other words, they are based on ascriptive identity rather than self-definition on the part of those so described. Does the notion of ethnicity sidestep this problem?
- Do those with an assumed common ethnicity acknowledge a common *group* label?
- Beyond the issue of separate group labels, is it legitimate to talk about minority ethnic groups when referring to those known to suffer from racism and discrimination?

And finally (to reiterate a fundamental point):

- Does not the idea that there are distinct groups based on ethnic difference lead, at least potentially, to precisely the sort of distinctions we have sought to eradicate?

These questions in large part define the agenda of this chapter.

What is ethnicity?

As with 'race', the precise nature of ethnicity is highly contested terrain. In this case, however, the debate surrounds competing theories rather than its fundamental ontological status. But, as with 'race', the term tends in practice to be deployed extremely loosely, to imply commonalities of language, religion, identity, national origins and/or even skin colour. Bulmer (1986), along with many sociologists and anthropologists, sees the core element as to do with 'memories of a shared past', a sort of collective memory of a people. But there are a number of problems here.

Are we talking about a form of **primordialism** based on recognized 'facts' of history (assuming these can be determined and are part of the sedimented knowledge of a people over generations) or, rather, different understandings of history? Are these simply 'imagined communities' in the sense in which Benedict Anderson (1993) used the term? What role might ethnic mobilization play here? Recalling the Balkan wars of the 1990s, we heard a great deal in the media and political discourse about Serb, Croat and Bosnian identities. In cases where (say) Serb and Croat had lived happily side by side for decades and even intermarried, suddenly there were social divisions of catastrophic proportions. One plausible interpretation for this turn of events is that their separateness was to a point 'manufactured' by leaders bent on deploying ethnic mobilization to achieve wider political ends. What is incontestible is that they were seen to draw on fragments of history (a partial history): memories of (say) a 'greater Serbia' fusing a reconstructed and bolstered sense of ethnicity with nationalism. As is known all too well, 'ethnic cleansing', a terrible euphemism for genocide, was the result.

It might be argued that ethnicity, rather than being essentially primordial, has more to do with situation or context. This **situational** interpretation suggests that we have highly complex and multi-dimensional ethnocultural identities. The essential point is that different aspects of our identity (not necessarily rooted in heritage) emerge in different social contexts. A simple example, often remarked upon in the literature, is the case of South Asian youth. At home they may speak Urdu, Hindi or Punjabi and dress quite happily in accordance with their family's wishes. In the public sphere, however, they may have carved out a rather different persona, with Anglo-Asian or African-American-Asian overtones. Black street styles are common in most towns and cities in Europe and the US, irrespective of an individual's family origins or heritage.

In so far as these appear to presage wider alliances amongst minority groups, they may be seen as threatening. In the course of research in Bradford in northern England in the 1990s, local council officials spoke to me in rather nervous tones about the increasing popularity of gangsta rap amongst the city's Muslim youth. This was seen as a socially cancerous process which threatened to envelop swathes of disaffected young people irrespective of putative ethnic background. In the sphere of popular music more generally, prominent UK-based bands such as Apache Indian and Asian Dub Foundation are important for having defined a public cultural space for contemporary Asian youth.

The key question, however, is whether this represents ethnicity, or merely lifestyle or a sort of off-the-peg identity. It is perhaps not ethnicity in the classic sense as applied by key thinkers such as Barth (1969), for whom ethnicity is about the processes surrounding boundary maintenance. But it is arguably a major component of contemporary cultural formations and, potentially at least, about future **group** formations. As we shall see later, it is associated with who one is and, crucially, with whom one identifies and socializes. Current debates as to whether the celebrated (white) soccer player David Beckham is really 'black' are a case in point. Those who make this claim, including many within the black community, do so on the basis of his adopted persona and prior associational patterns whilst growing up in London. The argument is therefore that, irrespective of his evident phenotypical traits, he is nevertheless culturally (and ethnically?) black.

This raises the rather obvious point that there are certain aspects of who we are which we cannot change. One example, drawn from Malik (1996b: 9) will serve here.

> There is a scene in Woody Allen's film *Bananas*, in which our luckless hero, played by Allen, bemoans the fact that he dropped out of college. 'What would you have been if you had finished school', someone asks him. 'I don't know', sighs Allen. 'I was in the black studies programme. By now I could have been black.'

The point here is that who we are is partly a product of our heritage, who we think we are and also how others perceive us. Boundaries are arguably the outcome of these negotiated constructs. But, the bottom line is that although a white person can associate with those who are black, it is the immutable fact of skin pigmentation which above all else determines treatment on an individual basis. Only those who possess, or who appear to possess, certain phenotypical characteristics experience the full force of racism.

A further interpretation sees ethnicity as constantly changing, not permanently anchored in history, either 'real' or imagined. As with the situational variant, it arises from social interactions of various kinds, and draws inspiration from global, national and local contexts. This is the essence of **cultural hybridity** and of **diasporic identities** which are seen by many as integral to contemporary transnational communities (Cohen 1994, 1997; Back 1996). The core argument is that major political fissures across the globe, especially since the late 1980s, have generated not only a very different mapping of nations and ethno-national groups but also an ever-increasing flow of migrants with meaningful roots in a number of countries and even continents.

What we have, therefore, is a complex fusion of language, culture, religion and attachment to place. Some would see ethnicity as layered. As Fenton (1999) argues, some aspects are global. We all belong to global communities along, say, linguistic or religious lines; for example, the English- or French-speaking world, world Jewry or the followers of Islam. The difference between these examples is that the historical forces which generated linguistic hegemony were not necessarily conducive to the development of forms of collective identification on ethnocultural lines; indeed, they were always rather more likely to have the opposite effect. Recent conflict in the Middle East, however, has demonstrated in the clearest possible terms that the same is not true for Islam. Islamic identity clearly transcends national borders, and supersedes other forms of self-identification such as nation or region.

Perhaps the best way of viewing ethnicity is as something which is multi-dimensional and stratified. The borders between those of different putative ethnicity, in so far as they can be discerned, are subject to negotiation and re-negotiation and, as a result, constantly shifting. Our examples drawn from contemporary culture and political economy show how other global or transnational factors are part of an 'ethnicity-making' process.

The central feature of nationalist agendas is an attempt to undermine forms of ethnic identity which acknowledge these wider forces. In the UK, the clearest example of these came from Norman (later Lord) Tebbit, ex-cabinet minister and Chairman of the Conservative Party in Margaret Thatcher's administrations in the 1980s. His infamous 'cricket test', in which migrants to the UK of, say, Indian or Pakistani origin were expected to support the English cricket team rather than that from their homeland was part of a crude strategy to coerce people into adhering to a narrow Anglocentric identity. One can clearly be both Asian and British, and many other things as well. Transnational migrants, and their descendants, will in most cases have a complex sense of 'home'. Parminder Bhachu's *Twice Migrants* (1985), those who (largely at the behest of colonial administrations) migrated to East Africa from the Indian subcontinent before settling in Britain, normally feel strong affinities with at least two, in many cases three, countries and continents.

Seen in these terms it is obvious that ethnicity is not amenable to simple empirical investigation and measurement. This is not, however, to endorse the anti-essentialist or poststructuralist positions fully. To say something is complex and shifting does not imply rejection of the idea that there are 'real', discernible groups (a function of both ascriptive and self identity). We shall see shortly how sociologists, social anthropologists and policy-makers have attempted to research ethnicity empirically. First, however, we turn to the thorny question of ethnic group formation.

What is an ethnic group, and how is it formed?

Much of this discussion about the nature of ethnicity concerned the making, and re-making, of bonds between people. There are a series of key questions here. What are the motors behind the making of an ethnic group? What binds these individuals together? Are there occasions when the term 'ethnic group' merely represents a loose collectivity of people associated with a common (socially constructed) label?

Defining ethnicity in the way we have suggests that it would be extremely difficult to define distinct 'ethnic groups'. If ethnicity has primordial elements but is constantly changing, situational and/or multi-layered then how might 'groups' emerge (as distinct from loose collectivities)? The fact remains that 'groups' are made both from without and from within. Often they are the product of centuries-old conflicts and alliances, or based on common claims on territory. Where nations are the product of a fusion of groups with quite different cultural traditions, language and even religion, wars of liberation or regime change may lead to the emergence (or re-emergence) of a myriad of groups with quite separate agendas. The recent war in Afghanistan, for example, revealed a complex system of 'ethnic groups' occupying various regions of the country: primarily the Uzbeks, Tajiks and Pashtuns. Although formally designated as an 'alliance' (as indeed they were in the narrow sense of opposing the Taliban), they were always likely to take this opportunity to press individual claims for recognition (and representation in any new government). The fall of the Soviet Union was accompanied by intense conflict as groups fought to gain independence and control of what they saw as occupied territory.

In the US, migrant groups such as Mexicans, Puerto Ricans, Cubans and Chinese would in general define themselves in these ethno-national terms. It is clear, however, that these groups are different in sociological terms from those discussed in the previous paragraph. The question is: in what ways are they different? It is clear that what gives them their group status is not a collective territorial claim.

We need to have some way of explaining how ethnic groups are formed and how group labels appear. It will become evident that in many cases the latter are the result of a complex dialectical process with both external and internal influences. Particularly problematic is a determination of the empirical content to which a label refers, especially when the latter may be the subject of considerable contestation by those who ostensibly share the same label. Underlying these difficulties is a historical process of ethnicity-making.

A useful way of getting to grips with the major dimensions of this is to use Eriksen's (1993) schema, as modified by Fenton (1999: 32–3). (The astute reader will note that this tends to simplify and 'freeze' groups in ways that contradict some of our prior arguments: we shall return to this issue later.)

> **Urban minorities** – examples here would be the migrant worker populations in American and European cities and in the economies of newly industrializing societies (for example Indonesian workers in Malaysia) and trader minorities (such as Chinese merchants in the Caribbean).

> **Proto-nations or ethno-national groups** – people who have and make a claim to be nations, and thus make a claim to some form of self-governance while being incorporated within a larger state. The obvious examples here would be the Québécois in Canada, Kurds in (and around) Turkey and the Basques (or Catalans) in Spain.

> **Ethnic groups in plural societies** – these are the descendants of populations who have typically migrated as coerced, voluntary or semi-voluntary workers, and have come to form distinctive, and sometimes large, minorities in the new context (for example the Chinese in Malaya). It is noted that they rarely make a claim for separate ethno-national status but form a distinct segment of a nation state system.

> **Indigenous minorities** – peoples dispossessed by colonial settlement. Obvious examples would be the Aboriginal peoples of Australia, the Maoris of New Zealand and the island peoples of the Pacific, such as the Hawaiians. In addition, there are the native American peoples of North, Central and South America.

> **Post-slavery minorities** – the 'black' African descendants of people formerly enslaved in the New World, of which black and African Americans are the obvious example.

In this final case, Fenton rightly argues that the picture has been considerably complicated by intermarriage, with 'mulatto' and 'mixed race' (sic) groups often forming partly distinct populations. This provides a clear hint, if one were needed, that group formation represents a constant process of evolutionary change. Fenton argues that an exploration of the social, cultural and political trajectories of these groups provides an insight into the significance of ethnicity in the modern world. This is absolutely correct. But an overriding focus on the history of particular 'ethnic groups' has its dangers, in particular the (at times) highly partial histories which form the core of social anthropological 'knowledge'.

The dangers of the 'ethnicity paradigm'

Because of this, some words of caution need to be added at this point. As was argued by Blauner (1972), and subsequently reinforced by Jenkins (1986a, 1987), much of the older social anthropological literature has been problematic in the sense of lacking a nuanced approach to power and stratification. This was partly due to a tendency to look at the experiences of single putative groups in isolation, partly a lack of reflection on the precise significance of external structural factors such as racism and discrimination. Particular problems arose because of the dominant focus on 'culture contact', 'boundary maintenance' and inter-ethnic rivalry.

The key points may be summarized quite simply:

- **Too much emphasis placed on internal strategies, hopes and aspirations: too little on the external social context**. In more theoretical terms, social agency tended to take precedence over structural forces, that is the forces of social regulation. We shall see many examples of this in the area of housing and residential patterns in particular (see Chapter 5).
- **'Race'/ethnicity also tended to take precedence over class and social stratification**. This was even a problem with analyses which deployed what were, in other respects, quite sophisticated models based on plural society theory (see Kuper 1974). As noted earlier, critical realism has performed a highly useful role in warning sociologists of the dangers of slipping into monocausal explanations (Carter 2000). If the analytical focus of a study is ethnicity and ethnic group formation, it is all too easy to suggest, if only by implication, that these factors (and not others) are the principal determinants of substantive variations in material outcomes.
- In general, there was also **too much emphasis on 'tradition' and on 'traditional customs' clashing with the modern (assumed superior?) world**. One outcome was the suggestion that young people from migrant households faced a particular crisis. They were viewed as being caught 'between two cultures', the traditional world of home and the Western (that is, 'modern') world beyond its confines. One prominent text published in the late 1970s (Watson 1977) adopted this notion as its title. It is essentially an anthology of social anthropological studies focusing on different migrant groups. It contains an interesting example of the traditional–modern ('first

world') dualism – in Nancy Foner's research on female Caribbean migrants to the UK. The latter are seen as having gained extensive new freedoms simply by virtue of their move to the metropolis, most notably in the area of consumption, for example car ownership, and expansion of their social world via pubs, restaurants and the like. (A further important problem, noted by Carby 1982a, stems from the notion of tradition. Much of what passes as tradition is in fact little more than the end product of earlier struggles: in many cases value systems imposed by imperialist and colonial powers. This should serve to remind us of the constant volatility of sociocultural forms, and formations.)

- **Ethnic essentialism, static values and the presumed uniqueness of the group** constitute a final series of problems. One often gets a sense that the group concerned is not only a uniform whole but is also frozen in aspic (for all time). Difference is prioritized over diversity, and the uniqueness of a group's experiences is accentuated (or even fetishized). Although this has the advantage of highlighting key variations in cultural forms and practices, it also has the effect of concealing important commonalities of experience. In other words, the subjection of all minority groups (and, in particular, the poorer members thereof) to various forms of racism and discrimination often recedes into the background. The effect of this prioritization of agency over structural constraint (whilst a useful antidote to accounts which take the diametrically opposing, similarly simplistic view) is a neglect of one of the key dimensions of everyday experience. A fully rounded account must reflect the complex dialectical relationship between various forms and levels of agency and a myriad of 'structures'/forces of regulation.

Naming difference: problems of nomenclature

Despite difficulties with the definition of ethnic groups arising from their formation and re-formation, those wishing to make sense of contemporary social relationships and structures of inequality have to resort to some form of descriptive categories. The problem is that there are many different, and often incompatible, ways of 'slicing' social reality, and each is likely to be less than ideal.

Whereas some ethnic labels emerge through a process of self-definition, untainted by explicit external forces, most, as implied by the earlier discussion of group formation, are not. The issue of nomenclature is important for two main reasons. First, those who generate the emergent categories are invariably members of superordinate groups (which, of course, also includes academia). Second, and partly as a result of this, application of the labels may act to weaken further the position of subordinate groups. For these reasons, both the process of categorization and the labels themselves should be subjected to scrutiny. This applies even where groups appear on the surface to accept the conventional descriptors.

Explicit 'race' categories such as negro or negroid have long been assigned to history, at least in social science and political discourse. With well-nigh universal agreement, these discredited notions have been superseded by the generic term 'black'. This was no accident, and certainly was not the result of a spontaneous change of heart by politicians, policy-makers or statisticians. It was a response to civil rights activity, and especially the emergence of Black Power in the US. Thus, social agency on the part of subordinated peoples was the key to the change. But this new focus on a particular phenotypical feature, a notional skin colour, was accompanied by a further unfortunate tendency. This was the discourse of colour. North Americans still talk of 'persons of color' to refer to those who are not 'white'; in other words 'the other'. In apartheid South Africa it was used to refer to those, largely of South Asian or 'mixed' origin, who did not fit the polar categories of white and black. This implicit colour banding, which represents an atavistic tendency in the sense of mirroring early theories of 'race' hierarchies, also applies in certain official statistics in Britain, as will be seen below. The term is certainly seen as offensive by those it claims to represent.

If the generic term 'coloured' is rejected, then what are the alternatives (from the perspective of those wishing to develop an emancipatory, or at least non-oppressive, discourse)? An understandable desire to avoid any reference to 'race', however oblique, led in Europe to the notion of 'ethnic minorities'. There were two problems with this. One, it was seen by many as simply a euphemism for 'races', despite the absence of any explicit reference to this concept. Second, it was increasingly seen as extremely insulting to those so described. It did, after all, appear to suggest, as we saw in Chapter 1, that only 'minorities' have an ethnicity. No one referred to the existence of ethnic majorities, or the ethnic majority. For this reason, sociologists tended to replace this with the admittedly similar-sounding 'minority ethnic groups'. It is worth repeating the point from the opening chapter, that this immediately suggests both that there are indeed majority groups which also possess an ethnicity and that the focal point is on numerical size (notwithstanding the concerns expressed in the Parekh Report – Runnymede Trust 2000: xxiii).

In the UK the term 'West Indian', normally applied by social scientists and policy-makers up to the early 1980s to refer to migrants from the Caribbean of African origin, was replaced first by Afro-Caribbean and then by Black-Caribbean or African-Caribbean. This is an interesting case for two reasons. One is that rejection of 'West Indian' emanated from a desire to rid the language of a term with colonial roots and replace it with one (African-

Caribbean) that reflects both contemporary geography and historical reality. The second point reminds us of the 'durability' of labels. Many to whom the new term refers still adopt the old label. It also lives on in public consciousness in obvious ways, most notably in sport, for example through the cricket team from the region: West Indies.

This illustrates both the socially constructed origin of ethnic labels, and their continually contested nature (from both within and without). Sometimes they may essentially represent convenient collectivities of individuals with certain commonalities of geography or language; on other occasions, they may describe those who can be characterized more readily as representing a group, or group-like, entity.

Are ethnicity and ethnic group measurable?

This raises one of the key questions for the current volume. Is it possible to identify the essence of ethnicity empirically and, more to the point, can we then develop a robust measure of ethnic group membership? Our earlier discussion of the nature of both concepts implies that this is not an easy task. But to do so is a prerequisite for any analysis (the current volume included) aiming to assess levels of inequality between various population groups, and then identify the underlying causes (remembering that ethnicity is only one of a number of different factors likely *a priori* to contribute to observed differentials).

As the core requirement is large-scale data, the obvious focal point is national census data. The first thing to note here is that not all states undertake censuses, and of those that do not all ask a question on ethnic origin or group. In mainland Europe, for example, the Netherlands fall into the former group, relying instead on national registration data supplemented by more locally generated data. The French government undertakes regular censuses but retains the view that to ask about ethnicity would be to contravene a core tenet of the constitution. Going back to the formation of the Republic, there has been a more or less consistent assumption that all citizens of France, irrespective of colour, ethnicity, religion and national origins, have equal rights *de facto* as well as *de iure*. To suggest otherwise would be to imply the failure of successive governments to achieve the freedom, equality and fraternity at the core of republican philosophy. However, increasing evidence of inequalities and the growth of the Front Nationale, a political party promoting an explicitly anti-immigrant and anti-minority agenda, has drawn attention to the need to address issues of 'race'. European legislation is also now forcing a change of heart.

The US census asks about ethnic origin, but the problem here is that the Bureau of the Census has been pressured by increasingly vocal minorities to respect the distinctness of more and more 'ethnicities'. The upshot is that it has become ever more difficult to make meaningful comparisons, especially over successive censuses. In Canada, there is also a question about ancestry. What this does, in theory at least, is provide a much clearer picture of the primordial dimensions of ethnic identity. For this reason, it was considered by the Office for National Statistics in the run-up to the 2001 Census in Britain. It was ultimately rejected on the grounds that this would be too difficult an exercise, and would probably lead to data of questionable quality (because of the twin problems of reliability and validity). In the event, the form contained a modified version of the question from the previous census (1991) supplemented by a new question on religion. The three questions are presented in Figs. 3.1 to 3.3.

Fig. 3.1   Question on 'Ethnic Group' from the GB Census of Population, 1991.

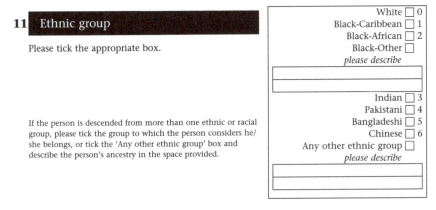

A key question is whether we have a measure that enables us to assess both levels of material inequality between putative ethnic groups and the implications of ethnic diversity. The latter is important not just to sociologists, but also to policy-makers exploring the needs and aspirations of those who wish to define their ethnicity in a particular way. At best, the answer is a highly qualified 'yes'. The reasons are not hard to discern. As we have said, ethnicity is a highly complex and contested notion. The census is based on a brief self-completion questionnaire, where the only assistance comes via a local enumerator. Categories need to be fairly parsimonious and questions easy to follow. The major problem for the analyst is that the ethnic group question is inevitably Janus-faced (Ratcliffe 2001a). Even a casual glance at the 1991 version illustrates this.

Given our earlier discussion about the nature of ethnicity, one thing is clear. Whatever the question does measure, it certainly is not ethnicity. 'White' is clearly a pseudo-'racial' term based on phenotype, 'Black-

Fig. 3.2   Question on 'Ethnic Group' from the GB Census of Population, 2001.

8 **What is your ethnic group?**
◆ Choose ONE section from A to E, then
✓ the appropriate box to indicate
your cultural background

A   White
☐ British   ☐ Irish
☐ Any other White background,
please write in

B   Mixed
☐ White and Black Caribbean
☐ White and Black African
☐ White and Asian
☐ Any other Mixed background,
please write in

C   Asian or Asian British
☐ Indian   ☐ Pakistani
☐ Bangladeshi
☐ Any other Asian background,
please write in

D   Black or Black British
☐ Caribbean   ☐ African
☐ Any other Black background,
please write in

E   Chinese or other ethnic group
☐ Chinese
☐ Any other, *please write in*

Caribbean' also prioritizes phenotype and conflates a variety of island origins and language groups (most obviously Anglophone and Francophone peoples). 'Indian', for example, brings together under one label those of many different religious, linguistic and regional backgrounds, including Bhachu's *Twice Migrants* (1985) hailing from East Africa. The key points are that assumed skin pigmentation takes priority over self-defined ethnicity, and an undifferentiated 'we' is contrasted with a slightly more differentiated 'other'.

The 2001 variant clearly recognizes the need for a more sophisticated listing of groups. But the demand for data comparability over the ten-year

Fig. 3.3 Question on Religion from the GB Census of Population, 2001.

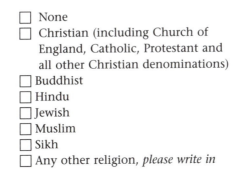

10 What is your religion?
◆ This question is voluntary.
◆ ✓ *one box only.*

☐ None
☐ Christian (including Church of
    England, Catholic, Protestant and
    all other Christian denominations)
☐ Buddhist
☐ Hindu
☐ Jewish
☐ Muslim
☐ Sikh
☐ Any other religion, *please write in*

period reduced the scope for change. Twenty-first-century realities forced the inclusion of a 'mixed' section, and the notion of joint identification with Britain on the part of those of minority origin is also acknowledged. The problem is that the focus remains on ascriptive rather than self identity, and although we now have a slightly more nuanced form of categorization, the analyst is unable to distinguish, for example, between those who define themselves as 'Asian' and those who opt instead for 'Asian-British'. There is also a rather unfortunate, albeit unintentional, atavistic allusion to Social Darwinian notions of 'racial purity', with the White category followed by the 'Mixed' category, divided into 'White and . . .', prior to a reference to those who are (purely?) 'Black' or 'Asian'.

The religion question may permit a rather more precise fix on ethnic background, but here again there is a totally undifferentiated 'we' in the form of 'Christian', and a much more detailed listing of the assumed 'other'. General opposition to the question also led to a remarkably successful Internet campaign encouraging the disaffected to enter 'Jedi Knight' in the 'write in' section, on the grounds that if sufficient numbers did so this fictitious category would become officially recognized.

Despite these quibbles, the measures, taken together, provide what is in pragmatic terms a useful slicing of social reality. The labels they deploy are almost universally accepted, or at least recognized, by those to whom they are intended to refer. It is clear, however, that they are much better as a basis for investigating material inequalities than they are in determining possible ethnicity-specific needs and aspirations.

We have looked at these issues in some detail at this juncture because most analyses, and indeed most non-census investigations, tend to use these or parallel descriptors. One simply has to bear in mind constantly, then, that they do not represent an unambiguous, essential social reality: we are effectively compelled to use them warts and all.

Further reading

Clearly, the literature on ethnicity, ethnic group formation and ethnic mobilization is vast. The following account must therefore be seen for what it is, namely highly selective and indicative. It divides contributions into classical theorizations, modern reformulations of these debates and, finally, substantive accounts relating to contemporary Britain.

In the first category is a book already recommended in the previous chapter. Rex and Mason (1986) contains a series of extremely useful essays by internationally renowned proponents of rational choice theory, plural society theory and sociobiology. The essay by Richard Jenkins also presents a useful antidote to the crude forms of theorization based on, and celebrating, ethnic difference. The Rex and Guibernau reader (1997) provides an excellent survey of theoretical debates, ranging from the classical to the more contemporary.

If the reader is looking for a cogent sole-authored text providing an analysis of the relationship between ethnicity, 'race' and class using comparative material from selected societies across the globe, s/he could do far worse than Fenton (1999). A highly readable alternative to this would be a more recent book by the same author (Fenton 2003). For those interested in competing interpretations of multiculturalism, there is Parekh (2000).

A central theme of the chapter was the rather elusive quality of ethnicity and ethnic group formation. The reader was also warned of the dangers of (over-)essentializing ethnicity. To understand the true salience of these arguments, it is advisable to look at contemporary empirical examples. Two of the best, Back (1996) and Baumann (1996), present lively accounts of contrasting communities in London. Both deploy ethnographic methods in insightful ways to illustrate the shifting sands of ethnic identification and racialization processes and the complex relationships between ethnicity, 'race', class and gender.

For a very personal view of the essence of Britishness, there is the provocative contribution by Yasmin Alibhai-Brown (2000). This explores what it means to be a Muslim growing up in contemporary Britain. As with the Parekh Report (Runnymede Trust 2000), it also provides an excellent introduction to the issues covered in the remaining chapters of the current volume.

PART II
SITES OF EXCLUSION

4 Transnational Migration, Immigration Control and the Treatment of Refugees and Asylum Seekers

Whereas Part I of the volume was concerned with the emergence and continuing social significance of various forms of difference, Part II focuses on the sites within which these differences assume substantive importance. We have seen, for example, that ascriptive role allocation associated with essentialized forms of difference in the guise of ethnicity or 'race' can have severe implications for subordinate(d) groups. These have been charaterized in broad terms as exclusionary forces. Adopting this rather narrow sense of 'exclusion', we would hope to avoid some of the obvious problems inherent in the notion of 'social exclusion'. Exclusion seen in these terms encompasses all those forces of social regulation normally referred to as ethnocentrism, racism, racialization and discrimination.

This means that in many respects the immediate focus will be on the 'structure side' of the structure-agency dualism (that is on the factors that are constraining rather than enabling). Agency here refers, of course, to that exercised by (and/or on behalf of) subordinated 'minorities' and not that of actors from superordinate groups. It is important to realize that this approach is adopted essentially as a pedagogic device. Substantive arguments are rather easier to present if this somewhat artificial division is entertained. Perhaps the best way to think of the resulting analysis is as a kaleidoscope. We sharpen the focus on structural constraints in this section, and agency (in particular collective agency) in the next. To counter accusations that this generates an unwarranted simplification, two strategies are adopted. First, an appropriate emphasis on the efficacy of agency *at the level of the individual* will be maintained throughout the analysis, including the case where this is an intrinsic feature of a constantly changing, multi-level and multi-faceted 'structure'. Second, a system of cross-referencing will be adopted, so that the essence of later debates about the efficacy of *collective agency* is brought to bear at appropriate points.

Various sites of exclusion form the basis of current concerns; in other words, arenas in which exclusionary forces are seen to operate. In later chapters, there will be detailed explorations of exclusionary processes in, for example, the housing, education and labour markets. For the moment, however, we turn to a much more basic, and logically prior, site of exclusion. This concerns the experiences of migrants seeking entry to a particular country or region. Exclusion in this case is seen in a very literal common-sense guise.

International migration is central to debates about exclusion on grounds of 'race' or ethnicity for a number of reasons. For one thing, defining who is to be admitted has a direct relevance to the project of defining the nation. Put simply, it is central to decisions about who, for example, is (at least potentially) Australian, British or American. These decision-making processes also have implications for minorities currently resident in the country in question, either directly by hindering family reunification or indirectly by driving a wedge between citizens of different origins. In so far as it implicitly distinguishes between groups of citizens, it can be linked to more general inequalities and differential citizenship rights. The racialization of immigration in effect constitutes an exclusionary process with much wider ripple effects.

Defining the nation cannot, of course, be taken out of historical context. In the case of ex- or post-colonial powers, historical relationships invariably influence both the nature and likelihood of certain migration flows and the subsequent response to such population movements. Even if we wish to focus on social inclusivity in the context of individual societies or nation states, it is clear that a much broader perspective is required. The present chapter needs first of all to ask two fundamental questions:

- How can we explain transnational migration processes?
- Is immigration control inevitably exclusionary (with regard to 'race'/ ethnicity)?

In order to tease out the nuances of these debates we then focus in some detail on migration to the UK. This demonstrates the intimate link between most significant migration flows and the demise of empire. The most notable exception was a direct consequence of the comparatively recent upsurge worldwide in the flows of refugees and asylum seekers. This in turn was primarily a direct result of major political upheavals first in Eastern Europe and the Balkans and then in Iran, Afghanistan and Iraq.

Explaining migration

In explaining why people migrate, some writers make a distinction between actions which are forced, or involuntary, and those which are voluntary (van den Berghe 1967). This is very appealing at a superficial level, in the sense that there is obviously a clear distinction between the 'migration' of slaves from

Africa and (say) today's 'economic migrants'. In the former case, agency (on the part of the slaves) plays no discernible part; in the latter, it plays a much larger role (though to characterize the process as 'voluntary' may be misleading). Sometimes migration is the result of a highly individualized decision-making process – for example, the professional person who plans to leave the UK to further her or his career in the US. Interesting though the latter process is, we are much more concerned here with explaining collective movements of historically subordinated peoples.

As we saw in the discussion of ethnic group formation, the movement of slave and indentured labour has had a major long-term impact on the societies involved. Indeed, the legacy is to be seen in all former colonial societies. The current chapter, however, focuses on more contemporary movements of people, often from the colonial periphery to the metropolitan core, but, more recently, to the richer countries of the North from the poorer South and areas of the world riven with political divisions and conflict. As will be seen, the significant point about the latter is that the essence of these divisions (at least on the surface) is difference, interpreted in ethnic, religious and/or ethno-national terms.

So how do we as social scientists explain why people migrate? At the risk of oversimplifying what is an extremely complex field of debate (Castles and Miller 1998; Castles 2000), three broad approaches may be discerned from the literature. These may be labelled classical (or rational) economic, (neo-)Marxian and subjectivist. In summary form, these are as follows:

Classical economic model

This essentially derives from classical supply–demand economics. In the migration literature it has become known as push–pull theory. The idea, put simply, is that if there is a shortage of labour in one place its price will tend to reflect this fact. Given a surplus of labour elsewhere, its price is correspondingly low. The argument is then that the rational economic actor in the latter location will tend to migrate to the place where labour is needed. Labour will thus be pulled in by the promise of relatively well-paid work. Unemployment and low wages, by the same token, are construed as push factors.

These arguments are very much in evidence in some of the best-known accounts of post-World War II migration to Britain (Peach 1968; D. Lawrence 1974; D. Smith 1977). Views differ as to the relative importance of particular socioeconomic conditions, and as to whether or not specific factors are causal or merely permissive. As with most analysis of this nature, suggested push and pull factors go beyond the merely economic. In the case of migration to Britain from the Indian subcontinent, for example, political factors, such as the instability, conflict, and indeed genocide following partition in 1947, feature prominently. Sociocultural traditions such as the system of primogeniture are also seen by some to play their part (D. Smith 1977).

(Neo-)Marxian models

Marxian or neo-Marxian explanations of migration accept certain elements of the rational economic model. Specifically, they would agree that economic imbalances between societies are indeed linked with population movements of the kind witnessed (say) between the Indian subcontinent and the Caribbean to Britain from the late 1940s onwards. Where they would differ is in the substantive importance attached to the historical reasons for these imbalances, and their characterization of those who constitute the pool of migrant labour.

Specifically, they would argue that colonialism and its legacy go a long way towards explaining contemporary disparities between the economies of the metropolitan 'core' and those of the colonial (or postcolonial) periphery. It is further argued that workers in the latter societies effectively constitute a 'reserve army of labour' waiting in the wings to be called upon by the core economy. These workers are then characterized as a lumpen- or sub-proletariat (or underclass) who are then subjected to exploitative labour market conditions in the receiving society (Castles and Kosack 1973; Sivanandan 1976, 1982). They are simply elements of what was often labelled the New International Division of Labour (NIDL).

It is further argued that it is the receiving society which always wins in such transactions and the sending society which loses (Berger and Mohr 1975). Rather more sophisticated accounts within this broad framework include Miles (1982, 1993) and Phizacklea and Miles (1990). The key feature of these works is the salience attached to the issues of 'race' and ethnicity. In more conventional Marxian accounts considerations of political economy are paramount, and it is therefore class and not these other forms of social division/stratification which are the main drivers of the theoretical model. Miles and Phizacklea at least accord 'race'/ethnicity a partially autonomous role.

Subjectivist explanations

The striking thing about these two explanatory paradigms is that they give primacy to external structural, or regulatory, mechanisms. Whether it is the economic system (or its state at a particular historical juncture), the prevailing political climate or sociocultural traditions, the individual is seen as being propelled by larger forces outside his or her control. These authors would clearly concede that given the same external stimulus, not all social actors will behave in the same fashion, but (with the notable exception, amongst the above authors, of D. Lawrence 1974) they are less concerned with the accounts of individual migrants.

Forms of explanation characterized here as subjectivist place much greater emphasis on listening to the stories of individual people as to why they took the, often momentous, step of leaving the country where, in most cases, generations of their families had lived. In terms of the UK literature, probably the classic showcase of this mode of analysis is the edited collection by Watson (1977). Watson is very much in accord with Piore (1979), who argued that you cannot treat migrants like shirts, that is, as a commodity simply to be moved at will from one place to another. The essays present accounts of the lives of members of different migrant groups who have made their home in Britain. In keeping with the title of the book, the focus is on people who find themselves 'between two cultures'.

All three approaches, and their sub-variants, have significant defects, however. To focus primarily on the subjective experiences and views of migrants is to elevate the epi-phenomenal to the level of theory. True, the accounts of individuals often provide useful insights into a world beyond their statements and life experiences. But they clearly do not, and cannot, constitute representations of the world itself.

Marxian accounts, by definition, provide macro-level explanations. But these invariably fail to capture the complexity of real-world social relations, especially when the latter are not reducible to class position in a fundamental sense. They also tend to be overly deterministic. To include Indian doctors migrating to the UK in the 1960s, even if only implicitly, as one segment of a sub-proletariat is clearly a nonsense. This is so however much one might want to argue that they were subjected to discrimination and exploitation by the National Health Service (and were a specific target of immigration policy, a sort of labour pool in the subcontinent).

The rational economic model has an obvious appeal. One can study migration flows in relation to levels of labour market activity in various countries, and find statistical evidence to support the theory. But one is still left with a rather static, non-social, mechanistic (and, importantly, ahistorical) economic model which is also far removed from the decision-making arena of individual actors and their families.

One might have thought that it would be extremely difficult, if not impossible, to provide a synthesis of these very different forms of explanation. For one thing, they embody very different social ontologies, in particular the apparently insurmountable divide between individualism and collectivism. There are few serious attempts to bridge the methodological divide: but see D. Lawrence (1974) and Ratcliffe (1981: Chapter 1). The latter book in particular attempts to distil the essence of the various economic models, turning then to meso- and micro-level data to make sense of very different decision-making processes of migrants and their families (or indeed non-migrants, those who decide to remain). Probably the fairest conclusion, however, is that no ultimate explanatory model (for all migrations and for all time) is feasible; the world system is simply too complex and, of course, constantly evolving in unexpected and unpredictable ways (not least under the influence of active social agents).

Contemporary theorizations tend to focus much more on two factors. The first concerns the global movement of capital and the irrelevance of the specificity of space and location given the emergence of the IT-based transnational corporation (Castles and Miller 1998). The second reflects the major political transformations of the past few decades. Here, massive population movements can be linked directly to the aftermath of wars in the Balkans, dissolution of the former Soviet Union and, post 9/11, wars in Afghanistan and Iraq. These have begun to raise much larger questions about a twenty-first-century global mission on the part of the US and the relations between followers of two of the world's major religions, Islam and Christianity (Sarder and Davies 2002).

Immigration control as exclusion

In an obvious, even trite, sense immigration control is necessarily exclusionary. All 'receiving' societies impose entry conditions defining who is, and who is not, permitted to enter and settle. The key question for the current volume, however, concerns the use of 'race', ethnicity and other related factors in such policies and practices. As noted earlier, the latter are of particular importance in that they are invariably seen as cementing a definition of the nation. This is, of course, an arena of contestation, and will vary over time with the state of global politics and political economy, in addition to more local concerns.

Until relatively recently the Australian government relied very heavily on a policy which restricted immigration to those defined as ESB, namely those from an English-Speaking Background (Inglis 1994, 2001). This was clearly aimed at restricting the entry of migrants from South East Asia and all others deemed to lack the defining criteria of the new Australian citizen. In the process of nation-building, then, Australia was, in effect, deploying a exclusionary strategy on the basis of ethnicity and 'race' (albeit through the medium of language). It defended this policy on the grounds of social cohesion, its multicultural policies having run into serious problems.

Despite a black presence for many centuries, most would argue that Britishness is normally conceived in quite specific ethnic or 'racial' terms. To Alibhai-Brown (2000) and others there remains a problem in reconciling difference: in other words hyphenated identities, such as Asian-British or

Black-British, have still not become sedimented in the national psyche. In part this is a direct by-product of immigration debates, policies and practices. But then the latter are in turn largely a result of the historical relationships between Britain and its colonies and, more importantly, a failure to re-evaluate the relationship between the citizens of the respective countries. It is this circularity which continues to represent a fundamental barrier in the quest for a more inclusive society.

To illustrate this point, further reflection on an earlier example would be fruitful. In Chapter 2 there was a brief reference to urban unrest in Liverpool in 1919. May and Cohen (1974) saw this conflict as a consequence of colonial exploitation, colonialist discourse and the creation of an international division of labour. Migration resulted largely from the war needs of the metropolitan economy, but brought to Britain black people from the colonies whom whites had learnt to regard as inferior. Such antipathy was then compounded by the *real politik* of labour market relations. Sailors recruited cheaply in the colonies were seen as undercutting the wages of white labour; colonial workers signing up in Britain were seen as direct competition, which in turn exerted a downward pressure on wages.

There were also signs of housing stress, in that there were heavy concentrations of migrants in relatively poor neighbourhoods close to the docks. Although some in authority saw this as useful in that such 'containment' would help them in keeping a watchful eye on the 'problem', others foresaw serious dangers. The spatial segregation of groups was viewed by them as constituting a potential threat to stability in that strong social ties may well develop between the disaffected in such poor areas.

If one adds to these concerns mutual animosity arising from popularized forms of Social Darwinism and eugenics, there was always the potential for social conflict. Newspapers of the day, for example, made much of the propensity of black sailors to form relationships with local white women. So not only were the former taking 'our' homes and jobs, they were also taking 'our' women. Forgotten was the forced miscegenation at the root of slavery and colonial exploitation. The perceived threat here was to the 'purity' of the white 'race'. Its likelihood was seen as assured by the alleged lasciviousness and sexual prowess of the black male and the apparent keenness of white women to form relationships with them.

The key point, then, is that as early as the first few decades of the twentieth century, the influx of black colonial labour was seen as deeply problematic. This was so despite the obvious immediate gains in the sense of providing a replacement labour pool. Attempts to solve this problem by voluntary repatriation (when labour was no longer needed) proved a total failure, as migrants simply refused to be discarded at will (especially under the terms offered by the government of the day).

These events provide a useful backdrop to our later debates, in particular those surrounding the exclusion and inclusion of migrants on grounds of 'race', ethnicity and culture.

The racialization of immigration control in Britain

The Liverpool example illustrates the way in which immigration discourse becomes racialized at particular historical junctures and under certain economic conditions. Post-World War II immigration to Britain is very much a case in point. Although commonly argued to be a *laissez faire* period (in immigration terms), the late 1940s and 1950s are notable for furious political debates behind the scenes about the alleged dangers of resorting to 'coloured' labour from the colonies (Carter, Harris and Joshi 1987; Solomos 2003). It was largely these concerns that lay behind the European Volunteer Workers (EVW) initiative. The then (Conservative) government clearly felt that although southern and eastern European workers had little in common with their British counterparts in terms of language and culture, they were preferable to those from the colonies, who usually spoke English, often knew British customs and traditions, but happened not to be white. But the seriousness of the labour shortage, combined with a decline in the labour supply ultimately generated by EVW, forced a rethink.

Even Enoch Powell, who, as demonstrated by later pronouncements, was implacably opposed to immigration from the black Commonwealth, was party to this process. As Health Minister in the mid-1950s he was responsible for a nurse recruitment drive in the Caribbean. There were also, in truth, many other migratory forces at work, once again giving a lie to the label of *laissez faire*. As early as 1948, London Transport had targeted Caribbean labour, as evidenced by the much-heralded arrival in that year of the S.S. Empire Windrush (M. Phillips and T. Phillips 1998). Elsewhere, large multinational corporations with operations in the colonies, such as Birmid Qualcast (India), used these links to recruit labour for their plants in the UK. All of this is well documented in the literature (Hiro 1971; D. Lawrence 1974; Sivanandan 1976; D. Smith 1977; Solomos 2003). Because of this, there is little need to develop the arguments here, beyond adding that disparate elements of the earlier theoretical approaches to migration feature in this material (see the further reading suggestions at the end of the chapter).

The main point of reviewing these events in early post-war Britain is to draw attention to the fact that the racialization of immigration debates predates the introduction of formal immigration control by well over a decade. It took widespread violence in Nottingham and Notting Hill in London in 1958, however, to bring matters to a head. Suddenly the hostility to black immigration, which previously had been confined to memos between ministers and government departments, came out into the open. Politicians (largely

Conservative at this time) blamed immigration policy for the unrest and called for an immediate halt to the entry of workers from the Commonwealth. Others pressed for a more cautious approach, arguing that although there appeared to be little demand for labour at that time, shortages may appear at some point in the future. For this group, a system of controls would represent the more appropriate response.

The Labour Party in opposition opposed calls for cutbacks, especially if they were to be targeted specifically at the Commonwealth. Hugh Gaitskell, whilst leader of the Party, argued that this would be immoral. Also, as will be seen in Chapter 10, as early as 1951 members of his Party had been pressing for legislation to address discrimination and violence against migrant communities (without success). The first Commonwealth Immigrants Act appeared in 1962. It did not represent a complete ban on immigration, nor did it formally impose numerical limits on the numbers of migrants from Commonwealth countries. What it did was to introduce a voucher system structured in such a way that it could easily be used to tailor migrant cohorts in future years. Category A vouchers were for those with a job offer in the UK (and their prospective employer had to justify the appointment). Category B vouchers were intended for those with qualifications or skills in short supply in the UK. For those who failed to satisfy the conditions of either, there were C vouchers available on a first-come, first-served basis. As Sivanandan (1976) points out, this effectively amounted to a tailoring of immigration to the needs of the UK economy. It was clear to everyone, not least the migrants themselves, that it was likely both that the final voucher category would be abolished sooner rather than later and that number limits would be imposed on A and B vouchers.

Both happened in 1965 but not, somewhat ironically, under a Conservative administration. Hugh Gaitskell had died and Harold Wilson, as the new leader of the Labour Party, was now Prime Minister. Rather than marking a major shift in position of the Party leadership itself, it could be argued that this tightening-up of immigration controls was a response to two factors. Wilson had a narrow majority in parliament, and was conscious of the presence of many in his own Party who were unsympathetic to the liberal view on immigration. More important, however, was the second factor.

In the previous year a by-election was called in the formerly safe Labour seat of Smethwick in the West Midlands. Labour's candidate was a highly respected ex-government minister from the liberal wing of the Party, Patrick Gordon-Walker. In the event he was defeated as a direct result of a policy adopted by local Conservatives. The infamous slogan which carried their candidate, Peter Griffiths, to victory was 'If you want a nigger for a neighbour, vote Labour'. 'Playing the race card', as this approach has become known, has arguably left an indelible mark on the Labour Party. This single incident demonstrated that on the 'race' issue, as with direct taxation and their relationship with the trade unions, they were extremely vulnerable. The fact that the opposition knew that toughness on issues of 'race' would pay dividends, of course, speaks volumes for the sentiments of the British people as a whole. So, racialization of the polity is both a reflection of common-sense 'race' discourse and an ultimate source of its (re)generation and reproduction.

The 1962 Act as amended by the 1965 White Paper targeted citizens of Commonwealth countries, but not those with UK passports. Fears of mass immigration of South Asians from East Africa in the wake of the Africanization policies of Kenya's leader Jomo Kenyatta led to an immediate response from the British government. The problem for those in favour of stricter controls in this case was that Kenyan Asians held UK passports (a goodwill gesture in recognition of the role they played in the former British colony). Mainly of Indian origin (Bhachu 1985), they had been given a stark choice: opt for Kenyan citizenship and relinquish your UK passport or retain your existing nationality status and prepare to leave the country that had been home for generations. In so far as the latter's new destination of choice was Britain they were soon to find themselves potentially stateless.

The Commonwealth Immigrants Act 1968 used lineage criteria as the basis for determining who had 'substantial connections' with the UK (Layton-Henry 1992; Solomos 2003). Patriality rules, enshrined in immigration law from this point, determined who out of all those with UK passports was 'really British'. From 1968, therefore, full rights of settlement in the UK were no longer accorded automatically to those in possession of a UK passport. Those who failed to meet the new criteria would have to apply for one of a limited number of vouchers.

This offended liberal opinion on the grounds that it appeared to display state-sponsored discrimination, even racism. Even many Tory traditionalists on the liberal wing of the Party were uneasy, not least because many potential migrants were deemed to have served the colony well and were affluent, Westernized people with 'valuable' professional and/or entrepreneurial skills. Supporters of the new Act argued that large-scale immigration threatened attempts to integrate and assimilate migrants already settled in Britain. Some on the political right even tried to argue that it was discrimination on grounds of geography not 'race', because there were many whites who would also be affected by the Act, for example the Welsh community in Patagonia. But the vast majority of those potentially affected were non-white, and there was no evidence of a likely influx of members of the Welsh diaspora.

This episode illustrated just how quickly the British state could move in cases where an issue was seen as particularly pressing: the Bill went through both Houses of Parliament in a matter of a few days. Many saw the passing of the 1968 Act as marking the final demise of the 'liberal moment'. Roy Jenkins as Home Secretary, however, defended the overall policy strategy, projecting his vision of British society as one where cultural diversity could flourish in an atmosphere of mutual tolerance. Much was made of the fact that the first Race Relations Act had been passed in 1965, and alongside the tighter immigration controls of 1968 there was a new Race Relations Act with more robust measures to deal with discrimination against minorities (see Chapter 10). The problem was that the combination of anti-immigrant rhetoric and tougher immigration controls sent a very clear message to those already settled in the UK – a message totally at odds with the inclusionary vision projected by the anti-discrimination legislation (and Jenkins' pious rhetoric).

It is argued by some that by the time the next immigration Act had been passed (in 1971) the UK effectively had a contract labour system (Sivanandan 1976, 1982). Those who did not meet the patriality rules but were permitted to enter the UK were limited to a maximum four-year contract, with the possibility of renewal subject to employer references. This, of course, conferred immense power on employers. And at any time in the four years the migrant worker could be deported if his/her presence was not felt 'conducive to the public good'. The possibility of being given 'indefinite leave to remain', and even of acquiring British citizenship (in the longer term), is likely to ensure compliance with contract conditions.

A new Nationality Act, which came into effect in 1983, was described by the then Conservative government as merely tidying up ambiguities in nationality law. Others saw it as yet another immigration Act in disguise, not least because political debates at the time persisted in dwelling on the 'continuing problem' of immigration. Once again based on lineage, what the Act effectively did was to deny settlement rights to some UK passport holders: it even denied the automatic right to UK citizenship for those born in the UK. What was happening in effect was a narrowing of the legal construction of Britishness.

Another rather less visible facet of immigration control was the treatment of female migrants. They were conventionally seen in the role of dependant, despite the evidence of large numbers of female primary migrants, especially from the Caribbean (Foner 1977). It was this perception of the role of women that guided policies on male fiancés living outside the UK. The assumption appeared to be that a woman should be 'where her man is'. An ideology of this nature clearly undermines the right of women to reunite with their partners in the UK. Successive governments through the 1970s and 1980s tightened, and then slightly loosened, the rules. WING (1985) argues, for example, that lobbying from white feminists amongst others won important concessions, but the changes (based once again on patriality) tended to benefit white, and not black, women.

In terms of the mainstream literature, it was rare to see serious discussion of gender issues in relation to migration: important exceptions being Parmar (1982), Morokvasic (1983), and Phizacklea and Miles (1984). Morokvasic bemoaned in particular the fact that sociologists in general had either failed to enhance the visibility of women or (where women were visible) had distorted their experiences. Her core thesis contains a warning about the dangers of treating migrants merely as genderless units, and a more specific argument to the effect that a female migrant's structural position is in general weaker than that of a male with ostensibly similar claims to settlement and/or citizenship rights. Parmar (1982) rightly draws attention to the fact that it is not only policies that can oppress women, but also the ways in which those policies are translated into practice. She highlights notorious cases in which Asian women have been subjected to X-rays and vaginal tests at Heathrow Airport, supposedly as part of the process of satisfying officials of their right to enter the country.

Immigration policy and the treatment of refugees and asylum seekers

Following the effective cessation of large-scale primary migration from the 'black Commonwealth' in the early 1980s, attention turned to the question of refugees and asylum seekers and in particular how numbers entering Britain could be controlled. And with Britain's membership of the European Union came a new series of concerns. It was clear that Britain would be under pressure to permit free movement of labour from other EU member states. British politicians, for their part, never believed in the viability of the policy known in some circles as 'fortress Europe', whereby as internal borders are lowered external borders are made more secure.

The Carriers' Liability Act 1987 had already effectively dealt with the 'problem' of undocumented workers arriving by air. This was because the responsibility for checking entry visas was passed onto the airlines themselves, turning their staff into surrogate immigration officials. Heavy fines would be levied on airlines for any passenger arriving at a UK port of entry without appropriate documentation.

The only other viable means of entry into the UK is from mainland Europe, that is by ferry or through the Channel Tunnel. So-called Eurosceptics had always perceived the latter as a threat to the sovereignty and spatial integrity of the UK. But these concerns were heightened with the introduction of the new Article 8A (amendment to the Treaty of Rome). Coming into effect on 1 January 1993, this said that:

> The internal market shall comprise an area without internal borders in which the free movement of goods, persons, services and capital is ensured ...

Kenneth Clarke, as the then Home Secretary, was adamant that immigration checks would remain (a position also adopted by every subsequent Home Secretary). In practice, anyone looking 'suspicious' (more often than not of non-European origin and/or appearance) is much more likely than others to be challenged. (The facility for internal checks, via identity cards, remains a live option.)

In the wake of massive social transformation in Eastern Europe and protracted wars in the Balkans, the number of refugees and asylum seekers increased markedly. The essential aim of the 1993 Asylum Act was to deal with the burgeoning number of applications, difficulties in arriving at firm decisions, long delays in processing claims and the large number of applicants granted exceptional leave to remain in Britain while their cases were being processed. But, as Cohen (1994) argues, rather than simply 'streamlining the system', as government claimed, it effectively criminalized asylum seekers and their children (via fingerprinting), abolished the right of appeal in the case of visitors and students refused entry, and removed rights to housing. A new right of appeal against an immigration officer's decision was undermined by the insistence that an appeal had to be lodged in 48 hours, with a hearing, in most cases, within five days. Draft regulations accompanying the Bill also suggested that failure immediately to apply for political asylum, 'failure to make prompt and full disclosure of material factors' (and the destruction of travel documents en route), would be held against the applicant.

Fekete (2001) argues that in the early 1990s asylum seekers had essentially the same rights as all Britons, but that this position was first undermined by the 1993 Act and then taken further by the 1996 Immigration and Asylum Act. The New Labour Government's strategy, expressed in its 1998 White Paper (interestingly titled *Fairer, faster, firmer*), was to 'minimise the attraction of the UK to economic migrants' by removing access to social benefits and making cash benefits as small as possible. This is what was behind the introduction of vouchers (see below). The key 'new idea' was that all funding for support of asylum seekers would be brought into a single budget managed by the Home Office. As a result, since the passing of the 1999 Immigration and Asylum Act, responsibility for the housing and welfare of destitute asylum seekers has passed to the Home Office (the body, of course, responsible for immigration control). This apparently innocent modification in administrative arrangements in fact masks a radical shift in ideological terrain.

The administration of immigration control: refugees and asylum seekers

Under the UN Convention on Human Rights 1951, those who have a 'well founded fear of persecution' must be given asylum. The increase in political instability around the world over the past few decades has meant that the numbers seeking asylum have grown markedly. By the end of the millennium there were around 20 million displaced persons around the world. In 2000, there were 75,000 applicants for asylum in Britain. Most (79 per cent) are refused initially, but those with a good case appeal against the Immigration Officer's decision, and around a third of these decisions are overturned.

The Oakington Reception Centre is one of the places where 'fast-track' asylum seekers are sent whilst their cases are decided. Ninety-nine per cent of these applications are refused. These cases are considered 'easy' in that applicants are persons from countries on the 'Oakington list', meaning that they are considered stable and 'safe'. Poverty, destitution and even the *genuine* fear of persecution are not sufficient: persons seeking asylum must have a *well-founded* fear of persecution. Applicants are told that their case is easy to decide and that their placement in Oakington is simply so that (1) they can be accessed easily when they are required for interview, and (2) they can be provided with legal advice and support. In the political rhetoric of the day, conditions were likened to a holiday camp, in that they have free movement and leisure facilities. Most are detained there simply so they may be deported more readily.

Those given 'leave to remain' had the right, as new citizens, to a reasonable standard of living, respect and a secure and stable environment (that is, the total negation of their recent past). For a variety of reasons, this did not conform to their actual experiences:

- **The voucher system**. Until the system was finally abolished in 2002, asylum seekers were stigmatized by having to pay for food and clothing with vouchers rather than money. Many complained that this led to abuse and maltreatment; others even likening it to the yellow star with the label 'Jude' used in Nazi Germany in the 1930s.
- **Forced dispersal**. Despite the blatant denial of asylum seekers' wishes, this has been defended on the grounds that it reduced pressure on housing in certain areas, principally London, and that it minimized the likelihood of local hostility. In fact, it has often failed on both counts: witness the return of many to London following the rejection of housing offered by resettlement agencies, the harassment of Kurdish refugees and, ultimately, the murder of a 22-year-old Kurdish man in Sighthill, Glasgow.
- **Poor housing**. Many saw themselves as having been 'dumped' in housing not wanted by anyone else (such as Sighthill, a soulless social housing estate of decaying high-rise blocks on the edge of the city – see Power 1997).

Current issues: asylum seekers and combating terrorism

Under the New Labour administration elected in May 2001 asylum procedures were substantially streamlined, with more government money. Many
feared that in the quest for 'efficiency' the interests, and indeed rights, of
asylum seekers would be further compromised. This fear was very real as the
two major political parties had, during the run-up to the election, vied for the
dubious privilege of being seen as tougher on immigration control. Ironically,
the Conservatives' proposal that *all* asylum seekers should be housed in secure accommodation in the form of detention centres was subsequently
espoused by New Labour. But the most radical shift in policy in the wake of 9/
11 has been the re-centring of the debate around the issue of 'terrorism'. The
bogus asylum seeker has now become the potentially *dangerous* asylum seeker.

Previous legislation on terrorism (such as the Prevention of Terrorism
Act) was geared to tackling the 'Irish problem' or, more specifically, the activities of so-called dissident Republican/Nationalist groups. With the introduction of the Terrorism Act 2000, however, the focus shifted to those
refugees and asylum seekers who may constitute a threat to Britain's interests.
The purpose of this was to authorize the Home Secretary to form a list of
proscribed organizations, whose members would thereby constitute a target
for surveillance and possible deportation. Since 9/11 the Home Secretary's
powers to deport suspected dissidents without the need for lengthy legal
proceedings have been increased. Whilst being acknowledged in government
circles as conflicting with key provisions of the recently enacted Human
Rights Act, it is defended as merely a temporary, emergency measure. The
cynic might point out that this is exactly what had been said about the
Commonwealth Immigrants Act 1962.

Further reading

Many of these themes will be picked up again in subsequent chapters, as they
are at the core of debates about exclusionary processes in housing, education,
employment and the policing of minority communities. For the moment, we
reflect briefly on what is a daunting body of literature.

For clear, concise and extremely readable accounts of migration to the UK
(and subsequent controls), it is difficult to better Cohen (1994) and Solomos
(2003). The Cohen book deals with the asylum controls of the early 1990s in
the context of defining Britishness. The new, updated edition of the standard
text by Solomos provides a very useful historical and political backdrop to
immigration debates and includes a critical discussion of contemporary politics and policies.

For a challenging discussion of how the question of asylum links to debates about 'social exclusion' and citizenship rights, there is a recent journal article by Lydia Morris (2002). This somewhat theoretical account can be supplemented usefully by a recent special edition of the journal *Race and Class*. This contains the Fekete article (2001) noted earlier in the current chapter and will appeal to those looking for a lively, politically committed account of the experiences of refugees and asylum seekers over the past decade.

5   Spatial Segregation and Housing Inequalities

Spatial segregation and its implications are currently very much at the top of the policy agenda in the UK; housing inequalities, curiously, rather less so. Whereas the social implications of communities living 'parallel lives' (Cantle 2001; Ouseley 2001) continue to exercise the minds of those wishing to end 'social exclusion', housing was rarely mentioned, let alone considered as meriting a chapter, in the Parekh Report (Runnymede Trust 2000). It is the contention of this book, and that of Ratcliffe (2005, forthcoming), that housing is absolutely pivotal both to 'the future of multi-ethnic Britain' (to quote the title of the Parekh Report) and to the prospects of greater inclusivity.

Before addressing these very specific concerns, however, it is necessary to give further consideration to the concept of spatial segregation, and, perhaps more specifically, 'spatial exclusion', in a broader theoretical context. This is followed by a discussion, largely based on UK and US debates, of the ways in which ethnic/'racial' settlement patterns emerge. This will be seen to raise for the first time a direct example of the complex interplay of structure and agency operating in an urban environment. Others will emerge as we move on to consider education and labour market issues in subsequent chapters.

Spatial segregation as social exclusion

In so far as spatial segregation arises primarily, or even exclusively, from a situation where macro-structural forces predominate, it perhaps represents the ultimate form of 'social exclusion'. In Nazi Germany a policy of what would probably now be labelled, euphemistically, as 'ethnic cleansing' resulted in mass genocide. This began with a process of marking out 'the other' through the enforced wearing of the Star of David with the inscription 'Jude', and ended with the 'final solution' as represented by the death camps. It was also at this time that the term ghetto, still routinely used in the US literature, came to represent the most extreme form of enforced segregation. An obvious example was the Warsaw Ghetto, where systematic enslavement and starvation wiped out the hapless inhabitants.

Mass genocide had also been a direct, and sometimes indirect, result of centuries of slavery and colonialism. The role of the British and Spanish colonial powers provide many examples of the way native peoples were wiped out by a combination of brute force and disease, to be replaced by a slave, indentured or, in the case of Australia, convict labour force (Fryer 1988). Where Aboriginal peoples remained they were confined to 'homeland' territories, segregated from colonial populations. Such segregation was justified, as in the case of the Nazis, by an ideology that mocked, demonized and/or vilified the 'race', ethnicity, religion and culture of the 'lesser peoples'.

In Chapter 3 we discussed the case of the Balkans, where gobbets of an invented past were deployed in the course of ethnic mobilization. Here, Serb, Croat and Bosnian Muslims, who had for generations lived side by side and had even intermarried, became mortal enemies almost overnight (Ignatieff 1994; Davidovic 2001). Serbian nationalists were essentially using historically specific enmities in pursuit of a process of systematic 'ethnic cleansing', amounting in effect to forced spatial segregation, murder and genocide. The breakdown of the former Soviet Union, where Russification had provided the mortar to fuse those of many different nations, cultures, religions and languages (Ziatdinov and Grigoriev 1994; Hesli and Kessel 2001), culminated in the emergence of outright war, most notably in Chechnya.

The case of the state-controlled ghetto under the Nazi regime was an extreme version of two familiar forms of *de iure* segregation. The system of Jim Crow, which came into being in post-Reconstruction America, was essentially designed to prevent equal status contact between the 'races', that is the former slaves and whites largely of European origin. More will be said about this in Chapter 9: the key thing to note here is that its supporters argued that separate facilities for the subordinate group(s) were not necessarily inferior. In practice, of course, they always were. Blacks lived in vastly poorer housing with scant facilities, and were denied access to decent health and welfare services. Every aspect of their lives bore the imprint of racialization: they were segregated at home, at school, at work, at leisure and at prayer.

The philosophy of 'separate but equal' also underpinned the official justification for apartheid in South Africa. A strict system of 'racial' categorization defined the rights of respective groups to live in particular areas. Spatial segregation, along with the imposition of separate facilities, was integral to the process of 'racial'/ethnic subordination that was at the heart of apartheid. Marxian commentators argued that capital was able to exploit the policy to the full, being able to rely on the ready availability of pools of cheap labour in the so-called 'homelands' and the shanty towns which grew up around the major cities (Wolpe 1988). To the plural society theorist it was the classic case of structural pluralism (Kuper 1974), differential political incorporation with total spatial segregation between communities defined in terms of 'race'/ethnicity.

Even with the demise of legalized Jim Crow, segregation remains a central feature of American life. But *de facto* segregation of urban blacks is not universal, outside the South at least. It is, however, sufficiently so for Marcuse (1996) to talk about the 'outcast ghettos' of poor black communities. The very use of the term 'outcast' suggests a systematic limitation of life chances, in other words a form of structural exclusion from the sort of opportunities open to non-blacks.

In Northern Ireland, segregation between Protestant and Catholic stems not from external legal pressures, but from the very real fear of violence and abuse which might accompany the crossing of lines marking out the territories between the communities. Interestingly, however, Doherty and Poole (2000) suggest that the capital, Belfast, has always been segregated, rather than having become so as a direct consequence of 'the Troubles' over the past few decades.

What these examples tell us is that segregation takes many different forms and can arise from a number of different structural constraints. The latter clearly vary along a continuum from genocidal forces at one extreme through various forms of separation by law to the *de facto* segregation of communities arising from a combination of poverty, the fear of violence, harassment or ostracism. The final structural force has usually been labelled 'racial steering'. This is a process, usually linked to institutional processes in the housing market, whereby individuals are directed towards an area where others of a similar ethnic heritage are already concentrated.

Reasons for segregation are in practice rather more complicated than this analysis suggests. As will be seen later in the chapter, agency on the part of minority groups also invariably plays an important part (and not simply in a reactive sense). Successful explanations embrace a complex, and ever-shifting, system of interaction between a variety of social forces.

In so far as segregation in most contemporary Western nations may be a consequence of at least partial compliance, even collusion, on the part of minority groups, an obvious question to ask is whether it even matters. Irrespective of the society concerned, it could be argued that the answer is the same: yes. For one thing, as noted earlier, separate tends to be associated with unequal. Minority groups rarely acquire access to housing and quality of built environment that matches those of the superordinate group(s). Even if this is achieved, there is a strong case for the promotion of social intermixing of those of differing ethnic, cultural or religious heritage. Spatial segregation is rarely accompanied by such mixing (hence the 'parallel lives' idea). Spatial integration, on the other hand, whilst not in itself implying social integration (let alone assimilation), nevertheless makes this more likely.

One point is worth singling out for particular attention, not least because its ramifications will be felt throughout the remainder of the current volume. This is that the segregation of minority communities invariably acts as a powerful symbol of their 'racial'/ethnic subordination. Quite apart from poorer housing, it tends to limit access to key resources both directly, through a lack of availability of good schools, medical facilities and job opportunities, and indirectly through what has become known in the UK as 'postcode discrimination'. Precisely the same issues were recognized in the US as early as the 1960s (Blauner 1972).

Ethnic and 'racial' segregation in the US and UK: the historical legacy of slavery and colonialism

As the examples in the previous section have amply demonstrated, segregation is invariably embedded in historical social processes. Sometimes, as in the case of the Balkans and the former Soviet Union, age-old ethnic divisions had largely become absorbed, or at least submerged, within universalizing socialist philosophies only to become resurrected in the late 1980s and 1990s. Violent conflict and segregation were a direct result of ethnic mobilization holding out the promise of (say) a prosperous Serb future. This was a future based on the myth of a glorious past, and associated with the idea that a once proud and distinctive identity could first be reborn and then restored to a hegemonic position. The genocide in Rwanda in the mid-1990s was interpreted in the media as a dispute between the Hutu and Tutsi populations for control of the country. A rather more nuanced historical analysis would probably lay the ultimate blame elsewhere, to the abiding legacy of colonialism in cementing division and discord.

In this section, we focus on two case studies which illustrate contrasting patterns of segregation historically: the US and the UK. The first point of note concerns the term segregation. Thus far, the discussion has tended to focus on situations where the spatial separation between communities is 'total'. In most contemporary societies, the term segregation tends to refer to far less clear-cut settlement patterns. There are in fact many different ways of measuring the phenomenon quantitatively, the two most common being the Index of Dissimilarity (ID) and Index of Segregation (IS) – see, for example, Peach and Rossiter (1996). Crucial to both is the level of spatial scale: in general, the smaller the geographical unit (on which the index is based), the larger the apparent level of segregation. This highlights the potential dangers of making careless comparisons based on different measurement/estimation procedures. The technical details are beyond the scope of the current volume (for further details, see Taeuber and Taeuber 1964; Massey and Denton 1988 for US examples, and Peach and Rossiter 1996 for UK cases). In this text levels of segregation will simply be described by what Howard Becker (1970a) called quasi-statistics, such as 'high', 'medium' or 'low'.

The one major contrast between the US and UK is in the levels of segregation between black and white populations. As Peach and Rossiter (1996) argue, nowhere in Britain does the level of segregation between minority ethnic communities and whites come close to that routinely found in the US in respect of African Americans and whites. Certainly, in some of the northern towns and cities in England, segregation levels between Muslims of Pakistani and Bangladeshi origin and whites are very high, especially at a highly localized level (Rees and Phillips 1996). Levels elsewhere in the UK (for similar groups) are medium to high in a mere handful of localities. Unlike in the US, where the African American middle class is almost as segregated as the poor urban black, high levels in the UK are essentially confined to the relatively poor working-class segments of these populations. There is increasing evidence of suburbanization, even ex-urbanization, of the South Asian middle class, albeit with some evidence of re-clustering in these new settlement areas (Phillips and Ratcliffe 2002). The African-Caribbean population is comparatively dispersed, with concentrations in a small number of localities in major urban locations (for example Brixton in London, Handsworth in Birmingham and Moss Side in Manchester).

The obvious question at this point is why spatial assimilation is so little in evidence in the US, relative to the UK. This might appear especially surprising given the early theorizations from the Chicago School, most notably in the form of Robert Park's 'race relations cycle', suggesting that (social and spatial) assimilation would occur over time. The short answer is that Park got it wrong. He severely underestimated the historical legacy of enslavement, on the part both of the slaves and those who had sanctioned and perpetuated the system. Jim Crow, and now *de facto* segregation, are the fruits of a society reluctant to accept blacks as equal members of society. This, in turn, invokes a desire for separatism on the part of significant sections of the black community, irrespective of class and wealth (see Chapter 9).

As is acknowledged throughout this volume, it would be foolish to suggest that the UK is fundamentally different when it comes to underlying feelings about minorities. Racism is rife, as is the exclusionary behaviour associated with it. But the fact that, with the important exception of domestic slavery, the enslavement of Africans did not take place on British soil is directly relevant here. Slavery, in the UK context, was essentially pursued 'at arm's length' (given the prevalence of absentee landlordism – O. Patterson 1967), and colonialism also 'happened elsewhere'. Also, as noted in the previous chapter, despite a 'black' presence for centuries, numbers have, until the last half-century, been comparatively small. This, combined with the diversity of migrant cohorts, has undermined any tendency towards the formation of communities with common ethnic, cultural and religious heritage.

It has already been implied that segregation, as well as tending to consolidate divisions between communities, is associated with the limiting of life chances. To address this problem, the US Department of Housing and Urban Development (HUD) in Washington DC formulated a programme called 'movement to opportunity'. Recognizing that segregation levels were not falling and were not likely to do so in the foreseeable future, it has promoted schemes aimed at the dispersal of poor urban black communities. Such attempts at social engineering have not yet been mooted in the UK, except as a panic, 'on the spot' response to the urban violence in northern England in summer 2001. But this is partly because of a lack of unanimity as to the need for, and desirability of, such a step.

In so far as concentration emerges not solely as a result of external forces, one question in particular needs to be asked. Is it not central to the notion of an 'inclusive' society that people should be able to determine, as far as possible, where they live? Policy-makers may espouse the notion of 'mixed communities' as the ideal urban social landscape of the future, but such a scenario clearly cannot be imposed in a market economy. What one can do, and is being done in a number of UK towns and cities, is to promote housing developments (and tenure options) in such a way as to appeal to the widest spectrum of potential residents.

Explaining housing inequalities in the UK

We shall return later to the vexed question as to whether the segregation of communities, at least on the UK (rather than US) scale, is necessarily a bad thing *per se*. First, however, more discussion is needed as to how segregation arises and evolves. More specifically, there needs to be an evaluation of the nature of housing inequalities between communities, and of how and why they are sustained.

The first point to make is that the substantive linkage between ethnicity and housing is rather more complex than often suggested by the literature. Carter (2000) reminds us of the potential dangers of accounts which impute or imply a crude causal relationship between one's heritage and a number of material positions (for example in education or the labour market). Although it is possible to reach exactly the same conclusion from a quite different theoretical position, he adopts a critical realist perspective to an analysis of social inequalities. Applying this in the current context reminds us that one's housing position may be determined by a host of factors besides ethnicity or 'race': class, wealth, gender and age being obvious candidates. (This suggests a clear role for multivariate analysis, given the appropriate data.)

Housing position is used here in a holistic fashion to denote quality, size, tenure, location and the nature of the surrounding built environment. In other words, it is about place and space rather then simply bricks and mortar. In explaining housing position, we are therefore also attempting to explain locational factors, including the level and nature of segregation between majority white populations and minorities. As suggested by earlier comments, the relationship between ethnic settlement patterns and class is radically different from that in the US.

Despite certain concerns about ethnic essentialism (see Chapter 3), the UK analyst is limited by the data available. In nationwide studies, this effectively means using census data. As we have seen, this permitted in 1991 a breakdown of South Asian groups into Indian, Pakistani and Bangladeshi, and 'Black' groups into Black-African and Black-Caribbean. There were also residual categories in both cases, and a separate classification for those of Chinese origin.

Considering ethnicity in isolation for the moment, there were clear differences between the housing and segregation patterns of the three South Asian groups. Those of Indian origin were much more likely to be in detached or semi-detached properties, and were less segregated from whites than other Asian groups. Their owner occupation level was much higher than the population average of around two households in three, but was less than the comparable figure for the Pakistanis. The Bangladeshis exhibited a much lower level of home ownership but in other respects were similarly placed in housing market terms (to those of Pakistani origin). They were more likely to be housed in older urban terraced housing (or in flatted accommodation in London) and to be highly segregated from white Britons. Both groups were also much more likely to be living in severely overcrowded conditions than those of Indian origin. In urban locations where Bangladeshis share territory with Muslims of Pakistani origin there is growing evidence of subtle micro-geographies featuring high levels of inter-group segregation (Ratcliffe 1996b).

Both major black groups were much more likely than the general population to rent their property. This was also associated with high proportions of flatted accommodation. In geographical terms, the Black-African group is heavily concentrated in London; the Caribbeans also have significant populations in Birmingham, Liverpool and Manchester. The one thing that the black groups have in common with one another is that they are much less segregated (than the Asians) from local white populations. Where high levels of segregation are in evidence, these are restricted to very small neighbourhoods. This also applies to the UK's Chinese populations. Largely due to their distinctive economic niche, they tend (outside the major urban 'China-towns') to live in dispersed pockets, and in private rented property rather than social housing.

This brief summary of differences in housing market position, endorsed by newly emerging data from the 2001 Census for England and Wales, suggests that explanations will not be straightforward. This is indeed the case. In fact, it could be argued that some of the finer details have thus far eluded even the most tenacious of researchers. There have been many attempts over the past four decades, but most have focused on the tensions between 'choice' and 'constraint'.

In essence this is a reworking in a substantive context of the structure-agency dualism. Those favouring constraints-based explanations argue that the dominant factors are those which reduce housing options for minorities. Primary among these are racism and various forms of discriminatory policies and practices in market institutions, but may also include a fear of moving to certain areas (because of likely racist harassment) or cultural factors (such as familial or religious obligations). On the 'choice' side of the argument are those who suggest that it is not so much a question of people being compelled to take certain actions: they make informed (in some interpretations 'rational') choices, often linked to their ethnic and cultural heritage. The following examples illustrate the key elements of these very different modes of theorization.

As an example of the constraints model, we take a brief look at arguably the most cited study in British urban sociology. Rex and Moore (1967) focused on the housing of migrant groups in Sparkbrook in Birmingham at a time when these communities were in the process of consolidation. Primary immigration had begun to slow in the face of the controls discussed in the previous chapter, but the brakes had not yet been firmly applied. Inflows from the Caribbean were less marked, but there was evidence of significant chain migration from the Indian subcontinent.

The authors suggested that there were limits placed on the housing careers of migrants by external forces. They said that minorities (irrespective of ethnicity) were denied rental accommodation by systematic discrimination, and were refused mortgages by the high street banks and building societies. In operating 'red-lining', the policy of refusing to offer loans on properties in certain locations, would-be lenders argued that their actions were based purely on financial considerations (and not on characteristics of the applicant). They would add that all applicants, and not just black households, would be affected. The reality, as Rex and Moore rightly identified, was that the vast majority of those competing for what were invariably the cheapest homes in run-down urban areas were new arrivals from the Commonwealth. With private rented accommodation difficult to find and low-income home ownership also rather difficult, there were only two remaining options. One was council housing, the other was the 'lodging house'. Residence qualifications made the former difficult, in the short term at least. When council property was offered, it was likely in practice to be of a poorer than average quality, most likely a 'patch-and-prop' (an older property purchased by the council for renovation – often completed in a fairly cursory manner).

The lodging house phenomenon was in many ways the cornerstone of the analysis. Rex and Moore claimed that desperate migrants were effectively forced to buy large Victorian villas which, although once the homes of the rich, had long out-lived their usefulness, being far too large for the modern family. As to the question of how fairly impoverished migrant households could afford such houses and, more importantly, obtain the necessary mortgages, there was a simple answer. 'Fringe' banks were all too willing to offer short-term loans at exorbitant rates of interest. This meant that to pay off the loans lodging house proprietors would be forced to let rooms at a high rent to those whose options were severely curtailed: namely other migrants. This accounts for the emergence of pariah landlordism: migrant households being exploited by others with a limited range of options. The Rex and Moore analysis was ultimately flawed by a statistical error that exaggerated the numbers of these larger houses, but their general point was well made.

Theoretically, the study was particularly interesting as it attempted to combine classic Weberian theory with the ecological model of the city developed by Robert Park and Ernest Burgess of the Chicago School. Rex and Moore were concerned to understand the ways in which major cities change in the wake of large-scale immigration. The idea that migrants held a relatively weak position in the housing market (compared with local whites) seemed to them to accord with a Weberian interpretation of class, with its focus on competitive processes in markets. As the latter was not limited to the social relations of production, they developed the theory of 'housing classes' (1967: 234). The great appeal of the theory lay in its simplicity, the housing class categories being simply an elaboration of standard tenure categories. This attracted a great deal of criticism, not confined to Marxian thinkers. Some felt that it was really more about housing position than about access, and that the existing categories failed to distinguish between, for example, very different categories of home ownership. John Rex responded to these more sympathetic critics in his study of Handsworth a decade later (Rex and Tomlinson 1979). Housing classes reappeared but in a rather more nuanced form, and there was an attempt to woo Marxian theorists by a slightly modified interpretation of class (1979: 132).

Although there was clearly an element of agency on the part of migrants, it was a heavily constrained form of agency. In contrast, Dahya (1974) saw this as distorting the life projects of migrants. His view, endorsed in large part rather more recently by Lewis (1994), was that South Asians came to the UK with particular aims, and made housing choices congruent with them. Single men came first, and high-density living in cheap urban dwellings was part of a strategy of accumulating money to remit to kinfolk in the subcontinent prior to their return. When this 'myth of return' (Anwar 1979) was abandoned and families were reunited in the UK, they lived in tightly knit communities as a bulwark against a culturally alien environment, and developed a local infrastructure of shops, mosques, community centres, and so on. Ballard and Ballard (1977) argue that although 'racial' discrimination was undoubtedly in evidence, such forms of agency should be given prominence, even priority, in any analysis of settlement patterns.

The appeal of the choice-constraints model lies in its simplicity. As in other substantive arenas such as education, health and employment, individuals are faced with a series of enablements and a number of factors which limit the free exercise of social agency. Elements of both sides of the equation change over time as a result of legal and policy interventions and of more general processes of social change. Residence requirements, for example, have largely disappeared and the introduction of Race Relations legislation (discussed in detail in Chapter 10) has outlawed 'red-lining'. It has also had some impact on 'racial steering', the process whereby minorities are presented with a limited range of options by officials working for estate agents or the social housing sector. Even though vestiges of such exclusionary processes continue, and others have simply been driven underground (by anti-discrimination legislation) as covert rather than overt operations, housing market institutions are in general conscious of their legal obligations.

The housing market has undergone a series of radical transformations since the days of the Birmingham studies. The further increase in home ownership, boosted by the sell-off of council housing under the 'Right-to-Buy' provisions of the Housing Act 1980, has been accompanied by the growth of housing associations (now known as Registered Social Landlords – RSLs) and a change in landlord of much of the remaining local authority housing. With a significant increase in the UK-born components (now comprising over 50 per cent in most cases), minority communities are also very different in demographic terms, with considerable evidence of social (and spatial) mobility in towns and cities around the UK (Modood et al. 1997; Phillips and Ratcliffe 2002).

The problem with the choice-constraints framework is that it works best in the case of the individual sovereign actor facing a series of known and identifiable enablements and constraints. Given this perfect knowledge about possible scenarios, the actor is then assumed to engage in a 'rational choice' process. This would be fine if the real world of decision-making operated in this way: but it rarely, if ever, does. Housing decisions tend by their very nature to be household-, or more broadly kin-, based. They are negotiated choices (Ratcliffe 2000).

The choice-constraints framework is, however, sufficiently flexible to incorporate the impact on decision-making of other forms of difference such as class, wealth, age/generation and gender. This is excellent as it enables the researcher to distinguish the likely relative effect of these factors on an individual's (or, forcibly stretching the approach, a household's) power in the housing market. The major problem with this form of analysis is that it is both extremely static and insufficiently anchored in structural terms. The 'actor' is rather narrow and wooden; the structural constraints are often empirical (or even empiricist) abstractions with uncertain links to an underlying social essence.

One solution to this was suggested by Philip Sarre and his colleagues

(1989). They argued that Giddens' structuration theory provides for a more dynamic mode of analysis focusing on the two-way interaction between actors and the wider social structure. In the broadest interpretation, the latter is conceived of as constantly changing at micro-, meso- and macro-levels. The shifting nature of the structure then presents the actor (broadly conceived) with an ever-changing series of enablements and constraints. Engaging with ever-new, or renewing, structures in turn impacts on the actor-market nexus.

As an example, we can imagine a scenario where estate agents systematically discriminate against minority communities. This limits the choices available to the latter in the short term, but considered in another way it provides, ironically, a possible niche for the minority entrepreneur. Little start-up capital is needed to open an estate agency, indeed there are large numbers in places such as Bradford which are run from the front living rooms of small inner urban terraced houses. The point is that the meso-level 'structure' is now different, and the options open to the potential house buyer or renter are materially different. If this process results in significant inroads into the profits of mainstream agents, one would expect to witness a transformation in the ways in which they, in turn, do business in the future.

This approach certainly seems to offer more in theoretical terms than the previous orthodoxy. It might also help us to grasp, rather better than hitherto, why the experiences of different minority groups, and certain subgroups thereof, are so much at variance. The remaining challenge is to link, in a sufficiently nuanced way, individual- or household-level data with material shifts at the different levels of structure.

The 'parallel lives' phenomenon

In this final section of the chapter we return to the question of how segregation impacts on the inclusivity agenda. The first point to make is that spatial concentration presents obvious benefits for migrant groups, especially where language and/or cultural distinctiveness marks them out from the general populace. In the slightly longer term, advantages accrue from the development of the local infrastructure to meet their needs and aspirations.

The most pressing problem lies in the fact that, unlike in the US, concentrations have almost exclusively been in the areas of poorest housing and environmental quality. Many of the houses owned by Bradford's Muslim residents, for example, are literally unfit for human habitation and also often overcrowded (Ratcliffe 1996b). Living and growing up in such dwellings poses a number of direct and indirect threats to life chances. It is linked to generally higher levels of morbidity and mortality. Local schools tend to be poorly resourced, with low levels of measured performance in terms of key leaving examinations. This in turn compromises an individual's job prospects. Less visible is the impact of postcode discrimination, or what has been labelled 'geographies of exclusion' (Sibley 1995), on such key matters as insurance (Cebulla 1999) and access to health and welfare services.

The other dimension of the segregation debate is its long-term social ramifications: the so-called 'parallel lives' phenomenon. The argument is that in areas such as inner Bradford, young Muslims of Pakistani or Bangladeshi origin meet few, if any, white Bradfordians at school or at work (assuming they avoid unemployment) due to labour market segmentation. Crucially, the groups also tend to have distinct, and non-overlapping, social networks. Cantle (2001) and Ouseley (2001) identify this as something for policy-makers to address urgently, especially in the post-9/11 world heralding in-creasing levels of Islamophobia and of paranoia surrounding the perceived threats posed by terrorism and the influx of refugees and asylum seekers. It is apparent, therefore, that the issue of segregation is pivotal to every chapter in this section of the book.

In theoretical terms, it is clear that although ethnic segregation in the UK is not solely a function of class, those who live in highly segregated areas are nevertheless drawn from the poorest sections of their respective communities. Some commentators have suggested that the UK may be heading for a US urban future, with increasing 'racial' tensions in urban areas perhaps accompanied by increasing levels of segregation. There is, however, little, if any, evidence for this assertion. Recent research in Bradford (Ratcliffe et al. 2001; Phillips and Ratcliffe 2002) suggests that, largely as a result of demo-graphic changes, working-class Muslim communities are spreading from the inner urban areas to contiguous areas with better housing and environment. Others, admittedly rather fewer in number, have acquired the means to migrate to more distant suburbs formerly the sole preserve of white Bradfordians.

Both of these tendencies are, of course, likely to provoke hostility from some local whites. The same applies in the case of refugees and asylum see-kers, who are often the unwitting victims of wrongly conceived and badly enacted policies. One example will suffice. Thanks to a complete failure on the part of the local authority to discuss re-settlement plans with their existing tenants, asylum seekers moving onto Bradford estates in the late 1990s faced considerable resentment and anger from many of their new neighbours.

It is not yet clear from emerging evidence on the selective re-clustering of minority groups in middle-class areas whether this form of segregation is a function of the policies and practices of housing market institutions (for example via 'steering') or a desired option (or a combination of both). But in so far as segregation arises from unrestrained choice (or somewhat compro-mised choice in the case of less desirable areas), this raises a more general question for those who suggest that segregation is inconsistent with a socially cohesive, and inclusive, society. Is it not the very essence of social inclusivity (even from a basic human rights perspective) that citizens have the right to choose their place of abode? To attempt to deny this right on the grounds of some alleged greater good accruing to the nation as a whole would be a difficult position to defend.

Conclusion and further reading

If one wanted to draw out a single message from this chapter, it would be a warning against the dangers of simplistic theories linking ethnicity to housing and spatial patterns. It should have become abundantly clear that other forms of difference are central to a successful explanation. In so far as ethnicity *is* a key variable, we have to ask ourselves what it means to say that ethnicity *explains* housing position. What is it about one's ethnic identity or background that accounts for a given outcome? To offer a simple example, it is often argued that 'Asians' are especially likely to favour owner occupation over the alternatives. This raises the rather obvious question as to what precisely it is about being 'Asian' that (allegedly) propels them towards this tenure option. Is it (say) to do with cultural or religious traditions, or perhaps a particular mode of economic organization in the country or region from which they migrated? Whilst some of these factors may play a part, the principal reason for observed differences in housing market outcomes appears to be far more prosaic. It has much more to do with variations in familial and household structure and the limitations of existing social housing provision (Ratcliffe 1997).

Although most standard texts on 'race' and ethnicity in the UK discuss housing issues, few devote whole chapters to the subject. Modood et al. (1997) and Mason (2000) constitute notable exceptions. Pilkington (2003) touches on the subject only briefly. Solomos (2003), whilst giving wide coverage to urban conflict, ignores housing. Sadly, the same applies to the Parekh Report (Runnymede Trust 2000), as noted earlier.

One recommended text is Somerville and Steele (2002). This relates housing debates to the discourse of social exclusion and mixes more theoretical essays with discussions of important contemporary issues such as the housing of refugees and asylum seekers. Boal (2000) addresses the question of ethnic spatial patterns and incorporates the work of contributors from many societies around the world. This helps to provide a broader comparative perspective.

Probably the best text from a theoretical viewpoint is Harrison with Davis (2000). This provides an excellent contemporary sociological overview of the choice-constraints debate interpreted within the structure-agency framework. It also contains a properly nuanced account of the impact of 'difference within difference' on housing outcomes, notably the key issues of gender and disability.

6 'Race', Ethnicity and the Educational System

Introduction: the key issues

When we think about the prospects for a socially inclusive society, education readily comes to mind as a pivotal issue. Not only does it hold out the prospects of social mobility for all young citizens, irrespective of class background, gender and heritage, it also provides a context in which issues of diversity can be tackled. This is why Touraine (2000) saw the moulding of apprentice citizens within the school system as central to the inclusivity project.

Unfortunately, this ideal of an emancipatory and socially integrative education system is far from being realized in most societies around the world. This certainly applies to Britain. To understand why this is the case, it is helpful to reflect on some of the key points from our earlier discussions. Most important amongst these is the direct and indirect legacy of a history of slavery and colonialism.

As was seen in Chapters 2 and 3, images of 'the other' have long become part of sedimented, common-sense knowledge. People generally feel they know something about the nature and essential character of the 'African' or 'Asian', even in the absence of direct experience through social contact. Such discursive forms are not fixed in time, but are subject to an ongoing dialectical process involving both reformulation and reproduction. Crucially, this 'knowledge' has a direct impact on contemporary social relations. It also inevitably intrudes into the educational process.

We have seen that the eugenics movement essentialized difference between peoples, suggesting that populations could be categorized into those with genetically, and socially, desirable attributes and those who lacked these qualities. In extremis such ideas have led to genocide. More routinely they have resulted in the hierarchization of groups within societies. Such has been the ultimate legacy of two related forms of theorization which still have their adherents in academic social science.

The first is the suggestion that there are natural differences in intelligence between 'races'. As noted in Chapter 2, the 'race' and IQ debate, as it became known, first came to prominence in Britain with the work of Hans Eysenck (1971). Its main adherent in the US at this time was Arthur Jenson (1969). The significance of this for debates about education, of course, was that if it is nature (and not nurture) which determines ability, one would expect to see differences in group performance levels irrespective of the precise quality of education delivered. This would also 'explain' why some 'races' achieve rather less than others in the labour market.

A plethora of contrary research evidence through the subsequent decades appeared to have discredited this thesis (Montagu 1999; Miles and Brown 2003). It re-emerged in even more insidious form in the 1990s, however, with the work of Charles Murray. His book, co-authored with Herrnstein (1994), re-ignited the controversy about the Bell Curve, the normal distribution alleg-edly representing the spread of IQ across a notional population. The sur-rounding debates acquired massive political significance in that the African American population was alleged to suffer from inferior inherited in-telligence. Whilst it was conceded that some from this group would in-evitably have above-average intelligence, this failed to prevent it being seen as endorsing the notion of a black underclass. The lack of 'inclusive fitness' (to compete effectively) was then linked, as noted earlier, to character flaws such as fecklessness and welfare dependency.

These ideas spread readily to the UK, where there had long been much fertile ground politically. The late Sir Keith (later Lord) Joseph, whilst a government minister in the 1970s, seemed to embrace eugenics. And in the first half of the 1990s successive Conservative governments pursued an un-ambiguous neo-liberal agenda, appearing to welcome the opportunity to debate Murray's ideas. Whilst in the UK, Murray portrayed the country's so-cial problems in much the same light as those in the US. He used the terms 'New Victorians' and 'New Rabble' to characterize Britain's urban underclass (see Lister 1996).

The second form of theorization threatening to endorse 'victim-blaming' discourse was sociobiology. Its adherents, including Pierre van den Berghe (1986), argued that social scientists had to be willing to accept some un-palatable 'truths' about the nature of biologically driven human behaviour, and should have no qualms about undertaking research which might gen-erate politically sensitive findings. Denying that sociobiology was little more than a 'new' form of biological determinism (ignoring the cultural dimension to behaviour), van den Berghe suggested that there was no reason why culture could not act as a marker for biological difference. He has even intimated that 'natural' does not necessarily mean 'unchanging'. But opponents argued that the naturalization of phenomena such as altruism and xenophobia was tan-tamount to denying the efficacy of human agency. Furthermore, the theories generated by this group of writers were intrinsically untestable (and hence unfalsifiable), with the inevitable effect that many socially and politically dangerous ideas could be left on the research agenda in perpetuity.

The legacy of these ideas for debates about educational inequality is clear. To suggest that 'racial' or ethnic groups possess different levels of intrinsic ability naturalizes differential performance. It was precisely this notion which underpinned the 'underachievement thesis'. In this case, however, there was an additional dimension to the argument. Cultural deficit theory led to the idea that young black males of African-Caribbean origin were also handicapped by a culture which downplayed the role of the father figure (Lawrence 1982b).

These ideas will re-emerge in various guises in the next section of the chapter, which focuses on the roots of ethnic inequalities in the experience of education. We then move on to look at two key policy developments which sought to redress them: Multi-Cultural Education (MCE) and Anti-Racist Education (ARE). Of interest here are not just the policies themselves, but the theoretical positions on which they are ultimately based. Both strategies were widely derided and disparaged by the free market, neo-liberal administrations led by Margaret Thatcher from 1979 to the early 1990s. We examine the political forces that sought to undermine any educational policies appearing to deviate from 'traditional' values and methods.

The result was lingering problems with disaffected minority pupils, especially African-Caribbean males, leading to relatively poor school-leaving qualifications and high suspension and permanent exclusion rates. But there is another side to the educational landscape. Increasing numbers of minority students were succeeding (despite these problems), gaining access to higher education and employment commensurate with their abilities and aspirations. These contrasting trajectories form the basis of the concluding sections of this chapter, and the chapter to follow. Where appropriate to the argument, reference will be made to societies other than Britain.

The roots of educational inequality in Britain

In tracing the roots of educational inequalities in Britain, it is important to situate these debates firmly in the context of historical and political processes. As noted earlier, although there has been a black presence in Britain for centuries, numbers were small prior to the late 1940s. Up to that point there had been little public debate about the implications for the system of a multi-ethnic school population. With immigration from the disparate societies making up the New Commonwealth, a number of issues were raised.

The first was language. Many children from the Indian subcontinent had a first language that was not English. Those from the Anglophone Caribbean were seen as presenting a somewhat different 'problem'. Many of these children spoke various forms of patois. This was generally regarded at the time as an unacceptable form of English. More significant in many ways, though, was the fact that many teachers saw its use as undermining their authority. The accusation, as Carby (1982b) suggests, is that it was being used as a mode of resistance to the disciplinary code of the institution. In other words, the children stood accused of *opting* for a form of English that was incomprehensible to their teachers. This is particularly interesting in that it reflects a common theme in the characterization of black as distinct from South Asian students. Whereas the latter were, and to a large extent still are, viewed as conscientious and respectful, African-Caribbeans (especially males) have been viewed as more likely both to be confrontational (having 'a chip on their shoulders') and to lack the necessary application to their studies.

The second issue links directly to the migration process and the settlement patterns that accompanied it. As we saw in the previous chapter, the majority of early migrants (irrespective of ethnicity) moved into inner urban areas. This meant in effect that residential segregation was accompanied by segregated schooling; though the precise ethnic mix might vary significantly from area to area.

As far as educationalists were concerned both represented major problems for the system. A more enlightened perspective would have led to a recognition of the potential for a richer teaching environment, but this was a time in which assimilationism was the dominant policy paradigm. Significantly, concentrations in particular schools of those whose first language was not English were seen as threatening the performance of local (white) students. Extra resources were therefore directed towards the teaching of English, and under Section 11 of the Local Government Act 1966 a local authority with a sizeable New Commonwealth population could recruit additional teachers (part-funded directly by central government).

As in the US, bussing was seen as the solution to the imbalance in the ethnic composition of school populations (Carby 1982b). But, as in the US also, this was both extremely unpopular and its application rather patchy. Bussing across the city led to objections from migrants about the disruption to their children's teaching day, and many white parents were unhappy for their children to study alongside (artificially) inflated numbers of African-Caribbean and South Asian pupils.

It was clear by the mid-1960s that the policy of assimilation was not working (Troyna and Carrington 1990; Mason 2000). Coinciding with the rethink of immigration policy geared to the limiting of numbers was the idea that integration did not necessarily mean assimilation (see Chapter 4). Cultural pluralism was now the watchword. As far as the school system was concerned, this meant the introduction of Multi-Cultural Education (MCE).

Promoting change: MCE and ARE

The idea behind MCE was that if pupils of different heritages understood more about each other's ethnic, religious and cultural backgrounds this would bring two benefits. It would result in a healthier and more productive learning environment and would bring more long-term benefits to the society as a whole. This was extremely laudable. The problems lay in its application and its omissions, most notably a failure to recognize the pervasive significance of 'race' and racism.

Rather than undertaking a radical overhaul of the curriculum and re-thinking aspects of school ethos and culture, most authorities endorsed variants of a policy characterized by Troyna and Ball (1985) as the 'three Ss' – Saris, Samosas and Steel bands. This approach is well illustrated by the following statement from the government's Select Committee on Race Relations, 1968–9, cited in Carby (1982b: 194):

> ...much can ... be done ... to create better understanding of the national and cultural background of immigrants.

Its recommendations included:

> Specific teaching about the countries from which the immigrants in a particular town come. Here material direct from those countries can be displayed in the classroom by immigrant children. Children in primary schools in Hackney or Brixton, for example, could be taught West Indian songs, or children in Wolverhampton be taught Indian art, jewellery and costumes. This would help bring the immigrant children into the life of the school.

Although its adherents were for the most part well meaning, in practice this approach did little more than essentialize cultural difference and generate crude caricatures of 'Asian' or 'West Indian' culture. Radical-left critiques saw it as essentially an exercise in social control (Carby 1982b) – luring minority children into acquiescing in their own exploitation by appearing to respond to their needs. Others attacked the policy from a quite different perspective, suggesting that it represented unwarranted 'special treatment' for minorities. Both were presented with ample ammunition for their critiques. There were stories of teachers being sent on fact-finding trips to the former colonies to observe cultural differences for themselves. For critics on the Right, such 'profligacy' merely compounded concerns about the extra expense incurred by changes to curricula. Others, of course, saw the trips as an eerie reminder of much earlier forays into the former colonies by missionaries and anthropologists.

On the positive side, MCE did at least constitute an official systemic response to the increasingly diverse school population. It made a conscious commitment to respecting the belief systems of faiths other than Christianity. It also helped to bring about a greater sense of relevance to classroom discussions about geography, history, arts, music and the media.

The problem, as with the Black Studies movement in the US, was that new teaching material was essentially tacked onto the existing curriculum. It therefore tended to be seen as supplementary, rather that integral, to the existing syllabus. And crucially, it was often viewed as of more relevance (or even *only* of relevance) to the migrant, rather than to the 'indigenous', child.

The most significant problem, though, was that it did not address, at least directly, the main issue for schools. It assumed that racism was simply a question of ignorance; that with a concerted attempt to educate young citizens about the nature and value of cultural diversity, it would wither away. As has been seen in previous chapters, racism is far too deeply embedded in common-sense 'knowledge' (even amongst children) for this approach to bear fruit.

Racism is about power relations outwith the specific context of the school and the educational system. But its effects are also in evidence within schools, with instances of insensitive, ethnocentric and even racist behaviour on the part of teachers and other staff (Mason 2000: 71). This, combined with an ongoing debate about 'underachievement' on the part of minority children (see below), provided the rationale for the introduction of Anti-Racist Education (ARE).

MCE was never adopted in a universal fashion in English schools. Authorities representing the 'white highlands' were loathe to accept that they had a 'problem' in their area (that is, children of minority background). The argument that *all* children need to be prepared for entry into a multicultural adult society was rarely seen as persuasive, nor was the point that areas are not hermetically sealed (as 'white') in perpetuity. Its application was even patchy elsewhere. Given this, and in the absence of a strong lead from government, it was never likely that ARE would gain universal approval. It would, after all, entail a radical form of intervention into the culture and ethos of the school (as well as the curriculum).

Few authorities took a robust approach to ARE. Those that did were prone to attack from neo-liberal politicians. One such authority was Brent, in northwest London. Brent became the symbol of an 'extremist'/'loony' form of intervention in schools. Cross (with Brar and McLeod 1991) provides a dispassionate account of the authority's wide-ranging review of curriculum and school management. Rather then 'doing good by stealth', Troyna's characterization of the normal process of educational system evolution, Brent undertook a root and branch re-appraisal of the education delivered to local children.

They disposed of the remnants of MCE, symbolized most prominently by the suspension of a universally popular headteacher, Maureen McGoldrick (for allegedly making a 'racist remark' to a council official). What amounted to a local inspectorate was then set up to oversee the installation of teachers committed to ARE. The degree of radicalism, and the fact that even many

South Asian and African-Caribbean parents opposed the apparent system chaos, left the authority vulnerable to attack from even the mainstream media. Most notable here was a programme screened in 1986 as part of the BBC's long-running flagship documentary series *Panorama*. Entitled 'Brent Education Rules OK' this represented a savage indictment of a school system allegedly captured, and subverted, by a small clique of left-wing ideologues determined to impose their will irrespective of opposition from the 'voices of reason' (including Mrs McGoldrick and other proponents of MCE).

Some local authorities professed commitment to the idea of ARE, and undertook a more limited review of pedagogic practice and management style (Troyna and Carrington 1990). Others did little more than re-package and re-badge existing MCE policies. This led many commentators to argue that, although very different in theory, MCE and ARE tended in practice to differ little (Carby 1982b; Troyna 1993).

Backlash and retrenchment

A savage blow to the ARE cause was dealt by an incident in the playground of Burnage High School in Manchester in 1986 (Macdonald et al. 1989; Troyna and Hatcher 1992). Following a fight, a 13-year-old Asian boy, Ahmed Iqbal Ullah, was stabbed by a white classmate and died from his wounds. The focus of the subsequent inquiry turned to the school's ARE policy. Why, it was asked, had a policy aiming to defuse conflict between children of different ethnic backgrounds failed so abjectly in this case?

It was decided that the ultimate culprit was an unintended consequence (of the policy). Many white working-class boys were already disaffected by what to them seemed an alien school culture that regarded them as stupid and worthless. Being told by teachers operating the ARE policy that they were also racist had merely served to alienate them even further.

This provoked further national debate about the aims and objectives of ARE and how such policy might be implemented sensitively. But as early as the late 1970s there had been increasing question marks around the one issue which had been used to justify both MCE and ARE – underachievement. In 1979, the then Labour government sponsored an inquiry chaired by Anthony (Lord) Rampton. This was tasked to investigate the roots of educational un-derachievement, the premise being the 'fact' that young males of African-Caribbean origin performed consistently worse than other minorities. This had become so much part of common-sense knowledge that it had long been incorporated into the syllabi of prospective teachers, in the process becoming a self-fulfilling prophecy. Teachers had literally been trained to observe the problem, not question its existence.

Rampton endorsed the orthodox view, but argued that institutional racism was a serious problem to be addressed. This angered the incoming Thatcher administration, which sought to argue that 'racial'/ethnic (and even class) differentials were no longer a significant issue, being merely a fiction created by outmoded socialist dogma. Unfortunately for them, however, the 'race' issue would not go away. Serious outbreaks of urban violence in 1980 and 1981 were designated 'race riots' by politicians, media and (even) some in academia (see Chapter 8).

Rampton stepped down as Chair, allegedly because of disagreements with government. The agenda was subsequently taken up by Lord Swann (Troyna and Carrington 1990). His Commission endorsed the position on institutional racism taken by Rampton, but failed to say how schools might address the problem (apart from a number of comments on the curriculum – Mason 2000: 73). Worse than this, it individualized what was effectively a collective problem, by endorsing the use of Racism Awareness Training (RAT). On the basis of the 'rotten apple theory of racism', offending teachers would be taken out of the classroom and subjected to retraining. This is, of course, much easier to do than to address a collective institutional failure.

On the positive side, Swann championed the cause of targeted recruitment drives so as to increase the number of teachers from the minority communities. Extra resources would be devoted to this end. It also focused in some depth on the value of creating an atmosphere which emphasizes the value of cultural diversity.

Like Rampton, the Swann Report (1985) reiterated the facts of 'underachievement'. As Troyna (1988) rightly points out, however, the analysis was deeply flawed. The crude label 'Asian' was used to represent a large number of culturally and ethnically distinct migrant groups and, to compound the error, birthplace was used as the basis for classification. The lack of a serious analysis of the influence of social class also made it difficult to say how much differential educational performance could be explained by class rather than ethnicity (or, for that matter, some other factor such as gender or school attended). As Mirza (1992) argued, global data on those of African-Caribbean background conceals marked gender differences, young women performing consistently better than their male counterparts.

Class background clearly has a major influence on performance, both directly and indirectly. The middle-class child (irrespective of ethnicity) is likely to benefit both from a relatively privileged socialization and a more generously funded school outside an inner urban area. Because of what we shall learn in the next chapter, this largely explains why those defined (in conventional census terms) as 'Indian' tend to leave school with better results than their poorer Pakistani and Bangladeshi neighbours (irrespective of gender).

The real danger of the erroneous analysis from Swann, however, lay in its impact on those policies which sought to redress ethnic differentials in measured outcomes: MCE and ARE. As Troyna (1988) argues, the results seemed to justify the arguments championed by proponents of cultural deficit theory. If 'Asians' not only performed better than 'black' pupils, but sometimes (even) out-performed whites, then surely this casts doubt on the need for ARE (as racism would presumably impact upon Asians too)? Also, if those from different cultural and ethnic backgrounds achieved such different results, is it wise to treat all cultures as equally conducive to educational advancement (as MCE does)?

This reinforced both the stereotyping and pathologization of various aspects of minority cultures and practices (Lawrence 1982b) and played into the hands of the Conservative government, which had remained implacably opposed to the entire equalities agenda. They saw both MCE and ARE as examples of 'political correctness' and as unwarranted intrusions into traditional teaching methods and curricula. As a consequence, in the first half of the 1980s they pursued a 'softening-up' strategy (Troyna and Carrington 1990) in preparation for the introduction of a radical piece of legislation, the *Education Reform Act 1988 (ERA)*.

Local education authorities stood accused of squandering tax-payers' money on initiatives which failed to deal with what for them were the real issues. Black youth and their families were demonized for an alleged lack of (male) parental discipline. Asian migrants, on the other hand, were seen as holding back their children if English was not the first language spoken in the home or if they spent time out of the country visiting relatives in the subcontinent.

The fundamental idea behind the ERA was that local authorities could not be trusted to provide effective leadership in education. Standards would be restored by the imposition of a national curriculum that would spell a return to more traditional teaching methods and (British or, more precisely, English) values, and syllabi committed to the acquisition of core skills. Gone would be such things as 'anti-racist mathematics, whatever that might be ...' to repeat an oft-quoted jibe by Prime Minister Margaret Thatcher. Literature would mean **English** Literature (especially the classics by Shakespeare, Dickens, Brontë et al.); history would mean **English** history. Languages would mean modern European languages.

Although guidance notes from the then Department of Education and Science advised schools about the need to prepare pupils for adulthood in a multicultural society, this appeared very much an add-on to an already full curriculum. More significant still was the introduction of Local Management of Schools (LMS). This plan to devolve power to individual schools and their governing bodies would mean, of course, that the local authority would lose its former powers to influence education policy in its area. It would now be up to individual schools (assuming LMS approval) to decide whether or not to develop and implement equalities policies. In the context of scarce resources this was always unlikely. Much would also depend on whether a school's board of governors had a sizeable representation from minority communities (unlikely outside certain urban locations).

It was not until the year following the introduction of the legislation that the first major investigation of the influence of schools on the likely performance of minority children was published. Smith and Tomlinson (1989) assessed the significance of the 'school effect', dispensing in the process with some of the cruder explanations of the relationship between ethnicity and educational achievement. Although the findings are complex and open to misinterpretation, most notably the erroneous idea that the 'ethnic penalty' is a myth, 'disadvantage' being a function of the school attended rather than its ethnic composition (Gillborn 1990), it brought a greater sense of realism to educational debates. It confirmed what most professional observers already 'knew', that the education of minority children was being jeopardized by poorly funded inner urban schools, and enhanced *(but to varying degrees)* by 'better' schools.

As to what constitutes a better school, there are a number of key problem areas. In the interests of brevity, these can be summarized under four headings: effective leadership, steering, exclusions policy and rationing.

Effective leadership

This covers all aspects of the running of a school, but especially important is the combination of discipline, high expectations (of all pupils, irrespective of ethnicity, gender and class background), and the creation of a learning culture which genuinely respects diversity, in deed as well as in theory. This implies being aware of those elements of custom and practice which impinge negatively on minorities (for example dress codes, social activities, and so on). Bullying and harassment, and not just where minorities are the victims, need to be confronted firmly. The environment of the school must also be one 'in which minority ethnic group students feel psychologically safe' (Blair 2002: 190). More than this, Blair argues that the most effective leadership is one which is not afraid to use positive action to motivate minority students.

Steering

In the previous chapter we saw evidence of 'racial'/ethnic steering based on essentialist and determinist notions of ethnicity. Parallel processes remain common in schools even on the part of otherwise well-meaning teachers. High on the agenda here is the question of subject choice (Mason 2000). This goes far beyond obvious forms of stereotyping where, for example, the interests of African-Caribbean students are assumed to lie solely in sport (Mac an Ghaill 1988, 1992) and music. As Alibhai-Brown (2000) argues, South

Asian girls (and not only Muslims) still, all too frequently, face the problem that teachers assume they will be compelled by their families to leave school as soon as is legally possible (that is, when they reach 16 years of age); the corollary being that there is no point motivating them to achieve. The interviews conducted by Bradby (1999) shows just how false these assumptions can be. A more general issue is that option choices can be critical to the chances of appropriate forms of employment or further and higher education.

Exclusions

One of the major effects of alienation brought about by poor leadership and insensitive policies in the face of a polyethnic student body has been a rise in school suspensions and, more especially, exclusions. All the available evidence suggests that males of African-Caribbean origin are far more likely to be permanently excluded than any other group (Bourne et al. 1994; Gillborn and Gipps 1996; Runnymede Trust 2000: 152). But there is evidence that this is ultimately the outcome of a series of rather more insidious 'exclusionary' processes. Teacher training folklore, as was noted earlier, has embraced the notion that these children are to be expected to under-perform. This expectation (rather than evidence) has been shown to result in allocation to inappropriately low streams in key subjects. Role ascription, that is applying assumed group characteristics to individuals, then often associates poor performance with resistance to the aims of the institution (the children having 'chips on their shoulders'). Ostensibly similar behaviour on the part of white, South Asian or (say) Chinese students is much less likely to be interpreted in the same way or regarded as justifying a similar punishment (Ratcliffe 1999b).

Rationing

This problem has become even more serious in the wake of the 'GCSE 5 A–C economy'. The passing at grades A to C of five or more subjects at the General Certificate of Secondary Education (GCSE) has become the 'gold standard' for assessing achievement at the statutory minimum school-leaving age. At the same time schools are ranked in league tables on the basis of the proportion of students who achieve this standard. Many prominent educationalists have contested the validity of this crude measure as a core performance indicator, principally on the grounds that it does not convey any sense of 'value added'. In other words, it is simply not valid to use this statistic to compare the 'performance' of poorly funded and staffed urban schools with suburban schools with a more privileged student body. Gillborn and Youdell (2000) point to a rather more sinister consequence, however. Those students who are seen by teachers as destined to 'let the school down' (by failing to reach the standard) may receive less attention than those considered potential achievers. Even worse, there is now effectively an incentive to 'exclude' those considered disruptive, especially if they are likely to impinge on the performance of others. These points explain why the authors refer to the 'rationing' of education. Male students of African-Caribbean origin once again appear to suffer disproportionately.

Alternative educational futures: separatism or diversity?

Although we have largely focused in this chapter on state policies to redress 'underachievement', it is important to recognize that minority communities have developed local support strategies (usually with a rather broader educational remit). The Saturday school movement pioneered by African-Caribbean communities around the country was already in evidence in the 1960s (Rex and Tomlinson 1979). Mosques, temples and community centres have served a parallel function in the case of South Asians.

These developments were almost universally welcomed as a highly positive form of community self-help. The fact that they were examples of ethnically segregated schooling was not seen as a problem because they were simply supplementing the efforts of (integrated) state schooling. There has, however, been increasing demand over the last few years for separate schooling, largely, though not exclusively, from Muslim communities. This is justified on religious, cultural and pedagogic grounds. As Islam is about a whole way of life, it is not possible to separate the public from the private domain. It was also argued that the state school system was incompatible with Islam in a number of respects, not least in the area of gender relations. There were also concerns that sections of Britain's Muslim population were also increasingly prone to 'underachievement'. Such fears were very evident in Bradford, where discursive representations of 'Muslim (male) youth' closely mirrored those traditionally applied to 'black (male) youth'. Increasing pressure from the Muslim Association in the city led in 2000 to the establishment of Britain's first Muslim state secondary school (Wainwright 2000).

The more general question of whether this should be seen as setting a broader precedent presented government with an extremely tricky dilemma. There have been Church of England, Roman Catholic and even Jewish state schools in Britain for many years. It was therefore difficult to argue against the *principle* of faith schools. They also tended to perform rather better than average on the government's own performance indicators. Furthermore, the proposal seemed to accord with the spirit of social inclusivity and the more participatory democracy championed by Tony Blair. The subtext was that he was known (not least though the choice of schooling for his own children) to favour 'selectivity', contrary to many on the left of his Party.

There were very good reasons why this new form of separatism might not represent a desirable development, however. As noted earlier, acute spatial segregation in a small number of urban areas in England is accompanied by forms of social cleavage represented as 'parallel lives'. The problem for policy-makers was how to de-segregate schools, not how to sponsor the creation of more, in this case along religious lines. This became an even more pressing concern in the wake of the urban unrest in spring and summer 2001 and then the events of 9/11.

Realizing that her views would be highly unpopular with many fellow Muslims, Alibhai-Brown (2000) added to the voices of those opposing segregated schooling in the form of faith schools. Her view was that this would simply increase levels of distrust between communities and was not in the long-term interests of a cohesive, multi-ethnic Britain.

The government's position gradually became more equivocal. From an initial position of support for the idea of faith schools, ministers began to suggest that conditions might be applied prior to approval. The key argument was that school governors would not be permitted to operate an exclusionary policy with respect to those of other ethnic or faith backgrounds. In fact, a certain proportion of places would effectively have to be reserved for (in our example) non-Muslims. As to the argument that there were already many faith schools in Britain, the response was that these did not formally restrict entry to members of a particular faith community. Government ministers also suggested that, with the benefit of hindsight, the formation of such schools may not have been wise.

Since the events of 2001 there seems to have been a general change of tack by the government. Initially welcoming the celebration of difference (as well as diversity), the policy focus has shifted to modes of integration and, some commentators have suggested, even assimilation. Further enhanced by continuing inflows of refugees and asylum seekers, there is a renewed emphasis on the universal acquisition of English language skills and a commitment to an (as yet ill-defined) notion of Britishness.

Higher education as a vehicle for intergenerational mobility

Lest this discussion has suggested that Britain's minorities have suffered to the point where they have a much smaller chance of further and higher education, it should be pointed out that this was not even the case a decade ago (Jones 1993; Modood et al. 1997). According to Labour Force Survey data from 1988–90 (quoted in Jones 1993: 42), 60 per cent of South Asian males and 53 per cent of South Asian females were in post-compulsory education (PCE). These are far higher than the comparable figures for both white and African-Caribbean groups. Levels of degree-level education also compare favourably, at least if we focus on those of Indian and East African Asian origin (rather than South Asians as a whole). African-Caribbeans are seen to be lagging behind somewhat (Jones 1993: 43).

Steady progress has been maintained since this period. So the obvious question is: is access to a university education now similar for all groups? The answer is a *very* qualified 'yes', but there have in the past been instances where universities and colleges have been found guilty of adopting overtly exclusionary practices. A high-profile formal investigation into the admissions procedures at St George's Hospital Medical School in London (Commission for Racial Equality 1988) revealed clear evidence of discrimination. Because of the high volume of applications, a computer program was designed to act as a supposedly objective filter mechanism. But rather than selecting applicants on (measured) aptitude, it actually imposed negative weightings on the bases of 'race' and gender. Interviews (for candidates not already filtered out at this first stage) then displayed a further lack of even-handedness.

This provoked a national debate on admissions policies and practices in higher education. In particular, it drew attention to the need both for ethnic monitoring and closer scrutiny of the degree of discretion accorded to selectors at departmental level. This has led to a great deal more transparency in matters such as entry grade requirements, these normally being published in college prospectuses. The problem remains, however, that the sheer volume of applications to any one institution means that only a limited number of offers can be made for a given course. In the absence of interviews, judgements are based solely on UCAS (Universities and Colleges Admissions Service) forms submitted by candidates. In the typical case, where school-leaving results are pending, these judgements have to be formed on the basis of 'potential'. Much depends, then, on past results, a personal statement and a reference from the headteacher (normally).

In so far as decisions are unsupervised, the system is open to discriminatory behaviour of various kinds. Especially in marginal cases the reference can play a significant role. Tutors must then rely upon the impartiality of the referee. Shiner and Modood (2002) argue that there is no evidence to say that these disfavour minorities nationally, but the author's personal experience over a number of years suggests otherwise. A factor that certainly is likely to affect the chances of entry, at least to one of the more prestigious universities, is the presence of resits. Research has consistently demonstrated that minority candidates are much more likely than whites to retake examinations to achieve a higher grade (Shiner and Modood 2002). The reason is quite simple in most cases: minority students feel that they need to acquire better results than their white colleagues in order to compete successfully.

This brings us to the core of the debate. Minorities, despite their well-documented problems in the school system, are now entering universities at rates similar to, or in the case of some groups higher rates than, whites. The key differences lie in the type of the university they attend, and the subjects they study (Modood et al. 1997; Shiner and Modood 2002). Minorities are far more likely to enter the 'new' universities than the more prestigious, older universities (DfEE 1998). They are also more likely to study vocational subjects. This matters because career prospects tend to be deeply compromised (as will be seen in the next chapter).

As to the 'choice' of new university, it has been suggested that this might relate to a cultural bias that favours institutions in certain urban locations. More specifically, minority students (such as those of South Asian heritage) may wish to live at home and attend the 'local' university. This is a seductive argument in the sense that many of the ex-polytechnics which comprise the 'new' sector are in urban areas close to minority concentrations. It is ultimately unconvincing, however, since 'new' and 'old' sector institutions in major cities such as London, Birmingham, Manchester, Leeds and Liverpool lie almost cheek by jowl.

The true explanation is likely to feature a number of factors. The more prestigious universities are very 'white' institutions, in terms both of their ethos and personnel, students and staff. Their selection procedures and the lack of effective (ethnic) monitoring are probably also partly responsible for maintaining the status quo (Phillips, Law and Turney 2003). But the main explanations are likely to lie outwith the universities.

Schools play a significant role in advising students on the appropriate choice of college. There is mounting evidence that they, at times inadvertently, reproduce (in their pupils' attitudes) particular stereotypes about institutions and the sort of students who attend them. As with other forms of 'racial'/ethnic steering, this is often done in a sincere belief that it is in the pupil's interest. Ethnically segregated peer group interaction in schools then serves to consolidate attitudes and leads to the clustering of applications to certain colleges. The end result, of course, is the maintenance of yet another form of ethnic segregation.

Phillips, Law and Turney (2003: 3) quote one young Bangladeshi male as saying, when asked about the University of Leeds, 'it is not for people like us'. The challenge for this and other 'old' universities is to overturn such perceptions. More outreach work in schools is one way of achieving this, but little in practice is likely to change until there is a step change in the universities themselves. In the same way that schools need to ensure that the culture and ethos of the learning environment embraces a very contemporary and inclusive multiculturalism, universities need to do much more to become places where staff and students feel equally valued irrespective of difference (reflected in 'race', ethnicity, religion, gender, and so on).

Further reading

As with many other areas dealt with in this volume, the literature on issues of 'race' and ethnicity in education is vast. Most mainstream texts such as Mason (2000) and Pilkington (2003) provide useful summaries of the key debates. The Parekh Report (Runnymede Trust 2000) situates contemporary issues in the context of the broader 'race' agenda. It looks, for example, at the implications for the education system of recent legislation and of the findings of the national inquiry into the murder of the black teenager Stephen Lawrence in 1993. The reader edited by Gill, Mayor and Blair (1993) remains an extremely useful source for those interested in debates about MCE and ARE.

As to the IQ debate (referred to somewhat briefly at the beginning of the chapter), Montagu (1999) represents probably the best and most accessible rebuttal of the argument that there is a correlation between 'race' and (natural, inherited) intelligence.

Prior to his untimely death in 1997, Barry Troyna was probably the most insightful and prolific writer in Britain in this area. His work has the merits of both commitment and clarity. For a lively account of the politics of educational policy up to the end of the 1980s, his book with Bruce Carrington (1990) is difficult to better. In some ways, his mantle has now been taken over by David Gillborn. He edits the journal *Race, Ethnicity and Education* and has written two key texts on the major issues facing 'real schools' (1990 and 1995). His latest book, co-authored with Deborah Youdell (2000), confronts a series of controversial features of the current testing and league table culture within the school system. As noted in the chapter, the core argument here is that some minority children are the principal victims of a process of 'rationing education'.

For those wishing to compare the British experience with the US, there are some excellent chapters on school desegregation, multicultural education and self-segregation on college campuses in the reader by Steinberg (2000).

7 'Race', Ethnicity and Labour Market Differentials

Introduction: historical debates

Much of what has been said in earlier chapters already conjures up a picture of labour market responses to the influx of New Commonwealth migrants in the immediate post-World War II era. The grudging acceptance of the need for such labour on the part of governments in the 1950s tells its own story. The controls imposed from the early 1960s onwards were an attempt to maximize the economic gains to the UK, whilst minimizing the assumed negative effects in social terms. As was seen in Chapter 4, the aim from the mid-1960s onwards was to attract skilled and professional workers. Recent concerns about the influx of refugees and asylum seekers are ultimately predicated not on a rejection of the need for labour, but on the fact that this is considered to be the 'wrong sort' of labour (in terms both of skills and 'race'/ethnic background). This explains why there are simultaneous, and ongoing, recruitment campaigns aimed at attracting large numbers of nurses, teachers and others from various EU countries.

This does not imply, of course, that migrants have always acquired employment commensurate with their skills. Apparent distrust of overseas qualifications often concealed discriminatory behaviour. There were many cases in the 1950s and 1960s of South Asian bus drivers with university degrees (Hiro 1971; Brooks 1975). In the medical profession, many well-qualified senior hospital doctors found themselves in unpopular specialisms or working as general practitioners in poor urban areas with significant minority concentrations. Female nurses from the Caribbean were steered towards the lesser qualification of SEN (State Enrolled Nurse) rather then SRN (State Registered Nurse), thereby limiting their career options. Cooke et al. (2003) suggest that discrimination in the health service remains rife, despite the massive growth of medical staff of minority origin but now educated in British schools.

Even in the absence of direct discrimination by employers, migrants have been disadvantaged by a number of factors noted in Chapters 5 and 6. The complex interplay of constraining and enabling forces that resulted in the spatial patterning described in detail in Ratcliffe (1996a) entailed a number of consequences stretching far beyond questions of housing and quality of life. For those in inner urban areas (and especially those without access to a car), access to appropriate job opportunities (and the broader networks that facilitate them) can be severely compromised. For children, access to a well-resourced and academically successful school is less likely. Overcrowded and unhealthy living conditions reduce further the chances of academic success, which in turn reduce the likelihood of finding work opportunities beyond those generated by the communities themselves (in what has been labelled, rather disparagingly, the ethnic enclave economy – see the review of literature in Mann 2002).

This is by no means the whole story, of course. Indeed, a key point from Chapter 4 merits repetition here. For at least four decades there has been a sizeable professional middle class amongst New Commonwealth migrants, especially amongst those of 'Indian' and East African Asian origin. Many of these migrants never experienced life in poor urban Britain; others who did have long since followed a growing trend of suburbanization and ex-urbanization (Phillips and Ratcliffe 2002). There have also been remarkable changes in the employment patterns of Britain's minorities, quite incompatible with the existence of universally exclusionary forces (Iganski and Payne 1996; Modood et al. 1997; Mason 2000; Cabinet Office 2003).

This chapter opens with a summary of the current labour market position of Britain's minorities, and discusses the ways this has changed over the past few decades. It then asks the obvious question, namely: how can we best explain the existing differentials both amongst these groups (and gender components thereof) and then between them and 'whites'? We then explore the motors of future change. This will be seen to raise a series of important issues:

- the role of education, and especially higher education, in promoting labour market advancement;
- differential shifts in the attitudes of young minority women towards education and career; and
- initiatives geared to improving the career opportunities of minorities by addressing discriminatory processes, both at an individual and institutional level.

The current labour market position of Britain's minorities

The simplest way of summarizing the current labour market position of minorities in Britain is to say that, taken as a whole, they still lag behind the majority (white) population in many respects. But this requires an important caveat. Certain groups, most notably those of Indian and Chinese origin, compare favourably with whites; the African-Caribbeans, Pakistanis and

Bangladeshis (and especially males within these groups) continue to lag behind, often to a significant extent (Mason 2000; Cabinet Office 2003).

The first thing to say about this is that it is no coincidence that these 'winners' and 'losers' mirror closely those emerging from parallel exercises in the previous two chapters (in relation to housing and education). Much more will be said about this in the next section, but the key point to bear in mind is that there is no simple process of cause and effect at work here. There is a highly complex patterns of relationships between these factors, and with other factors not directly considered thus far, most notably health and welfare and the relative significance of informal social networks. Before we can attempt to explain ethnic differentials in 'labour market position', however, we need to have a clear idea of what the term means.

There are a number of interrelated components:

- Economic activity status
- Occupational distributions by type and status
- The level and nature of self-employment
- Income

Given the existence of a highly gendered labour market, and the possible influence of cultural factors in attitudes to work, all of these need to focus on the relative positions of men and women.

Economic activity status

The economically active are those who are either in work (in the formal economy) or seeking work. The economically inactive comprise those who for a variety of reasons are not seeking employment, the largest groups being students, the retired, the disabled or long-term sick and those defined (in the British census) as 'at home and looking after the family'. Because of the substantive complexity of these categories and variations in the measurement of some of the constituent items (such as the notion of 'seeking work'), economic activity rates must always be treated with great caution. Age-specific rates should also be used wherever possible given radical differences between the age pyramids of the migrant groups and those of the white population (Coleman and Salt 1996). The key point here is that the former are much younger populations (especially the Bangladeshis, who were the most recent migrant group from the New Commonwealth). This is not surprising in that migrant groups are invariably more youthful than the populations they augment, but it is nevertheless extremely significant in labour market terms. Much larger proportions are of working age, and they are each destined to increase as a proportion of the total working population (a point to be picked up again later – also see Cabinet Office 2003: 22, Figure 2.2).

As Pilkington (2003: 66–7) points out, there are significant differences in the economic activity rates of minority ethnic groups, but even more important are the gender differences. The majority (white) population has the highest rate, a fact that Pilkington attributes in part to the higher proportion of minorities in further and higher education. There is another key factor that he fails to mention, however. Rates of long-term limiting illness amongst those of working age are significantly higher amongst the South Asian groups, and especially the poorer inner urban (largely Muslim) segments thereof. (This provokes a series of questions about the causal chain here, the direction of causality between employment, poverty, housing and living conditions (Ratcliffe 1996b).)

In terms of gender, African-Caribbean women tend to have similar rates of labour market participation to whites, but significantly higher rates than the Pakistanis and Bangladeshis. Many of the former group, of course, came to Britain as *primary* migrants (as distinct from dependants), and Mason (2000) correctly identifies distinctive gender relations as an additional factor. Labour market participation amongst Muslim women has traditionally been low.

Researchers in the past have tended to focus in particular on the impact of various elements of traditional culture (Jones 1993), most notably marriage systems and *purdah* (Saifullah Khan 1977, 1979; Wilson 1979) and on the lack of a good command of English (Owen et al. 2000), associated with a lack of contact with non-Asians. Constraints on interaction with unrelated males have then been associated with 'sweat-shop' exploitation and unregulated homeworking (Hoel 1982; Allen and Wolkowitz 1987; Phizacklea and Wolkowitz 1995). With rapidly increasing numbers of young women educated in British schools, these arguments will become less and less convincing over the coming decades, even allowing for the ongoing phenomenon of transnational marriages involving the immigration of non-English-speaking females (Simpson 1997).

Even more significant are variations in unemployment levels. Once again measurement issues cloud the analysis somewhat, in that the definition of 'unemployed' varies radically. The International Labour Office (ILO) refers to those seeking work for the past month; the Census of Population for England and Wales enumerates those regarding themselves as seeking work in the week prior to the official census date; and the measure used by the current government is 'out of work and claiming benefit'. Not surprisingly, these produce marked differences in unemployment rates. In the current context, however, the pattern remains much the same irrespective of the measure one uses.

Overall, minorities (both male and female in all age groups) are much more likely to be unemployed than the comparable white group. To quote a government research paper (DfEE 2000: 11):

Unemployment amongst ethnic minority (*sic*) men is up to three times higher than for white men – and for ethnic minority women, four times higher than for white women. In particular, ILO unemployment rates for Bangladeshi men and Pakistani men and women are much higher than other groups. Unemployment rates decline with increasing age for both men and women, but are typically at least twice as high for ethnic minorities as for white people in each age group.

The more recent Cabinet Office Report (2003) tells much the same story, but also adds an important historical dimension. Comparing rates in 2000 with those from eight years earlier, it argues (ibid.: 26) that whilst differentials had narrowed, male unemployment rates amongst Bangladeshis, Pakistanis and Black-Caribbeans remained 10–15 per cent higher than their white counterparts.

Crucially, the picture changes little if we restrict the analysis to second-generation migrants. In fact, it appears that the differentials between whites and minorities (both male and female) have actually widened through the 1990s to the point where, for example, 'unemployment rates of second-generation Black-Caribbean and Pakistani men were over twice those of White British men of the same age' (ibid.: 32).

There are a number of current government initiatives ostensibly aimed at reducing unemployment levels amongst minority youngsters, but the evidence suggests that these are less than fully effective. The *New Deal for Young People* is a case in point. Although some research has pointed to positive outcomes in respect of increasing employability (Fieldhouse, Kalra and Alam 2002), DfEE (2000: 2) is more circumspect:

> Early evidence ... shows that a lower proportion of ethnic minority people than whites move into unsubsidised or subsidised employment (25% compared to 33% of whites) and a higher proportion into education and training (59% compared to 44% of whites), despite being better qualified.

What this actually means is that many relatively well-qualified minority young people are finding themselves on a scheme which similarly qualified whites usually do not need (either because they already have a job or are in full-time education).

Occupational distributions by status and type

Focusing first on professional and managerial-level posts, there has been a modest increase in the proportion of all minorities through the 1990s. But, if we look at the differentials between minority groups, and then compare these with whites, a familiar pattern emerges. Indian men, initially as a direct by-product of immigration policy, have for the past three decades displayed similar proportions in this grade of post to white males. But apart from the Chinese (who exhibit a distinctive occupational distribution, as will be seen later), the other groups lag far behind.

As pointed out by the report referred to above:

> Similar patterns are found in respect to women. However, certain groups of women have experienced more rapid progress than others: in 2000, 16 per cent of working Indian women were in professional or managerial jobs, slightly higher than White women, for whom it was 15 per cent; while 13 per cent of working Black-Caribbean women fell into this category.
>
> (Cabinet Office 2003: 29)

This pattern conceals major variations in job type and status (as the professional/managerial category is extremely broad). The relatively high figure for Black-Caribbean women, for example, is inflated by concentrations in relatively junior health service posts. A high clustering of doctors amongst Indian men (around 1 in 20 of all those in work) hints at a rather less diverse spread of occupations than is the case for white men. This is to be expected given marked differences in the pattern of courses followed at the higher education level. The big question is what this means in terms of a possible equalization of career profiles. In the medical profession, the evidence still suggests that progression to high-level posts, especially in coveted specialisms, is more difficult for minority doctors (Cooke et al. 2000). Elsewhere, the evidence also confirms that it is too early to discount the 'glass ceiling effect' (in respect of ethnicity and gender).

One highly significant issue deferred from the previous chapter is the effect of university and course selection on the career prospects of minority graduates. The concentration in vocational subjects such as medicine, law, business and management studies, and computing should ensure an increasing minority presence in well-remunerated professions. On the down side, there is evidence that minority graduates find it less easy than white students to gain suitable (graduate-level) work and relatively few are able to acquire jobs in 'blue chip' (top public) companies. Here, probably the key issue is the disproportionate numbers attending the former polytechnics, that is the 'new' universities. Many of the top companies restrict their recruitment fairs and the annual 'milk round' (trawl of universities) to the more 'prestigious' institutions.

Turning the focus onto the manual/non-manual split we, not surprisingly, see the obverse of this picture. According to Modood et al. (1997: 100), two-thirds of Black-Caribbean, Pakistani and Bangladeshi males are in manual occupations, as compared with 50 per cent of white males, and 52 per cent and 44 per cent of those of Indian and African Asian origin respectively.

As to the data on manual work, these figures conceal significant differentials in the rates of shift-working. Pakistani men have been much more likely than other males to work shifts; amongst women those from the Caribbean have consistently held this dubious privilege. But Mason (2000: 52) employs data from Jones (1993) to suggest that younger minorities were less likely than the previous generation to be working shifts. Although the explanation for this is not immediately evident (and probably involves a number of issues), a key factor has to be the impact of de-industrialization on those manufacturing industries in which these groups (and especially the older Pakistani males) were concentrated.

The level and nature of self-employment

For reasons to be explored in the next section of the chapter, some minority groups exhibit relatively high levels of self-employment. The Cabinet Office Report (2003: 31) says that 'Pakistani and Indian men have higher rates of self-employment than their White counterparts. Black self-employment rates, by contrast, have been consistently lower than all other ethnic minority (*sic*) groups'. In terms of the small business sector nationally, however, the proportion that is minority-owned is consistent with the overall size of this component of the population. To be more specific 'around 7 per cent of all small businesses (are) in ethnic minority hands' (ibid: 31).

Thinking now about the business sector as a whole, there are major differences in type and scale between minority-owned businesses and those typically found amongst the majority (white) population. A high proportion of minority enterprises are very small in terms of both personnel and turnover. They are also more likely to have required little start-up capital. At the smallest scale is the 'own account worker', the most immediate example in today's urban scene being the taxi driver who owns his own cab (most, of course, are male). Other obvious cases would be independent building workers, plumbers and window cleaners; rather less obvious would be the growing numbers of businesses run from home. A walk around the streets of towns and cities such as Rochdale and Bradford now reveals ample evidence of estate agencies and travel agencies run, quite literally, from the front room of small terraced houses.

Other modestly sized minority businesses reliant on individual or family labour are likely to be in textiles (as either manufacturer or trader, or both), catering, or the ubiquitous corner shop. These tend to be very much niche enterprises (Owen 1997; Pilkington 2003: 76). What is particularly significant about this is that, by the early 1990s at least, they were not in the 'growing service sector and high technology industries' (Owen 1997: 66, cited in Pilkington 2003). This being said, it would be wrong to assume that this position is not undergoing subtle changes. There is ample evidence around the country that many small businesses are becoming unviable, not so much because of declining profitability (though this clearly is a common problem) but because the younger generations of more highly educated minorities are increasingly unwilling to take on what are widely regarded as 'unglamorous' occupations. This applies in particular to South Asian and Chinese youngsters (given the pattern of business ownership). For this reason the 'open-all-hours' Asian-run corner shop is becoming an increasingly rare sight, with an estimated decline of more than 20 per cent over the past decade (Brown 2002).

Whether the young people turned off by these 'traditional' businesses nevertheless become entrepreneurs remains to be seen. The likelihood is that many will enter the professions, most notably (judging by the pattern of courses followed at university) the 'new' professions dominated by information technology.

Income levels

Taking all of these factors into consideration, it is perhaps not surprising that the average income levels of minorities (both men and women) lag significantly behind those enjoyed by whites. Also to be expected are massive variations between minority groups. The recent Cabinet Office Report (2003: 27) summarizes the key points as follows:

- In 1994 and 2000, Bangladeshi men were the most disadvantaged group, their average weekly net earnings being between 45 and 52 per cent below those of their White counterparts (£109 less in 1994 and £155 less in 2000).
- Over the same period, Indian men were least disadvantaged, earning 8 per cent less than Whites in 1994, but 3 per cent more by 2000 (£20 less in 1994 and £10 more in 2000).

Now, one has to bear in mind that there is significant 'internal' variation by, for example, class and location. Even more crucial are two key issues, however. These data tell us little about *household* income (and do not, of course, mean very much in the absence of parallel data on household size and structure). They also, by definition, tell us nothing about those households where no one is in paid work (in the formal economy). The latter point is particularly important in certain urban localities. Ratcliffe (1996b), for example, reported that in the mid-1990s around a half of Pakistani and Bangladeshi households in Bradford were in this position (by virtue of a combination of factors, but primarily unemployment, long-term illness or disability).

When households become the unit of analysis, the picture, as Mason (2000: 52–3) argues, becomes extremely complex. Pakistani and Bangladeshi households still emerge as the poorest of the principal minority groups (Berthoud 1998), and only the Chinese come out, unambiguously, as having similar incomes to white households. Even the Indian and African-Asian households are more likely to be living in poverty than their white counterparts.

Later in the chapter we will reflect on the likely future economic and occupational trajectories of Britain's minorities, drawing important parallels and contrasts with the US situation. For the present, however, the focus turns to attempts to explain the labour market differentials outlined thus far.

Sociological explanations for ethnic differentials in labour market position

The first point is essentially a reminder of an earlier argument. The 'groups' that form the basis of our analysis constitute merely one particular 'slicing' of social reality. It is, we hope, a more meaningful one than possible alternatives, but the 'minority groups' to which we routinely refer are only 'groups' in a highly qualified sense. We must also, taking on board the essence of Carter (2000), beware of unguarded remarks that impute, even implicitly, a direct causal link between 'race' (or ethnicity) and labour market position. The juxtaposition of these factors in previous sections of the chapter needs to be carefully scrutinized in what follows.

Sociological explanations of labour market differentials have taken a number of very different forms. First, there are a series of macro-analyses driven by a search for the ultimate causes of structural inequality. Prominent here are the underclass thesis, the notion of racialized class fractions, segmented labour market theory, and (various) theories of globalization. In contemporary analyses, some of these have been reinterpreted under the rubric, or rhetorical discourse, of 'social exclusion'. The common feature of all of these is that they are about what society and markets therein do to people. In other words, they largely deny the efficacy of social agency.

The second, and undoubtedly most common, form of analysis in the social science literature argues that the labour market position of minorities can be explained by direct or indirect discrimination, racism(s), or the presence of racialized market relations. Once again, these explanations lean heavily towards the idea of structural constraint, that minorities are in the position they are as a result of various forms of (external) social regulation.

The third approach concedes a more prominent role for agency on the part of minorities but argues that they suffer from various forms of 'lack', or deficit. Put simply, they do not possess the social capital to compete effectively. This form of analysis takes a number of forms: language problems, the lack of appropriate skills, faulty job search strategies, and so on.

The fourth, and final, approach argues that much of what we observe in terms of occupational patterns, is a direct result of (positive) social agency. The emphasis here is much more on achievements rather than deficits. In other words, discrimination is an unfortunate day-to-day reality to be confronted by minorities, but they are able to transcend this by virtue of a variety of strategies. The focus, then, is on the effective marshalling of cultural resources to secure a particular niche in the labour market. Cultural and ethnic difference are therefore factors to be celebrated as resources rather than actual, or potential, deficits.

Rather than representing an exhaustive list of explanatory models, these should be seen as representing notional points on a continuum from structural determinism to (a somewhat compromised form of) enablement and empowerment. As with the attempt to explain migration processes in Chapter 4, it will be argued that inherent weaknesses of each (given the sheer complexity of the empirical evidence) means that a more nuanced approach needs to be taken. (Given constraints on space, a greater emphasis than usual will be placed on the core readings listed at the end of the chapter.)

Beginning with the structural explanations, there is much to be said in favour of Pilkington's (2003) scepticism. As argued in Chapter 4, when these arguments were first outlined, the notion of an imported 'reserve army of labour' destined to fulfil the role of an underclass had a certain appeal. It was no accident, however, that the earliest forms of this model emanated from the US (Cox 1970), where the slave economy ensured a virtual 'caste line' between black and white portions of society. The fact that this 'color line' endures in twenty-first-century urban life, gives added weight to the notion of a permanent underclass (thereby explaining its continuing appeal in US social science). But, as will be seen in the final two chapters, this theorization ultimately fails even in the US case.

It certainly does not fit the UK experience of migration from the New Commonwealth. Major progress in economic and career terms by Britain's minorities combined with comparatively little evidence to support the notion of permanent 'exclusion' from the formal economy, fatally undermines the underclass thesis (Pilkington 2003). (If there is to be support for the 'theory', this would come from an analysis of the position of asylum seekers compelled to work illegally (usually at wages well below the statutory minimum wage) due to the denial of the legal right to work.)

As Phizacklea and Miles (1990) recognized, although these migrants often acted as a replacement labour force in low-status jobs that the indigenous population did not want, professional and skilled personnel were the main target of immigration policy. The Indian professional middle class was already a major feature of the UK social scene in the 1960s and 1970s, and not solely a result of more recent advances, a point not properly reflected in some key texts (Miles 1982; Mason 2000). What Phizacklea and Miles did, in developing the idea of racialized class fractions, was to argue that the weaker ideological position of minorities meant that even those who might appear to be 'winners' in career terms were not unreservedly so. But this still placed 'race' in a secondary explanatory role compared with class, and downplayed the efficacy of agency (by downplaying very real achievements).

Whilst it is undeniably the case that a large proportion of early migrants were employed in declining, increasingly uncompetitive industries, either as replacement labour or as a measure designed to compensate for under-capitalization (Duffield 1988), this could not be interpreted as a permanent feature of the labour market. De-industrialization undoubtedly had a disproportionate effect on these communities, contributing in the process to raised long-term unemployment levels amongst the older first generation. And inner urban deprivation combined with physical isolation from areas with a vibrant, burgeoning local economy, still combine to constrain the opportunities of many from the younger generations.

The globalization of economic relations is also, arguably, a core element in the widening differentials between rich and poor. But, in view of the evidence presented earlier, it would be difficult to sustain the argument that the contemporary UK labour market remains segmented along specifically 'racial' or ethnic lines. A degree of labour market segregation, partly as a result of the 'separate lives' phenomenon, is a necessary but not sufficient condition for this.

Leaving aside for the moment the issue of discrimination, we move on to consider the question of social capital. As Mason (2000: 55–6) argues, three reasons have been given for the disadvantage suffered by minorities: language, job skills and job search. 'Lack' in any, some or all of these has been seen by some as explaining labour market 'exclusion'. A poor command of English can, and clearly does, restrict access to many jobs, irrespective of status and pay (Modood et al. 1997). It does not, however, preclude the acquisition (say) of highly marketable IT skills (a fact that may well partly account for the concentration of Chinese students in UK degree programmes); nor does it explain why labour market differentials transcend generations (Mason 2000: 55).

The lack of appropriate job skills and qualifications can obviously impact on job opportunities, irrespective of ethnicity. First-generation migrants, as argued earlier, often came to the UK with degrees and diplomas from overseas institutions. Many employers either refused to accept these as equivalent to those awarded by UK universities and colleges, or were suspicious of their authenticity. Subsequent generations do not suffer this indignity and, as we have seen, display higher rates of Post Compulsory Education (PCE) than whites.

The 'underachievement thesis' retains an insidious presence, however, now being applied to other groups alleged to be replicating the experience of African-Caribbean males, most notably working-class Bangladeshis. This labelling process inevitably impacts on careers advice and subsequent employment prospects (Cross et al. 1990). As Mason (2000: 55) argues, the relationship between qualifications and labour market position is a complex one, varying between minority groups and job type (see also Modood et al. 1997). But the general pattern shows minorities faring worse (after controlling for qualifications) in both the likelihood of unemployment and job level. This probably also accounts for the higher than average level of qualifications possessed by minorities on the *New Deal for Young People* (DfEE 2000).

It has long been recognized that the effectiveness of a person's job search strategy is central to career prospects (Dex 1978/9). The Cabinet Office Report (2003: 43) suggests that some of the difficulties faced by minorities relate to two forms of social capital, 'bridging' and 'bonding'. It argues that because of strong community networks facilitated (especially in the case of South Asians) by spatial segregation, minorities have a high degree of bonding social capital. This results in the generation of jobs serving the needs and aspirations of these communities and contributes to thriving local economies. The more successful businesses are those for which turnover derives in the main from the majority population.

Bridging social capital, which requires broader links to job opportunities is seen as more of a problem for minorities. The idea is quite simple. Many well-paid occupations are in companies or employment sectors dominated by whites, largely because recruitment remains largely 'word-of-mouth' (Commission for Racial Equality 1982). The Cabinet Office Report (2003: 43) accuses the media as being particularly prone to this, strictly illegal, procedure (see Chapter 10). Conscious of the need to widen their appeal, the visual media seem to be taking at least some steps to rectify this. Whether the changes are market-led or a result of the possible threat of legal sanction the end result is positive.

Job search procedures may also be limited by neighbourhood and community factors. Those with social obligations to kin are known to impose limits on travel-to-work time (Thomas 1998; Owen and Green 2000). In so far as the range and frequency of employment opportunities in the immediate vicinity of inner urban areas is limited, these groups will suffer. As is well known, the areas in which South Asian settlement has taken place (with the important exception of the capital) have been those where opportunities for work were plentiful in the 1950s and 1960s. In towns like Bradford there has been little, in terms of inward investment, to replace the textile mills and ancillary businesses (Ratcliffe et al. 2001). The effects are even more serious for women (Mason 2000).

Some of these remarks have hinted at the presence of discriminatory practices. Deferring discussion of this issue once again, we turn to the fourth approach to explaining labour market inequalities: culture and ethnic difference. In the previous paragraph it was noted that some minority group members would exercise certain choices that effectively imposed limits on the range of available job opportunities. Earlier in the chapter, it was also argued that cultural differences might explain the massive differentials between, for example, the economic activity rates of African-Caribbean as against South Asian Muslim women, the particularly high rate of the former group being associated with an equalization of gender roles and the relative autonomy of the female (Mirza 1992).

Some would regard differential patterns both of university attended and courses studied therein, as due in part to 'traditional' cultural values (Shiner and Modood 2002). But is the popularity (say) of medicine amongst Asian students primarily a function of cultural difference, or rather the by-product of an awareness that there is already a large number of Asian doctors in the health service? This was, after all, a major aim of post-war immigration from the subcontinent. Today's students are also likely to know family members, kin and friends who work, or have worked, in hospitals or as general practitioners.

It has been suggested that there is also, amongst some migrant groups, a cultural predisposition towards self-employment and entrepreneurialism (Ballard and Ballard 1977; Cabinet Office 2003: 27) or, conversely, a negative predisposition in the case of others, most notably African-Caribbeans (Mason 2000). Others, whilst making no direct reference to cultural norms, nevertheless argue that migrants deploy traditional skills to exploit niche markets. In the case of the highly successful Chinese catering industry, therefore, it is often thought that these cooking skills were honed prior to arrival in the UK. In contrast, recent research by Mann (2002) demonstrates that this was far from being the norm. Most of those in the catering industry had no such prior skills. They identified the niche, learnt the appropriate skills, and then adapted various strains of 'Chinese' cuisine to suit British tastes, and, as with 'Indian' cuisine, invented some entirely new dishes in the process. The result is a commodification of invented tradition.

The big question is whether this development was the result of choice (irrespective of the causal chain) driven by external constraining forces (which may also, of course, be culturally based) or, perhaps, a combination of both. This leads naturally to the third mode of explanation: discrimination as exclusionary process. Ram (1992) argues that minorities in Britain set up small businesses essentially as a direct response to various forms of racism which restricted access to other forms of employment.

De-industrialization led to extremely high levels of unemployment amongst poor working-class migrants, and they undoubtedly found it extremely difficult to find alternative work. In the case of northern textile workers, the response of many was to acquire an inexpensive car and use it as a taxi (Kalra 2000). Others, in cities such as Bradford, entered catering, distribution and textiles. The common feature of most was that only relatively modest amounts of start-up capital were required. Had it not been for discrimination in the financial services sector (Ram 1992; Barratt 1999), this would have been less of a problem. In the event, it has led to many being dangerously under-capitalized, and therefore destined to operate at the margins of profitablity (Ward and Jenkins 1984).

Assessing the weight of evidence, it is difficult to escape the conclusion that discrimination, either direct or indirect, individualized or institutional, still represents a powerful constraint on the career prospects of Britain's minorities (Modood et al. 1997; Mason 2000, 2003; Cabinet Office 2003; Pilkington 2003). Sometimes this is quite subtle, for example steering by (say) careers officers (Lee and Wrench 1981; Cross, Wrench and Barnett 1990). As in many other cases it normally goes unrecognized, revealed only by the sort of experimental testing procedures used by Brown and Gay (1985) or by the uncovering of word-of-mouth recruitment as in the case of the CRE formal investigation of the Massey Ferguson plant in Coventry (Commission for Racial Equality 1982).

The fact that discrimination on the basis of 'race', colour, nationality or ethnic origin has been illegal since the entry onto the Statute Book of the Race Relations Act 1968 has in many cases simply had the effect of driving the process underground. Exclusionary policies and practices have become covert rather than overt. This applies not only to matters of recruitment, but also to other human resource concerns, such as training, promotion and disciplinary procedures. As will be seen in Chapter 10, to back up the non-discrimination legislation the CRE has developed a range of policy guidance documents geared to ensuring equality of treatment, starting with a Code of Practice approved by parliament as far back as two decades ago (Commission for Racial Equality 1984a).

So, where does this leave us in trying to develop an adequate model for understanding the labour market position of minorities? Racism and a panoply of discriminatory processes have to be placed at the core, but this cannot hope to explain the massively different experiences and achievements of the various groups. Migration to Britain involved extremely disparate groups with very different class, wealth, educational and skill backgrounds as well as radically different cultural traditions. These factors influenced their initial location in British society, in both spatial and material senses. The legacy of these remains all-pervasive, even half a century later.

As we have seen, spatial location influences access to education and then to employment. Irrespective of whether or not discriminatory mechanisms in the marketplace were initially to blame, those who remain in poor inner urban locations suffer a number of additional 'ethnic penalties'. Career prospects are often compromised through lack of local investment caused by the fact that these areas are not attractive to business (DETR 2001). Individuals from these areas may suffer negative treatment by potential employers, not just because of their 'racial'/ethnic identity but due to 'postcode discrimination', negative stereotyping of the 'type' of people who live in the area concerned.

Cultural factors also clearly play a constraining or enabling role in job search strategies, sometimes both. They also influence decisions as to whether or not, for example, women enter the formal labour market, and if so under what conditions. But the key point to remember is that cultures are not frozen in aspic. To assume, as some teachers have, that there is no point grooming Asian girls for higher education or a career because they are destined for marriage and a life of domesticity is obviously unacceptable (Alibhai-Brown 2000). Such essentialist thinking flies in the face of increasing evidence that Asian women (including Muslims) are delaying marriage, sometimes indefinitely, to pursue career goals (Bradby 1999). This is a parallel form of essentialism to that which blights the futures of many African-Caribbean males: in this case the assumption that they are destined to fail. This is cultural essentialism as social regulation.

What is clear from this analysis is that an explanatory model needs to incorporate a complex interplay of enabling and constraining forces, none of which can be assumed to be fixed temporally. To imply as some have that either racism(s) or cultural difference (or, say, religion – Cabinet Office 2003: 39) or some form of 'deficit' on the part of minority groups (on its own) explains labour market differentials is misguided.

Work and the future: towards a more inclusive Britain?

The historical legacy of earlier migrant generations has left an indelible imprint on the prospects of current generations of workers, and would-be workers. That much progress has been made is undeniable. The record numbers of minority students, both male and female, in colleges and universities demonstrate a high commitment to career advancement, in the face of a continued reluctance on the part of many employers to hire them.

The current government has announced a commitment to ending discrimination in employment over the coming decade (Cabinet Office 2003: 8), but it remains to be seen whether this will be accompanied by positive action. The portents are not good. Intervention into the human resource policies of private employers sits uneasily alongside the neo-liberal economic philosophy inherited from the previous administration. An espousal of the equalities agenda is therefore accompanied by a softly-softly approach to the promotion of change. As will be seen in Chapter 10, new legislation in the form of the Race Relations (Amendment) Act 2000, provides the potential for a more inclusive labour market. The key is a new statutory duty on public authorities not only to promote better 'race' relations but also to ensure that they, and all firms from whom they procure goods and services, do not discriminate on the basis of 'race', colour, nationality or ethnic origin (Orton and Ratcliffe 2003).

It is unrealistic to expect the equal representation of minority groups in all places of work across Britain, if only for the fact that spatial patterns are, and are destined to remain, somewhat disparate. Also, whether the result of 'choice', pragmatism or mere serendipity, employment patterns will differ even in the absence of exclusionary forces. What is required is an equal playing field, and that starts with the education system (at all levels) and the careers service.

Some have debated whether Britain is destined to witness a bifurcated future, in terms of the prospects for minority communities. Mason, for example, talks about patterns of change in terms of 'convergence or polarization' (2000: 59). We have already noted the problems faced by members of some groups concentrated, apparently irrevocably so, in poor inner urban locations. In sharp contrast are those groups who, taken as a whole, appear to be gaining parity with the white population.

Following the recent urban disturbances (to be addressed in the next chapter), some have even speculated that we are heading towards a US urban future. This is not justified by the evidence. The so-called 'outcast ghettos of the poor' (Marcuse 1996) have no parallel in the UK. The poor South Asian neighbourhoods in northern England are not characterized by the sort of resignation and despair witnessed, for example, in many US housing projects, nor are they places from which it is well-nigh impossible to 'escape'. Recent research (Phillips and Ratcliffe 2002) demonstrates continuing out-migration from inner Leeds and Bradford associated with social mobility on the part of all South Asian groups (admittedly at very different rates). Social mobility is particularly marked in the case of the younger generations.

Having said this, there are very serious problems to be addressed in what used to be called Britain's 'inner cities'. It is to these we now turn in the final chapter in this section of the book.

Further reading

Once again, there is a vast array of material covering the issues raised in this chapter. The Cabinet Office Report (2003), though not explicitly sociological, contains an extremely thorough appraisal of data on the current labour market position of minorities, and of the steps which could be taken to reduce the 'ethnic penalty'. Particularly valuable is the recognition that to do this necessitates changes beyond the immediate orbit of employment policies and practices (for example in the realm of education and training).

Of recent offerings from the social science community, Pilkington (2003) and Mason (2003) represent very accessible, and measured, appraisals of the debates around diversity and disadvantage. Equalities issues will be dealt with in more detail in Chapter 10, but there are a number of classic texts which are worthy of mention here.

Jenkins (1986b) presents an excellent account of how racism and discriminatory practices intrude into the recruitment and working lives of minority workers. As to equalities policies, the reader edited by Jenkins and Solomos (1989) provides a very useful review of the basic principles, and of many of the problems raised in the process.

8 Urban Conflict, Policing and the Criminal Justice System

Introduction: law and the inclusive society

To conclude this part of the book we move on from looking specifically at material inequalities to focus on the nature of civil society. Although housing, education and work are central to citizenship rights, so is equality under the law. In the UK, many rights are formally protected under the 'race relations' and human rights legislation (as will be seen in Chapter 10). But so were the rights of African Americans under the US constitution as far back as the mid-nineteenth century (with certain significant qualifications – see Chapter 9), and we have already seen evidence of the considerable gulf between the legal commitment to equality and day-to-day reality.

Until the introduction of the Race Relations (Amendment) Act 2000, the police were specifically excluded from the provisions of the anti-discrimination legislation (Commission for Racial Equality 2001). This was a significant omission. It meant that they were not formally required to have in place non-discriminatory human resource policies: nor were they required by law to promote good relations between communities and ensure that their service delivery was non-discriminatory. For their part, the police argued that both were unnecessary as they are servants of all the people.

The problem is that they are also *of* the people, in that in both individual and collective terms they embody the values of the society they serve. Key elements of 'policing culture', as well as the actions of individual police officers, will provide the focus of much of what follows. It will be suggested that, as with all cultures, this is subject to a constant process of modification as new understandings about the nature of their work and of the people they police become sedimented and routinized as everyday custom and practice.

This leads to one rather obvious, even trite, conclusion: that policing varies markedly at different historical junctures. What is being suggested here, though, is that there is much more to this than changes to formal operational policy and practice. It also varies in relation to local populations and 'space and place'. Long-standing segregation in particular urban areas inevitably means that a central concern of this chapter is on the ways in which urban minority communities are policed. In the event of unrest or conflict the role of the police is especially important, not least because its actions in themselves send out certain messages as to whom it views as the 'guilty party'. The latter in turn will interpret these actions in the context of their everyday experience both as citizens and as subjects of policing. Because an adequate understanding of these issues requires a historical perspective we begin with a brief overview of urban unrest in Britain.

Most political analysts would probably identify 1980 as marking the beginning of a spate of outbreaks of serious disorder, which were destined to last for around a decade and a half. These will be evaluated specifically in terms of how the state and its agencies responded to the threat to social stability. In 2001, there were a number of reminders that the underlying issues had yet to be addressed, or at least redressed. The events of 11 September later that year brought many of these issues into sharper relief. We therefore conclude the chapter with reflections on the response to these, much more global(ized), threats to social cohesion and the very essence of inclusivity.

The roots of urban conflict: historical and theoretical reflections

As we saw in Chapter 4, urban Britain is no stranger to public disorder. In 1919, a simmering resentment amongst working-class whites about what they saw as privileges accorded to (undeserving) black migrants led to widespread violence (May and Cohen 1974). One theme common to many subsequent events of this nature emerged. Incidents, in themselves fairly insignificant, escalated into a series of major fights and stabbings, with the police eventually resorting to the role of custodian (shielding groups of black residents for their own safety).

But for a relatively small number of port cities (in the main) there were few concentrations of black migrants at this time. Inter-war disturbances were largely associated either with poverty and class issues (for example the hunger marches and demonstrations) or with the rise of the British fascist movement in the 1930s, led by Sir Oswald Mosley (Rowe 1998).

With post-war immigration from the New Commonwealth, however, many of the earlier fears, anxieties and hostilities re-emerged. Politicians, for their part, did little to allay fears or to confront hostility to immigrants. Concerns were expressed by government ministers but, in the early to mid-1950s at least, these were largely confined to the private, rather than public, sphere (Carter, Harris and Joshi 1987; Solomos 2003). It was not until the 'riots' in Nottingham and Notting Hill in 1958 (M. Phillips and T. Phillips 1998) that senior Conservative politicians raised the spectre of further 'race' conflict in the event that the message of these incidents was not heeded. As to what exactly (in their view) the 'message' was, it was that immigrants were the problem and ongoing immigration the culprit (see Chapter 4, and Sivanandan 1976, 1982). Ignoring the positive contribution to British society from people who had been 'invited' to come here, the argument was that the violence would not have occurred had they not accepted the invitation.

The fact that the immediate catalyst for all of these disorders was a hostile act on the part of white residents did not influence the apportionment of blame. This is extremely significant. As will be seen, there is one constant in police characterizations of violent incidents involving 'black' and 'white' combatants. It is that they have had great difficulty in seeing whites as perpetrators and blacks as victims. In contrast, 'Asians' have been perceived, until relatively recently at least, as defensive-minded. In other words, they are essentially (by nature) peaceable, reacting physically only in response to violent acts perpetrated by others.

The major significance of the Liverpool disorders of 1919 lay in the racialization of discursive representations of the events. Deep-seated concerns about 'them' 'stealing' homes and jobs belonging to 'us' were complemented by fears about miscegenation (that is, black males 'stealing our women'). These (mis)constructions were given added salience by the ending of the Great War, returning war veterans expecting a smooth transition to civilian life. Despite the fact that many black migrants had also seen war service, they were seen as relatively undeserving. Any violence on the part of blacks was naturalized: as simply a product of their biological and cultural inheritance (May and Cohen 1974).

Systematic discrimination and racist attacks on post-war migrants severely undermined their *de facto* citizenship rights. Many studies from the 1950s and 1960s illustrated in graphic detail the problems many migrants faced in the search for housing and jobs (Richmond 1961; S. Patterson 1965; Rex and Moore 1967). Effectively forced into jobs that whites did not want and into the worst housing, most then found themselves the brunt of racist harassment and abuse (M. Phillips and T. Phillips 1998). Once again they were accused of draining the resources of the country and 'stealing' jobs and homes. Now, however, they were also held responsible for the decline of the areas in which they had settled. Overcrowding was seen as indicative of the way 'these people' live not the result of exclusionary treatment.

When tensions between the 'dark strangers' (S. Patterson 1965) and local whites exploded into violence, as they did in 1958, it was the former who were held responsible. These ideas ultimately led to the construction of 'black youth' as arch representative of 'the other' – an enemy within. Never clearly defined it conjured up all that was dangerous about immigration: young males with a different psychological and cultural make-up to the 'indigenous' white population. They were the 'self-excluded', beyond mainstream society, and irrevocably so. Gutzmore (1983), in a characteristically forceful essay, argued that the concept had been 'fabricated and manipulated' by the state as a means of justifying oppressive policing. A net effect was the criminalization of black Britons.

The vagueness of the concept made it all the more powerful as a re-presentation of what, for some, was wrong with British society (and, because of their 'youth', would become more so). 'They' therefore needed to be policed vigorously, and 'their areas' subjected to special policing strategies. It did not help their cause when sociologists appeared to reinforce the negative stereotypes, a point endorsed by Gutzmore. Cashmore and Troyna (1982) rightly problematized the concept, but the editors' own contribution interpreted 'the crisis' faced by black youth as in many ways of their own making. Implicitly making a distinction between Asian youth (who were not in crisis) and those of African-Caribbean origin (who were), the latter were argued to exhibit a 'violent proclivity', albeit one moulded by historical memories of enslavement. When a black sociologist, Ken Pryce (1979), also appeared to endorse the negative stereotypes of black males as hustlers and pimps, one was immediately reminded of Howard Becker's (1970b) famous question (about the role of sociologists): 'whose side are we on?'

Urban conflict and the official response: 1980s and 1990s Britain

It was somewhat ironic that the first major outbreak of disorder on mainland Britain since the late 1950s was in precisely the area about which Pryce was writing: St Paul's in Bristol. The police in-house journal welcomed the book, and the local force saw it as justifying their traditionally forthright approach to policing the area.

Writers in the *Race and Class* collective (1981/2) argue that the underlying cause of these 'riots' was 'years of harassment' of residents by the police, such that only a spark was needed to trigger violence. This was provided by a police raid on the 'Black and White' café in April 1980, 'one of the very few meeting places for black youth' (ibid.: 223). For two hours the police cordoned off the area, took away beer crates, and arrested the owner. The police were eventually forced to withdraw until reinforcements arrived. St Paul's was effectively a 'no-go' area for four hours (despite police denials): 130 people were subsequently arrested and around 90 charged with minor offences. All but one was found guilty.

William Whitelaw, the then Home Secretary, was sufficiently concerned about the events to propose a 'new look' at ways of handling disorders. In July, therefore, there was an attempted show trial involving 12 people. They were charged with 'riotous assembly', a serious offence carrying the possibility of a custodial sentence. In the event, the trial fell apart: three being acquitted for lack of evidence, five found 'not guilty'. The jurors returned a 'no verdict' decision on the remaining four. The Director of Public Prosecutions (DPP) decided not to order a retrial.

These events raised a number of important issues. They were widely characterized, and not simply by the media, as 'race riots'. The violence was thereby taken out of its material context, urban deprivation and aggressive policing, and associated with mindless, even random, acts of violence (that is, rioting). Central to this was the widespread image of the area as a black (largely Jamaican) area (Wallace and Joshua 1983). But the crowd contained a sizeable number of local whites who, unlike in Liverpool 60 years earlier, were also in conflict with the police. The 'race riot' label could therefore not be justified. But the events were undoubtedly racialized (or ethnicized), explaining why the presence of an ethnically mixed jury was seen as ensuring a fair hearing for defendants. Bristol was widely regarded as an example of 'urban rebellion', but also became a symbol of resistance for black youth (Race and Class 1981/2).

The next major outbreak of disorder occurred in Brixton, South London. In the wake (once again) of years of heavy-handed policing, the Met (Metropolitan Police) launched SWAMP81 on 6 April 1981. This was claimed to be an attack on 'muggings and street crime'. The scale of the exercise was extremely provocative, however, with 120 plain-clothed officers entering the area on a 'stop-and-search mission'. Some homes and cafés were raided. Altogether well over 100 people were arrested (some estimates being far higher).

By the Friday evening (10 April), police–youth relations were described as 'tense': so tense, in fact, that a very minor incident provided the spark this time. Police tried to arrest a black youth wounded in a scuffle in the street, at which point around a hundred youths released him. The police then called for reinforcements, and a 20-minute battle ensued.

The violence escalated, leading to the petrol bombing of police cars and the firing of a local pub. The police presence increased massively to prevent the creation, as they saw it, of 'no-go areas'. Many, however, were seen to be taking the law into their own hands. By the Sunday, the area was cordoned off. Four thousand police were estimated to be in the area, a thousand of them ringing the police station (armed with riot shields). Around three hundred people were arrested over the next few days.

What was the significance of these events? The first point to make is that, as with St Paul's, the 'rebellion' was not anti-whites but 'anti-police'. It was not simply a 'youth rebellion' either. According to a report in the *Guardian* (a respected broadsheet newspaper), it was not simply a question of 'youths' versus 'the people/community' (as some had tried to argue). The unrest was seen as having the 'backing of the whole Black community'.

As to the third point (the response of the government), Whitelaw ordered an urgent review of police riot gear. Significantly, he reiterated the 1950s argument that the problem lay not with racism in the Met, but with lax immigration policy. Ironically, this is precisely what Enoch Powell had argued, resulting in his expulsion from Edward Heath's government. But then this first Thatcher administration was rather different in ideological terms.

Widely trivialized in the press as 'copycat riots', violence broke out in Southall, to the northwest of London, and Toxteth, Liverpool, in July 1981. The former was the first major outbreak of violence involving mainly South Asian youth (and in a largely Asian area). It was also rather different from St Paul's and Brixton in that the immediate catalyst was unrelated (at least directly) to police actions. Incursion into the area this time was by a large group of skinheads who had ostensibly come to attend a concert at a local public house, The Hambrough Tavern. But they used this 'day out' as an opportunity to attack and abuse local Asian shopkeepers.

Asian youths responded by setting fire to the concert venue. The skinheads then withdrew under the protection of the police. One question remains largely unanswered. Why did the police allow the skinhead concert to go ahead in the first place (in such an area)? It was widely known that there was going to be trouble.

Although media constructions of the Liverpool 'riots' of July 1981 were dominated by images of violent blacks, more considered accounts focused on two issues: material conditions in Toxteth and the way the area was policed. The widely despised local police chief, Kenneth Oxford, claimed that 'it was exclusively a crowd of Black hooligans intent on making life unbearable and indulging in criminal activities' (ibid.: 226). But the revolt was not confined to young people: middle-aged women were found to be making petrol bombs. Nor was it a case of random violence (a 'riot'). As in Bradford, as we shall see shortly, attacks on property were seen as 'rationally based'. They included a bank, a racquets club 'used by judges', and local 'rip-off stores' (ibid.: 226). Police were bussed into the area from various parts of Britain, and this was the first time that CS gas was used on mainland Britain.

These and other, smaller, disturbances inevitably provoked a response from the government. Lord Scarman was appointed to head up an inquiry focusing on Brixton, but the remit was widened subsequently to incorporate Southall and Toxteth. Substantively, his remit was broad in that it was seen as covering underlying causes as well as immediate catalysts. He clearly recognized the significance of material deprivation (a position the government had rejected out of hand), but most of his analysis focused on the police. Underplaying institutional factors, he preferred instead to focus on the ethnic composition of the Met and the behaviour of individual officers (Lord Scarman 1982; Benyon 1984; Solomos 2003).

There were two key policy recommendations:

- The recruitment of more black police officers, and
- Expulsion from the force of racist officers, and the introduction of

specific training on the challenges posed by policing in a multi-ethnic context.

The aim was to inject a more 'consensus-based' approach. So, whereas the media deemed the 'riots' to be examples of 'mindless violence', 'hooliganism' and the work of 'outside agitators' (from the political Left), Scarman did at least offer some criticism of the Met.

There were clear parallels with the approach of the Swann inquiry into the educational performance of minorities. The latter, it will be remembered (see Chapter 6), advised an expansion in the number of black teachers. It also individualized exclusionary practices, subjecting 'racist' teachers to RAT (Racism Awareness Training). In both cases, however, the real underlying problem is systemic and institutional. Removing a few 'rotten apples' will not solve this. In so far as the problem lay with policing, it was to do with the collective culture rather than individual attitudes. This is partly about 'canteen culture', that is, the way rookie policemen become socialized into the job. But, as far as the Met is concerned, there were operational structures that could be deemed deeply problematic.

Since the early 1970s, under Commissioner Sir Robert Mark, they had used a 'race'-based coding scheme for the recording of crime statistics, namely:

IC1 White-skinned European Type
IC2 Dark-skinned European Type
IC3 Negroid Type
IC4 Asian Type
IC5 Oriental Type
IC6 Arabian Type

This was even used in a directly political vein to cast doubt on the hypothesis that black men are no more likely to commit offences than whites. Given this, it is perhaps not surprising that policing lacked even-handedness.

More generally 'consensus policing', as promoted by Scarman, was seen as part of the reason why the period from the summer of 1981 to mid-decade was largely peaceful. Other reasons cited by commentators were the cathartic effects of the 'riots', the introduction of social policy measures and increases in the political representation of minorities and their concerns (Solomos 1986). But, in truth, most of the changes were cosmetic. A high political profile, for example, was given to the so-called 'Hestletine initiative'. This involved the conversion of a large brownfield site (the disused docks area of Liverpool) into a garden centre – not very much use to local Toxteth residents given the notable absence of gardens!

The period of urban calm can be seen in retrospect as a false dawn. Hot on the heels of a highly successful carnival, violence erupted in Handsworth, Birmingham. This surprised many, as Scarman himself had singled out the local force as a model of sensitive, community policing.

Following this, there were major disturbances in Brixton and on the Broadwater Farm Estate in Tottenham, North London. In the latter case, the popular media had a field day in the wake of the death of a police officer (P.C. Blakelock) in street battles with local residents. The tabloids described him as having been savagely 'hacked to death' with a machete by 'hordes of Blacks'. This imagery was highly significant, representing the archetypal 'other': savage, barbaric and tribal. The man ultimately convicted of his murder, Winston Silcott, was widely believed at the time to have been a scapegoat. Indeed, he was subsequently freed on appeal.

The causal diagnosis was somewhat different this time (Gifford et al. 1986; Solomos 1987):

- Vicious cycles of inner-city deprivation;
- The social condition of young blacks, and youth in general;
- The problem of policing the 'enemy within'; and finally
- The events as symbolic of a 'riot-torn society'.

The focus was now on the various 'dangerous classes' of people that material deprivation bred. The late Bernie Grant, then MP for Tottenham, was seen as the arch representative of the 'enemy within' by failing to condemn Blakelock's murder. Indeed, the tabloid press reported him widely as saying that this was a case of 'chickens coming home to roost'. There were also stories of infighting between 'Asians' and 'West Indians'. The suggestion was that the very fabric of British life was in danger of unraveling. It conjured up a picture of what amounted to the very antithesis of the 'inclusive society' (though the term was not in vogue at this time).

There was renewed debate about urban policing methods and a greater level of consciousness about the need for sensitivity (at least amongst those at a senior level). Some would argue, though, that the major practical change at 'street level' was the replacement of heavy-handed, collective assaults on communities by the harassment of individuals through 'sus': the power to stop and search 'on suspicion' (that an offence might have been committed).

There was a grudging acceptance that material deprivation needed to be tackled. But the black-led report on the Handsworth disorders (West Midlands County Council 1986) claimed that the benefits of urban renewal and regeneration were not filtering through to minority communities. This was endorsed by a more wide-ranging review of policies and practices in the city as a whole (Ratcliffe 1992). Investment in the physical environment tended either to avoid areas of minority settlement entirely, or to have a relatively marginal impact on them. In some ways even more galling to communities suffering from much higher levels of unemployment, was the procurement of outside contractors to undertake the work.

Perhaps the most significant change in outsiders' attitudes to urban Britain, however, related to perceived changes in the nature of the dangerous 'other'. Whereas the African-Caribbean male had occupied this unenviable position for decades, in the late 1980s there was a new contender: the followers of a 'militant fundamentalist Islam'. The most prominent symbol of this was the Salman Rushdie affair.

Subject to a worldwide *fatwa* as a result of his book, *The Satanic Verses*, being regarded as blasphemous and anti-Islamic, Rushdie had unwittingly ignited a furore which had much wider implications than a clash of cultures or religious values (Samad 1992). At the very minimum it raised immediate questions about freedom of speech and the extent to which supranational legal systems could, or should, be accommodated by those of a particular (secular) nation state. Those who defended the *fatwa*, and more especially those who engaged in the public expressions of anger such as book-burnings, were branded dangerous 'fanatics'. They had effectively angered not only racists and bigots, but also those multiculturalists who sought to promote better relations and a greater understanding between Muslim and non-Muslim.

This, more than any other single incident, fuelled the rise in Islamophobia (Runnymede Trust 1997). The first Gulf War then exacerbated social tensions. In towns like Bradford, with high concentrations of poor, working-class Muslims, relations with local whites deteriorated further. Muslims often felt that the mores of the 'host' society were totally at odds with their core values; whites were suspicious of a community with which they had little contact.

Particularly offensive to Bradford's Muslims was the rise in prostitution in Manningham, the area close to the centre of the city where large numbers of South Asian migrants had settled since the 1950s. They accused local police of not doing enough to curb it, indeed they felt that the problem had been exacerbated as a result of police actions elsewhere. Local community action against kerb-crawling then brought them into direct conflict with the authorities. In the wake of the campaign, there was a minor incident involving a slight injury to a local Muslim woman objecting to the intervention of police officers into a game of street football played by youngsters. This sparked serious unrest involving attacks on businesses and property, and a number of arrests for public order offences.

Once again a question mark hung over policing methods, given the levels of distrust and anger on both sides. But two major reports (Bradford Commission 1996; Ratcliffe 1996b), the first specifically commissioned to look into the causes of the disturbances, painted a much broader picture. Quite apart from the extremely poor and overcrowded housing conditions suffered by South Asian communities in inner Bradford, there were major problems in relation to schooling and jobs. It was material disadvantage, made even more unbearable by constant abuse and harassment meted out by white Bradfordians (including police officers), which was at the core of the conflict. Other explanations, such as inter-generational conflict (a clash of value systems between the first and subsequent generations) were seen as largely peripheral.

The policing of black communities in the twenty-first century

The significance of the debate about inter-generational tensions was that it refocused concerns about 'black youth'. In the process, the latter seemed to take on the guise of a floating signifier, 'black' now seeming also to encompass South Asian, and more especially Muslim, 'youth'. Young people, not surprisingly, were more visible in the urban rebellions than their elders. Having, in the main, been born and educated in Britain they were understandably unwilling to put up the sort of treatment meted out to their parents and grandparents in the 1950s and 1960s.

The catalysts for the spate of disturbances in the summer of 2001 were the actions of extreme Right groups, especially the BNP (British National Party). It was an election year, and therefore they targeted particular constituencies where they thought they had some chance of success. The Pennine towns and cities of Bradford, Oldham and Burnley had sizeable concentrations of Pakistani and Bangladeshi Muslims (Rees and Phillips 1996). Significantly, they also had equally large concentrations of poor, disaffected working-class whites, for the most part living in contiguous areas. For many of these traditional Labour Party supporters, 'their' party had let them down.

Darcus Howe, in a TV documentary series for Channel 4 entitled *The White Tribe*, claimed that, quite apart from material disadvantage, they were suffering a sense of 'loss'. The loss in question was a loss of identity, a product not only of the demise of empire but also the relatively recent devolution of certain powers to Wales, Scotland and Northern Ireland. Put simply, it was a questioning of what it meant to be English in the twenty-first century, compounded by anger that the celebration of 'Englishness' (say) by the recognition of St George's Day was regarded as nationalistic and even 'racist'. Loss of identity was also seen by White (2002) as crucial to understanding the anger and resentment of whites on the Fitton Hill estate in Oldham, though here that loss was interpreted more in terms of a lack of religious conviction and the 'ethnic' transformation of space, community and neighbourhood: a 'loss of roots' (ibid.: 52).

The BNP in its election manifesto attempted to play down its anti-minority, racist stance, and instead present itself as a real 'Labour' alternative: the authentic voice of the white working class. Of course the 'real' voice of the latter is deeply infected by common-sense racism, a fact recognized by South Asians in areas targeted by the BNP. Even the *threat* of incursion provoked a mobilization of young Asians in Bradford at Easter 2001. Although the violence was limited in both intensity and duration, it provided a foretaste of what was to come later in the summer.

An application by the BNP to march through the city centre in July 2001 was formally rejected by West Yorkshire Police. There was a rumour, however, that this would not deter members of the Party (and also Combat 18, a group committed to racist violence) from travelling to Bradford, intent on provoking local Muslims in those areas where they are concentrated. This was enough to ensure that young Asians prepared for trouble. Stories abounded that weapons, even firearms, would be available for use if necessary. The Anti-Nazi League (ANL), for its part, declined to cancel plans for its own rally and counter-demonstration.

On the day itself, the taunting of Asians on the part of young white men drinking outside city centre pubs, provided the catalyst for serious unrest which lasted a number of days. Over three hundred people were injured and the cost in terms of damage was estimated to lie between 7.5 and 10 million pounds (Denham 2001). Rather than censure the extreme Right for extreme provocation, the Home Secretary, David Blunkett, instead blamed the violence on Muslim youth, whom he described as 'thugs'.

In Oldham, the BNP had already achieved remarkable success in the General Election of May 2001. Its chairman, Nick Griffin, polled 16 per cent of the vote in Michael Meacher's constituency of Oldham West and Royton, and they took 11 per cent of the vote in Oldham East and Saddleworth. Rather than withdrawing from the area following the election, however, they continued to leaflet local whites. They stoked up anger and resentment by claiming that local Asian areas were benefiting disproportionately from local council policy in relation to regeneration funds from central government. They also quoted local police figures suggesting that larger numbers of racist attacks were perpetrated by Asians (on whites) than vice versa. Both of these arguments were firmly refuted by the parties concerned. Council spokespeople denied the accusation of bias in the apportionment of funds; Asians claimed that the police statistics simply reflected the fact that it was not worth their while reporting attacks to the police, as no action would follow.

Serious disturbances broke out in Glodwick, an extremely poor area of run-down terraced owner-occupied housing. The vast majority of its residents were, and are, of Bangladeshi origin. Echoing responses to parallel incidents elsewhere, many residents complained about the police's handling of the conflict. Although the violence was sparked by incursion into the area by white youths, a disproportionately high number of Asians were arrested. It was a similar story in Burnley in July 2001, where a highly segregated Muslim population (seen, once again, as special beneficiaries of Council policy – Burnley Task Force 2001) bore the brunt of attacks inspired by extreme Right activists.

Although, as noted earlier, the government already seemed to have apportioned blame (with accusations of lawlessness directed at South Asian youth), there were two generic (national) inquiries into the background to the disorders (Cantle 2001; Denham 2001), and separate reports on Burnley (Burnley Task Force 2001) and Oldham (Oldham Independent Review Panel 2001). A further report, which was commissioned prior to both major disorders in the city, focuses on Bradford (Ouseley 2001).

There is no space here to discuss these in detail: this has, in any case, already been done elsewhere (Kalra 2003). We focus simply on core themes. Probably the key conclusion, as pointed out by Kalra (2003: 148–9) is that, unlike Scarman two decades earlier, none of the four reports discuss the hostility towards the police felt by many young people from minority communities. The dominant image of 'the police' is the 'populist view' (ibid.: 146), namely that they are effectively beyond, and external, to the society they are policing. In other words, they are simply dealing with problems not of their making. This clearly absolves them of any broader culpability for the disorders (though not, of course, for their actions on the streets once violence had erupted).

The police are seen instead as, at least potentially, the promoters of social cohesion. Cantle (2001), whilst commending their work during the disturbances, seems to suggest that they could do rather more to sort out 'the problems' of those communities. The 'problems' are somewhat decontextualized in a materialist sense, however, amounting to little more than the familiar patterns of criminalization and pathologization. Black (African-Caribbean) youth seem to be regarded as intrinsically violent and prone to criminality; South Asian (and, perhaps especially, Asian Muslim) youth appear to be associated with fraud and drugs offences (Kalra 2003: 148). Both stood accused of ensuring that certain urban areas were effectively off-limits to the police (so as to facilitate the activities of criminal gangs). In sum, the police were held guilty of under-policing minority areas, being overly tolerant to drug-related activities and deploying softly-softly tactics in relation to 'no-go' areas. As to poor, alienated white youth, they are pathologized as having 'no culture', but are alleged to share the same structural relationship with the police as minority youth (ibid.: 149). There is, therefore, an implicit denial of differential treatment on ethnic/'racial' lines.

The Stephen Lawrence Inquiry and its implications for policing and the criminal justice system

In assessing the degree of culpability of the police and the criminal justice system in terms of providing equality before the law, it helps first to ask what we mean by 'the police'. The term is used in at least four different senses:

- Structural position (as an arm of the state)
- Culture (of policing)
- (Local) policing strategies
- Individual police officers

If we think of policing in the broadest, structural, sense it is easy to see how it can be conceived of as 'above society'. It is clearly not responsible for material inequalities, nor is it responsible for the concentration of minorities in poor urban areas. In being required to maintain law and order, it clearly has a social control function that inevitably forces it into a conflictual relationship with the 'socially excluded'. Drugs, prostitution and theft are commonplace in many estates 'on the edge' (Danziger 1997; Power 1997), irrespective of ethnic composition.

The disorders of 2001 differed from the majority of those in earlier decades in so far as they involved inter-communal conflict. In the post-9/11 world, the police's responsibilities also extend to enforcement of new legislation on terrorism (dealing with a further 'enemy within'). And they ultimately have to face the consequences of hostility towards refugees and asylum seekers, not merely from whites but also from earlier groups of migrants (BBC2 2003b).

The question is how best to meet these challenges. Evidence presented earlier in the chapter suggests that in many respects they are ill equipped. A 'culture' of policing that criminalized blacks (principally African-Caribbean males) as 'muggers', drug dealers and pimps had too often been allowed to flourish (Hall et al. 1978; Gutzmore 1983; Kalra 2003). Local policing strategies were then predicated on these pathologizing stereotypes. This means that, irrespective of the attitudes of individual officers, the result is the same. The differential use by officers of 'Stop and Search' powers is effectively normalized by the cultural assumptions underlying the wider strategy: 'it makes sense to stop more blacks than whites because ...'. The empirical evidence demonstrates just how wide the ethnic differentials are (Home Office 2000, cited in Kalra 2003: 144).

One of the most damaging elements of police culture has been the refusal to see minorities (and especially African-Caribbeans) as victims. A fire in a house in Deptford, South London, in 1981 caused the deaths of 13 young black partygoers. Despite compelling evidence, the police refused to accept that this was an arson attack perpetrated by whites (M. Phillips and T. Phillips 1998: 324–48). In addition to this, there have been numerous suspected racist murders. One case, however, came to symbolize police attitudes on matters of 'race'.

A young black teenager, Stephen Lawrence, was the subject of a violent unprovoked attack by white youths in Eltham, South London, in 1993, while he was waiting for a bus. He died subsequently from the stab wounds he had sustained. His friend and companion (who was also black), rather than being seen as a key witness, was immediately suspected by police as the perpetrator. Thus, valuable time was lost to the investigation. This was compounded by what later transpired to be a catalogue of errors in police procedures.

Stephen's parents, Doreen and Neville, mounted a national campaign to pressure the government to order a formal inquiry. The then Conservative administration, led by John Major, refused. It was not until the election of New Labour in 1997 that the go-ahead for a national inquiry was given – with Sir William Macpherson of Cluny as Chair.

The resulting inquiry had a much broader remit than the murder itself. Ultimately, it went far beyond the Scarman Inquiry, not only by acknowledging 'institutional racism' but also by attempting to define and operationalize it. Macpherson (1999, cited in *The Voice* 1999: 10) refers to it as 'the collective failure of an organisation to provide an appropriate and professional service'. This surfaces as 'unwitting prejudice, ignorance, thoughtlessness and racist stereotyping'. 'Unwitting racist language' can emerge:

> because of lack of understanding, ignorance or mistaken beliefs ... from well intentioned but patronising words or actions ... from unfamiliarity with the behaviour or cultural traditions of people ... from racist stereotyping of black people as potential criminals or troublemakers. Often this arises out of uncritical self-understanding born out of an inflexible police ethos of the 'traditional' way of doing things. Furthermore such attitudes can thrive in a tightly knit community, so that there can be a collective failure to outlaw this breed of racism.

What Macpherson was trying to do here was to deal with various aspects of the *culture* of policing as well as suggesting (as Scarman had done) that there were racist officers who had no place in the force. He said that it was vital to get across the message that a racist officer is an incompetent officer. This was widely, yet wrongly, interpreted by the police as a slight on every member of the force, that is accusing all officers of being racist.

Another key area of debate for the Inquiry team was the concept of a 'racist incident'. They eventually settled on the following definition: 'A racist incident is any incident which is perceived to be racist by the victim or any other person.' Whether or not they constituted crimes in policing terms they were to be reported, recorded and investigated with equal (strong) commitment.

The problem with this definition, as was picked up by the Police Federation, is that it is rather vague and ambiguous. It could, theoretically at least, lead to a nightmare scenario where almost every incident might be seen by someone as racist. This would lead to a situation where serious cases might be drowned out by trivial and dubious ones especially, it was argued, because Macpherson had also proposed that measures be taken to encourage the reporting of such incidents.

There was a raft of recommendations as to how the police should deal with racist crimes. This was the most direct response to the spectacular failures of the Met in the Lawrence case. As to how we would know whether the police were making progress, Macpherson recommended monitoring procedures leading to a new set of Performance Indicators (PIs). These would include:

- The number of recorded racist incidents and related detection levels;
- Policy directives governing stop and search procedures and their outcomes;
- Achieving equal satisfaction levels across all ethnic groups in public satisfaction surveys;
- The nature, extent and achievement of racism awareness training;
- Levels of recruitment, retention and progression of ethnic minority recruits;
- Levels of complaint about racist behaviour or attitudes and their outcomes.

Reaction from the police was somewhat predictable: a mixture of quiet resignation, indignation and cynicism. Officers have complained that the recommendations have actually made them less efficient as a force. Many have claimed, for example, that it has made police officers wary of using their statutory powers to 'stop and search' for fear of being seen as racist. This is then alleged to lead to a rise in unsolved crime in certain urban areas (presumed to be due to the failure to apprehend black people).

There seems to be a stubborn reluctance to acknowledge serious problems. Significant numbers of serious injuries and deaths amongst black detainees (Runnymede Trust 2000), and differential sentencing policies and practices (Hood 1992; Kalra 2003) remain a major concern. A much higher proportion of black defendants is given a custodial sentence (controlling for type and severity of offence), a special concern being the disproportionately high incarceration rate for those convicted of first offences. These are major factors in the changing ethnic composition of the prison population. Although the UK is never likely to reach the current US situation where, at any one time, one in five African American males is in the criminal justice system (for example in prison, custody or on remand), there are worrying signs (Runnymede Trust 2000: 132). As Kalra (2003: 151) points out, there is also a high, and rising, Muslim male inmate population. In the wake of 9/11, arrest rates are likely to increase further, due to increased levels of surveillance of Muslim communities.

Conclusions and further reading

Macpherson focused attention on major problems in the police and criminal justice system, but in some ways even more important are its wider implications. Its recommendations led directly to pressure for enhanced anti-discrimination legislation, to incorporate the police and the criminal justice system for the first time. As noted at the beginning of the chapter, this aim was (partially) realized in the shape of the Race Relations (Amendment) Act 2000.

Macpherson's rationale was that institutional racism is an extremely serious problem throughout British society, and not simply confined to policing and the criminal justice system. The message generally is that active monitoring is the key to achieving real change. This means that organizations should keep records not only of racist incidents but also of all human resource matters, that is the entire process of recruitment, training, promotion and disciplinary procedures. Active monitoring requires much more than simply recording details: it means that the implications of the data must serve as a basis for action (see Chapter 10).

Explicit supplementary guidance was also provided where necessary. In the field of education, for example, the report said that the National Curriculum should be reviewed with the aim of increasing the emphasis placed on valuing cultural diversity and preventing racism. In short, it should better reflect the needs of a diverse society. It also proposed that the numbers and self-defined ethnic identity of 'excluded' pupils be published annually on a school-by-school basis.

There were also specific recommendations in the case of housing institutions. Much of this is enshrined within the new statutory duty on public authorities imposed by the Amendment Act. At long last, therefore, this held out the promise of real 'joined-up thinking' in the policy arena (a core element of New Labour rhetoric), contributing in turn to a greater degree of social inclusivity. This chapter, and indeed this section of the book, has shown just how far we have to go to achieve this end.

In terms of further reading on the 'racialization of disorder' in twentieth-century Britain, Rowe (1998) provides probably the most thorough account. Because of its relatively narrow subject area it presents considerably more empirical detail than standard texts, such as Solomos (2003), by their nature can.

On policing issues, a useful standard text would be Keith (1993), though some readers will undoubtedly be deterred by the author's rather opaque writing style. Viable alternatives are Cashmore and McLaughlin (1991), and Benyon and Bourne (1986).

In terms of more contemporary accounts, a good starting point would be Chapters 9 and 10 of *The Parekh Report* (Runnymede Trust 2000), supplemented by Kalra (2003). These will guide the reader through most of the key findings of, and issues raised by, *The Stephen Lawrence Inquiry Report* (Macpherson 1999).

PART III
COMBATING EXCLUSION

9 Civil Rights, Community Activism and Empowerment

Introduction: social agency and the promotion of inclusivity

The previous section of the book focused on sites of exclusion, so-called because they constituted substantive contexts within which the social significance attached to certain forms of 'difference' (the focus of Part I) was seen to have very real material effects. Our concern now turns to the negation of these exclusionary forces. This is critical to the quest for the equalization of *de facto*, as well as *de iure*, citizenship rights.

The sheer complexity of these forces, and the fact that the ideologies that underpin them are deeply embedded in normative value systems, means that this is clearly no simple task. Legislation has an obvious role, as we saw towards the end of the previous chapter, in defining a range of acts, both individual and collective, which are deemed unlawful. But they cannot, by definition, change thought processes in the direction of a more emancipatory world-view (except by inference). They may even have the opposite effect, of actually hardening attitudes. As evidenced by UK and US experience, 'political correctness' is an epithet routinely levelled at attempts to defend individual or group rights.

To say that social change needs to be driven from above is, to a point, demeaning to those subject to exclusionary forces. It could even be seen as an additional form of pathologization. There has to be a major role for social agency, and at a variety of levels. In the context of struggles against oppression on grounds of 'race' and ethnicity most thoughts would turn to the global anti-apartheid movement or the US Civil Rights Movement (CRM). But there are many rather small-scale actions that ultimately reap significant rewards. The case of Doreen and Neville Lawrence, discussed in the previous chapter, is a case in point. Ostensibly a single issue campaign, their mobilization of public sympathy and the media (including sections of it not normally known for taking a liberal stand on matters of 'race') was to prove crucial to the drive for a review of the police and criminal justice system, and ultimately a change in the law invoking, potentially at least (see Chapter 10), much wider gains.

Not only does this illustrate the power of micro-level agency, it also serves as a pertinent reminder of the dialectical relationship between structure and agency. One person's agency is ultimately transformed via the legislature into a regulatory mechanism that simultaneously constrains certain classes of behaviour and enhances the choices available to many. This in turn holds out the promise of more lasting ramifications in terms of the balance of *de facto* citizenship rights and material well-being between groups.

Once again for largely pragmatic reasons discussion of the efficacy of legislation as a force for social change is deferred to the next chapter. Whilst bearing in mind the synergy between this and social agency, we focus here on the latter. The starting point will be the struggle for civil rights in the US. We then move on to ask whether Britain has ever had a social formation that could be labelled a 'civil rights movement'.

Whatever the answer to this question, one might wish to argue that there is little to justify direct comparison with the US situation. This provokes the obvious query: why not? What is it about racism and racialization in the UK (and/or about UK society itself), that explains the markedly different forms which struggles for equality have taken?

Empowerment and civil rights: the US case

With the demise of plantation slavery and the end of a bitter civil war, came new hope for African Americans. From being the mere chattels of slave-masters, and therefore less than human, they were accorded certain inalienable rights, as US citizens, under the Civil Rights Act of 1866 (Pinkney 1975; Kitano 1985) and the Fourteenth Amendment (of the Constitution).

Kitano argues that, in the period of Reconstruction following the war, little thought was given to the social integration of the former slaves. Changes in the law also did little to undermine the belief of most European Americans (and not only in the South) that blacks were inferior. The consensus amongst historians is that the early phase of Reconstruction held out a glimmer of hope that *de iure* emancipation might also be accompanied by real material gains for African Americans. But small tenant farmers were almost as tied to the land as they had been as slaves, and were in some sense even more vulnerable, for example, in the event of crop failure.

The real threat to the new legal rights, however, came from those who wanted to suppress 'the uppity nigger', to make sure that he (sic) knew his place. This new wave of oppressive mechanisms adopted a number of guises. The newly bestowed voting rights were effectively removed by a swathe of eligibility criteria specifically designed to disenfranchise the vast majority of African Americans (Myrdal 1944; Silberman 1964). Lynchings also increased markedly following the civil war (Kitano 1985: 110), fuelled by the growth of secret organizations such as the Klu Klux Klan. If anything, Steinberg's (2000:

3) general historical assessment of the progress of African Americans as 'two steps forward, one step back' is a little optimistic in this instance.

To make matters worse, Jim Crow laws followed. These effectively introduced a form of US apartheid, later to be justified by the phrase 'separate but equal' (the same rationalization adopted by Verwoerd at the birth of apartheid in South Africa). The idea was at the core of a landmark judgement in 1896 in the US Supreme Court (in the case of *Plessey versus Ferguson*). It sanctioned the legal separation of the 'races', suggesting that there was no reason why this should necessarily result in inferior treatment for the 'Negro'. But in a society structured on the basis of class and 'white male power', this theory was never likely to be realized.

The struggle for civil rights was predicated on the desire to ensure that the Constitution was true to its promise. This was how W. E. B. DuBois interpreted the 'problem of the color line'. His Niagara Movement (founded in 1905), which drew on the support of like-minded whites, claimed immediate equal rights for blacks. The problem was that the National Association for the Advancement of Colored People (NAACP) which DuBois established (in 1910) following the demise of the Niagara Movement was, like its predecessor, seen as somewhat distant from ordinary working-class blacks.

Other prominent black figures, such as Booker T. Washington, took a very different view of the way forward. Although approving of DuBois' appeal to black pride, he felt that blacks needed to prove their case for equal treatment alongside whites (Silberman 1964). This strategy of 'self-improvement' would be achieved in the first instance by the acquisition of a humble trade. He appealed to whites to employ black staff, on the grounds that the latter would prove their worth by their loyalty and conscientiousness. Not surprisingly, this appealed to whites but drew severe criticism from DuBois on the grounds that it smacked of subservience, accommodationism and Uncle Tomism.

DuBois' basic philosophy became the guiding theme of the mainstream civil rights movement throughout the twentieth century: integration (with white America). Marcus Garvey, who founded the Universal Negro Improvement Association (UNIA) in 1916, took a diametrically opposite view. For him, there was no point in asking, or even pleading, white America for parity: they would never accede to it. His alternative was a separatist philosophy, the most radical variant being the 'Back to Africa Movement' (Silberman 1964; Pinkney 1976). To promote this (literal) separatism he founded a shipping company – *The Black Star Line*. His very direct appeal to black pride coupled with a highly flamboyant, charismatic presence attracted a mass following, with membership claimed to run into millions (in some 900 chapters worldwide).

The sheer size of the organization, and the presence on the streets of gaudily uniformed officials appearing to represent an alternative (black) government, worried white leaders. Whilst they tolerated DuBois' appeal to the 'talented tenth' (the small black middle class), UNIA's success in attracting ordinary working-class blacks was a different matter. Investigators undermined Garvey's business ventures, eventually imprisoning him for alleged fraud. On release in 1927, he was deported to the Caribbean as an undesirable alien.

The NAACP remained *the* voice of the civil rights movement but, largely because of its low-profile approach and narrow appeal, was seen by many blacks (assuming they had heard of it) as of little relevance to them. What made matters worse was that many of the issues which especially concerned ordinary blacks (such as low pay, housing and police brutality) were seen as class issues, and therefore beyond the remit of the NAACP.

Pressure for change following World War II increased as black war veterans, many of whom had fought alongside whites, resented their return to Jim Crow US. Although segregation was also rife in the army, many had experienced an 'integrated' working environment for the first time. The re-emergence of the 'uppity negro' angered whites, but a gradual process of change was undoubtedly underway.

In 1954, there was a landmark legal judgement that threatened to spell the end for Jim Crow. The celebrated case of *Brown v. Board of Education of Topeka, Kansas* ruled for the desegregation of schools. Whilst this was never likely to remove almost a century of Jim Crow overnight, it was perhaps the first major victory for the civil rights struggle. It also provided a crucial impetus for its activists.

The following year saw the Montgomery Bus Boycott, where Rosa Parks challenged the policy of segregated seating by refusing to move to the rear of a city bus. Her arrest sparked a lengthy boycott by the city's black population. This lasted until 5 June 1956, when the Federal District Court ruled that segregation violated the 14th Amendment of the Constitution. This did not lead to an immediate change in practice in that few blacks exercised their right to sit in the front section of the city's buses (largely a product of habituation and fear), but the principle had been established.

A young black preacher emerged as the figurehead of these protests – Martin Luther King Jr. King, despite some initial reluctance, became the President of the Southern Christian Leadership Conference (SCLC) in 1957. Committed to Ghandian principles, King and his fellow civil rights leaders orchestrated a programme of non-violent protest. Central to these were the 'sit-in movement' and the 'Freedom Rides campaign'. The former involved the refusal to accept segregated seating in public facilities such as restaurants and 'lunch counters', the latter a challenge to segregation on inter-state bus lines. Civil rights activists, which included many anti-racist whites (a key point), were subjected to violent attacks at the hands of those who wished to preserve the *status quo*.

It was clear, then, that changes in the law alone were not enough. This was emphasized in Little Rock, Arkansas, in 1956, where attempts to admit a small group of black children to a local school met with violent protest. Crucially, the local police and state troops refused to intervene, so President Eisenhower was ultimately compelled to federalize the state troops, to make them take orders not from the state, but from the federal, government.

A similar event some five years later, this time at the University of Mississippi, invoked the same response. There was an attempt to register the first black student. The state governor personally took control of the situation by preventing James Meredith from completing his registration formalities. Despite escalating violence between Meredith supporters and local whites, President Kennedy (JFK) was initially loath to intervene for fear of upsetting southern Democrat colleagues.

Echoing old divisions between South and North, the southern states were resisting efforts by the 'Yankies' to tell them how to conduct relations with descendants of 'their' former slaves. The depth of 'racial' antipathy could be gauged from the political climate of the time. When George Wallace was defeated in the governorship elections in Alabama in 1959, he complained bitterly that he had been 'out-niggered' that time. He ensured election in 1962 (on a Democrat ticket) by adopting an extreme racist platform (Marable 1991).

In many ways the key event in the civil rights struggles came in Birmingham, Alabama, in 1963. Police brutality sanctioned by the local police chief, 'Bull' Connor, provoked a mass demonstration of blacks. It was particularly significant for a number of reasons.

- It was the first time that the mass of poor blacks had been involved in a demonstration.
- It was the first international 'mass media event' (engineered by civil rights activists).
- The political ramifications were huge.

The level of violence used against ordinary black men, women and children caused a moral outrage not only in the US, but also internationally. By ensuring a high level of media interest (even prior to the outbreak of violence), civil rights workers had pulled off a masterstroke. Pictures were screened around the world, creating acute embarrassment for the government. The arrest and incarceration of civil rights leaders, including King himself, added to the already massive pressure on the federal government to take decisive action. Once again JFK was reluctant to intervene, worried about his electoral position (recall Wallace's election as Democrat governor the previous year). Ultimately, he was forced to act because of the wider political ramifications.

These events also led to a decision by the Kennedy administration to press ahead with a (federal) Civil Rights Bill. Perhaps rather more significant, however, was the broader political message conveyed to the black population. Mainstream civil rights activity (involving non-violent direct action) had achieved certain legal victories but little in the way of tangible results. Those restless for more fundamental, and rapid, change saw in the events of Birmingham an alternative way forward.

This provided an added stimulus to groups such as the Nation of Islam (a.k.a. the Black Muslims) under the leadership of Elijah Mohammad, and active involvement of a young Malcolm X. They flatly rejected the integrationist position adopted by the CRM. For them, whites were the embodiment of evil: separatism, black pride and a life governed by a quite distinct moral ethos were proposed. They won some high-profile recruits, most notably the heavyweight boxer, Muhammad Ali (formerly Cassius Marcellus Clay).

Malcolm, whilst initially embracing these values, left the Nation in 1964, convinced that its philosophy of a spiritually pure life devoid, for example, of smoking, alcohol and sex would not have mass appeal to urban blacks. The Muslims also seemed to be holding out the promise of a black future which, despite an adherence to separatism and a rejection of the essence of 'whiteness', seemed not that far removed from the 'American dream'. Malcolm adopted a more revolutionary stance, seeing capitalism as the real root cause of the historical oppression of blacks. His view was that capitalism was doomed and that the US was becoming increasingly unstable, with black leaders having lost control. He was shot dead within months of expressing these views.

As Ellison (1974: 244) argues, 'elements of black nationalism were ... absorbed by movements that had originally been both integrationist and non-violent. CORE broke with non-violence and accepted much of the radical ideology of the new left as well as the idea of black power at its 1966 annual conference.' Then in 1967 CORE and SNCC (the Student Non-Violent Coordinating Committee) edged out some of their white members (ibid.). Stokely Carmichael (of SNCC) said that black people were fed up of asking white society to give them civil rights and fed up of telling whites that they wouldn't be hurt (they simply wanted equality).

Despite being committed to furthering the cause of urban blacks, and in particular defending them against the excesses of the police, the Black Panthers also accepted the involvement of sympathetic whites. Founded in Oakland, California, in 1966 by Huey Newton and Bobby Seale, the Panthers worried white authority by the adoption of paramilitary uniforms and the open carrying of guns (Ellison 1974; Marable 1991). They were, however, scrupulously careful to stay within the bounds of the law in the latter respect. And they were much more than a defence force: they adhered to a radical self-help philosophy providing welfare facilities for poor black families, such as running breakfast programmes for children (Carmichael and Hamilton 1967; Killian 1968; Ellison 1974).

In 1968, there was a formal alliance between the Panthers and SNCC. This worried 'white power' to the point where the police intensified surveillance of these groups. They infiltrated the Panthers and the police used the intelligence gathered to launch raids on the homes of members and their sympathizers. As Ellison (ibid.) argues, by the end of the decade most of the major radical black leaders were dead, in prison or forced into exile.

But, what of the mainstream CRM, whose most prominent leader was MLK? The nationalists had rejected its integrationist philosophy and argued that King was asking too much of black people: non-violence plus non-hatred, and maybe even the love of one's oppressor. (In one of MLK's more famous interviews, he said it was possible to hate the deed but not the perpetrator.)

King had raised the profile of civil rights in the national consciousness through one of the best known events of the twentieth century: the Freedom March to Washington DC in 1963. Even more than the march itself, the day was to linger in the memory for perhaps the most eloquent and moving speech of the century. But in 'I have a dream' King was expressing views which few white Americans could find threatening. It was after all a 'dream' of a future halcyon, multicultural, integrated state. For now, the 'problem of the color line' was as seemingly untractable as it was at the beginning of the century when DuBois first used the term. And 'white power' knew this.

Many blacks, and not just those in organizations such as SNCC, were deeply sceptical of King's relationship with senior Democrats, not least with the President himself. For them, he was 'playing the white man's game': the Freedom March was little more than a media event. But they could not deny that political pressure from the CRM had contributed greatly to positive developments in the sphere of legislation. The 1964 Civil Rights Act outlawed Jim Crow in public accommodation. This was soon to be followed by the 1965 Voting Rights Act and the 1968 Civil Rights Act.

Interestingly, white America and these more radical blacks shared one important 'blind spot' in terms of MLK's wider philosophy. Beyond the core theme of integrationism was a deep emotional antipathy to the Vietnam War, to racism and to the forces which left large sections of the US black population in abject poverty. King's vision of an inclusive society, therefore, was also about a greater degree of material equality.

With his violent death on 4 April 1968, shot on the balcony of his Memphis motel room, came a collective sense of loss amongst both white and black communities. It could be argued that the white establishment had appropriated the King image, as the voice of reason and sanity in a violent and unpredictable world. In the wake of his assassination, the media (largely, of course, controlled by the same white establishment), avoided any reference to

MLK's attack on racism, poverty and war, and instead focused on non-violence as an end in itself. In Blauner's poignant words: 'the living exploit the dead, and white power exploits Black leaders and their philosophies' (1972: 35).

With King's demise and the suppression of black radicalism, the US was witnessing a familiar pattern. The obvious gains from civil rights activity (for example in terms of formal legal rights), a 'second Reconstruction' perhaps, were being undermined by reactionary forces. Lyndon Baines Johnson's replacement as President by Richard Millhouse Nixon, heralded a further period of white retrenchment. His adherence to a 'color blind' urban policy was particularly damaging to the black cause, in that it downplayed, or even denied, the significance of 'race' (Omi and Winant 1994). Under the presidency of Ronald Reagan there were massive cuts in urban grants and a further endorsement of the 'color blind' approach. The political shift to the Right also provided a massive stimulus to extremist organizations such as the KKK: its membership grew threefold during the 1980s.

The argument that 'race' was declining in significance compared to class (as a determinant of life chances) was not confined to the politics of the Right. It was the subject of a highly controversial book by a prominent black sociologist, William Julius Wilson (1978). For many black colleagues, this merely perpetuated the myth of black progress (Pinkney 1984). They argued that although there was now a burgeoning black middle class, we should not lose sight of the fact that there was also a massive urban black 'underclass', mired in poverty (Allen 1994, 2001; Marcuse 1996).

This increasing bifurcation, they said, could not be explained convincingly by class factors. Omi and Winant (1994: 28–30) point to the political interdependency of the two groups and labour market segmentation as evidence of the continuing salience of 'race' in the US social formation. They add four further points, all widely endorsed in the sociological literature:

- Cutbacks in welfare have impacted adversely on both middle-class and working-class blacks.
- The black/white unemployment ratio has remained remarkably stable since World War II (at around twice).
- Again since the War, the non-white/white income ratio has remained steady, at around 58 per cent. A study of wealth in the US in 1984 found that the average white family had ten times as much as the average Black family – $39,135 as against $3,397 (see also Oliver and Shapiro 1997).
- In higher education, the proportion of college-going blacks has actually declined since the early 1980s. The number of post-graduates has declined also.

Having said this, none of these writers would deny the massive progress made by blacks over the last half-century. Pressure from the mainstream CRM and the more radical forces of black nationalism, still represented by the Nation of Islam, has resulted in the outlawing of Jim Crow and the introduction of affirmative action (more of which in the next chapter). A combination of legislation and vigorous voter registration drives has also had a massive impact on the levels of enfranchisement.

In the old South, for example, the increases during the mid- to late-1960s were dramatic: Alabama up from 19.3 per cent to 61.3 per cent; Georgia from 27.4 per cent to 60.4 per cent; Louisiana from 31.6 per cent to 60.8 per cent and, most spectacular of all; Mississippi from a mere 6.7 per cent to 66.5 per cent (Marable 1991: 90). Rates still lag behind the equivalent figures for whites, but they have been sufficient to achieve a steep increase in political representation at the highest level. Despite electoral success in some major northern cities, only a few decades ago it would have been unthinkable to imagine that the mayor of Atlanta, Georgia, might one day be black – in 2003 this is now a reality. Two of the country's most senior and influencial political figures are black: General Colin Powell and Dr. Condoleeza Rice. (In terms of wider political representation, one important qualification should be registered. There are high levels of black disenfranchisement in some states, because of the exclusion of those with a criminal record. This, combined with well-documented polling station irregularities in key black areas, ultimately determined the election of the present incumbent of the White House, George W. Bush.)

In the 1960s, there were still all-white basketball teams in the South. Although there were black movie stars and pop idols, these were relatively small in number. And, whilst they regularly appeared in top venues around the country, they were also subject to the restrictions imposed by Jim Crow. The entertainer Sammy Davis Jr. is widely credited with drawing attention to, and ultimately undermining, Jim Crow in public space, by refusing to perform in Las Vegas unless he was permitted to enter the theatre through the front entrance (normally a 'privilege' reserved for whites).

In a television series recently screened in the UK (BBC2 2003a), Professor Henry Louis 'Skip' Gates Jr. of Harvard University drew attention to some of the major advances made by African Americans. Entitled 'America Beyond the Colour Line' (echoing once more DuBois' celebrated phrase), it assessed levels of progress in Hollywood, sport, politics, business and the professions. It drew attention to some remarkable success-stories with, for example, increasing numbers of black CEOs of major corporations, but also some lingering problems. Much had to do with the 'glass ceiling' effect, and the wider ramifications of the concentration of big capital and power in the hands of whites. Recalling the essence of an earlier point, attention was drawn to the fact that the black male prison population is higher than the corresponding figure for college attendance. And having a prison record is the norm, rather than the exception, in many public housing projects.

Elsewhere in the criminal justice system it is clear that some things are slow to change. Cases of police brutality, and overly hasty resort to the use of firearms, show no signs of disappearing. In cases such as that in 1992, where white police officers were filmed beating up Rodney King following a routine arrest, trial location and jury composition are critical. As in the case of the murder by police of a young black marine in Miami in 1980, the trial was moved to an all-white area and heard in front of an all-white jury. Acquittal of the defendants in both cases sparked serious disorder, as local blacks vented their anger. (It is worth pointing out at this stage that the current Home Secretary in Britain, David Blunkett, has dismissed suggestions that the ethnic composition of juries should be given serious attention. This issue was raised in the wake of the racist assault of a young Asian man, Safraz Najeib, by two top soccer players, Lee Bowyer and Jonathan Woodgate, then of Leeds United.)

Before moving on to consider community-based 'civil rights' struggles in the UK, we return to what remains a key theme of US debates: integration versus separatism. As will have already become very clear, the latter term has acquired a host of very different meanings. At one end of the spectrum is the 'back to Africa' movement: at the other, segregation 'by choice'. In the middle is a range of possibilities debated by black separatists from the 1960s onwards: from the implausible, a separate state (and state government), to very practical initiatives based on black-run business and self-help organizations.

The most interesting contemporary dimension of this arose in the course of 'Skip' Gates' documentary referred to earlier. Although Gates did not make this point explicitly, he found what could be termed spatial separatism with substantive economic integration. Impoverished urban African Americans have little choice but to remain where they are; in poor housing, highly segregated from whites. For affluent middle-class blacks, however, their very wealth and class position constitute enablements. In other words they could, if they so wished, live in desirable suburban areas attracting whites of a similar socioeconomic standing. But, as we know that middle-class African Americans are as segregated from whites as their working-class counterparts (Peach and Rossiter 1996), they clearly do not exercise this option.

The question is, why not? For those whom Gates interviewed, the answer appeared to be that they felt 'more comfortable' amongst those of a similar 'cultural background'. They also pointed out, quite understandably, that whites had been self-segregating for decades, and had shown no desire to live on 'their' estates. Being to all intents and purposes economically integrated into white America and its institutions, one could argue that much of their 'culture' (despite the prominent display in their homes of African and African American artifacts) is heavily imbued with 'traditional' (white) American values. Perhaps the invisible hand of Jim Crow lives on, and that it is not so much 'culture' as 'race' which influences key decisions such as location?

Has Britain ever had a civil rights movement?

Whilst it is clearly the case that Britain has never had a civil rights movement in the US sense, the exclusionary forces examined in Part II have met with a variety of responses from minority communities. In the same way that legal advances in the US were to a large extent a function of community mobilization, parallel legislation in the UK (see Chapter 10) did not emerge solely as a result of social agency on the part of isolated, enlightened individuals operating in a 'top-down' fashion. It was largely the product of a complex array of transformative pressures from below. We are concerned here with these processes.

Those writing about the struggle against racism and exclusionary forces in the UK rarely acknowledge the key role played by US movements. As Banton (1972) rightly points out, a UK branch of Marcus Garvey's UNIA opened as early as the 1930s. Then in 1964, following a visit to London by Martin Luther King Jr., the Campaign Against Racial Discrimination (CARD) was founded. The latter was established as a national pressure group, but it also encouraged the growth of local branches to give it a much more direct, grassroots presence.

But there were two forces that were to have a major impact on the organization:

- Influenced by the success of direct action and the rise of Black Nationalism in the US, there were disputes about who should be involved in the struggle against racism: in particular, whether whites had a part to play in this.
- With the simultaneous rise of pan-Africanism (again in the US), there were concerted attempts to widen the organization's goals to encompass a much more radical internationalist agenda.

Matters came to a head in 1967 when, prior to a major convention, there was a significant increase in delegates who appear to have joined CARD with a particular political agenda. The accusation was that this was a Trotskyite plot to turn the organization into a much more revolutionary body (Banton 1972: 21). The following resolution was put, and duly passed:

> CARD, realizing that racialism, racial prejudice and racial discrimination are manifestations of imperialism, will fight against imperialism in all its forms by all means at its disposal.
>
> (ibid.: 24)

Opponents argued that combating colonialism was a separate issue and a matter for other organizations. Crucially, the passing of this motion seemed to undermine attempts to organize locally, through local branches (though it could be argued that such a local mission is, in any case, incompatible with that of a national pressure group). The dispute about the involvement of whites, especially in the executive, further undermined it. Senior figures, such as the prominent civil rights lawyer, Anthony Lester, were irritated that people seemed to be flocking to join CARD without the slightest intention of putting in the time needed to produce results.

Many argued, however, that the real reason for the demise of the organization was that it had in a sense done its job. The Wilson government had introduced the first piece of anti-discrimination legislation, the Race Relations Act 1965 (see Chapter 10). Lester himself had been involved in this from the outset. The Race Relations Board was established and local voluntary bodies were set up around the country to act on behalf of minorities.

With the exception of CARD, there have been few national grassroots organizations of the sort seen in the US. Some, such as the Organization of Women of African and Asian Descent (OWAAD), were quite influential in the early days of post-war migration, only to dissolve into factional infighting. One enduring presence, however, has been the Joint Council for the Welfare of Immigrants (JCWI). It has successfully combined the role of national lobbyist on behalf of migrants, with that of providing advice on individual problems. Beyond this, there is the large non-'racial' body referred to in the previous chapter, the Anti-Nazi League (ANL). Others also drawing from all communities include the Campaign Against Racism and Fascism (CARF), Rock against Racism, and Kick Racism out of Football.

Whereas the NAACP has provided some continuity at a national level (indeed throughout the twentieth century), the only major generic 'pressure group' in the UK is in fact a quango (quasi non-governmental organization): the CRE. This was not established until 1976 and, crucially, was a result of legislation rather than being a *direct* outcome of community activism. So, whilst ostensibly acting as the independent conscience of the government it is also funded by it. This inevitably means that, as we shall see in the next chapter, its policy role is severely compromised.

In Britain, the momentum for social change has in fact been provided by a myriad of actors adopting a variety of strategies. These have included lobbying organizations, single issue campaigns, faith-based institutions, cultural groups, minority trade and business collectives, women's groups and youth groups, supplemented on an *ad hoc* basis by national research from academic social scientists and independent bodies such as the Policy Studies Institute (Ratcliffe 2001b). There are, in fact, many sources of, and roles for, social agency in opposing discrimination, racism and other forms of 'social exclusion'. The following typology should be regarded as indicative rather than exhaustive:

- **Locally based single-issue campaigns**. An obvious example of this would be concerted opposition to prostitution, and the perceived failure of the police to tackle it: this has already happened in Balsall Heath, Birmingham and Manningham in Bradford. A second might be collective action (say) to provide work or housing opportunities, or to win planning permission to build a mosque or community centre. An example of the former would be the Single Homeless Action Group in Handsworth (Birmingham), established to help (largely workless) black youngsters find accommodation.
- **The single issue campaign with implications far beyond the local**. Here the obvious case would be Doreen and Neville Lawrence's brave struggle to get justice in the case of their son's brutal murder. (They succeeded where the Deptford campaign failed (see Chapter 8, and M. Phillips and T. Phillips op.cit.: 323–48).)
- **Active involvement in local politics as a way of carrying forward an emancipatory agenda**. This can be extremely effective, in theory at least. The only problem is that those who come forward tend to be self-styled 'community leaders' with an underlying agenda quite different from the majority of their constituents, that is those whose interests they are supposed to represent.
- **The formation of local community/voluntary groups**. These can quite easily turn into highly effective political pressure groups. In a city like Bradford, for example, there is a myriad of organizations: from Asian youth groups to womens' groups to umbrella organizations involving all those of African and Caribbean origin. Elsewhere in Britain, the Southall Black Sisters have rightly achieved national prominence for their campaigning work on behalf of migrant women.
- In communities where religion is rather more central to the conduct of everyday life than it is to the average citizen in a secular society like Britain, **faith-based organizations** can play a vital role. In Bradford, the obvious example is the Bradford Council for Mosques.
- Up to the last decade or so (that is prior to the decimation of manufacturing industry), a variety of **workers' organizations** played a major role in local politics in areas like Handsworth (Rex and Tomlinson op.cit.; Ratcliffe 1981). Notable here were the Indian Workers' Association, Bangladeshi Workers' Association, and so on.
- The development of **minority-run media organizations**. There are now major national newspapers, magazines and radio/TV stations run by members of Britain's African, Caribbean and South Asian communities. These can be extremely effective in informing and then mobilizing people. Most major towns and cities with

sizeable minority populations also have extremely popular (minority-run) radio stations. (Quite apart from direct ownership, it is important to add that minority professionals are (slowly) gaining access to more significant roles in 'mainstream' media companies.)

The plethora of organizations and empowerment strategies in many ways mirrors the sociopolitical fragmentation of Britain's minority populations. As a means of promoting greater social cohesion more generally, the current government has begun to talk much more positively about introducing a form of 'neighbourhood renewal' that, theoretically at least, involves a more meaningful, constructive dialogue between local government and the citizenry, that is individual residents. The key word now is empowerment. There is also a rather belated recognition that 'dialogue' and 'consultation' in the past have, far too often, meant little more than the explanation (to residents) of proposed policies at public meetings. To make matters worse, the latter have conventionally been held at the local town hall: a strategy almost ensuring sparse attendance. It remains to be seen whether the 'new policy' amounts to more than political rhetoric.

Civil rights in the US and UK: two contrasting paradigms?

Despite the earlier arguments, there is technically a national civil rights movement in the UK. Indeed, the organization that bears this name has recruited some highly respected figures, most notably: Michael Mansfield QC (the Civil Rights lawyer), Lee Bridges (Professor of Law at the University of Warwick, and a member of the Institute of Race Relations), and Imran Khan (the key barrister in the Lawrence case). But the sad fact is that few have heard of it.

Earlier national organizations, such as CARD and OWAAD rose quickly to prominence, and then faded just as quickly. Like CARD, some local organizations, such as ACSHO (the Afro-Caribbean Self-Help Organization, well respected in Birmingham in the 1970s) even modelled themselves on elements of the US movement (in this case the Black Panthers – Rex and Tomlinson 1979: 257–60). But none gelled into an effective nation movement. The obvious question is: why not? Why has Britain never had a CRM on the US lines and scale?

At the risk of oversimplifying complex historical processes, one might suggest two main reasons. The first has to do with the legacy of the enslavement of Africans on US soil. As we have seen, Jim Crow effectively drew an indelible 'caste' line between 'white' and 'black'. The very fact that US scholars both reify 'race' (by rejecting the European convention of placing the term in inverted commas) and draw a clear distinction between race and ethnicity when talking about black and 'other' minority groups, is highly significant. For them and the majority of Americans, ethnicity is relatively fluid: race is not. The essentialization of difference in this rigid way, and the subsequent inferiorization of those who are ascriptively 'black', provide the background conditions for mobilization on white-black lines. None of these pre-conditions apply in the UK.

It is this solidarity in the US, and the corresponding lack of it in the UK, which also provide the second reason (for the absence of a CRM in the UK). But for the relatively small-scale exploitation of Africans for domestic slavery, the English institution was largely an 'arm's-length' process (best exemplified by absentee landlordism). Subsequent migration to the UK has taken the form of a continual process, with the absorption of many peoples over the past few centuries. More recently, as discussed in Chapter 4, post-war World War II immigration began with eastern and southern Europeans and continued with the arrival of New Commonwealth citizens. It is this diversity of ethnicities, nationalities and cultures which has always undermined attempts to unite minority groups under a national umbrella movement.

This diversity is also reflected at the local level, in the sense that UK towns and cities have very different ethnic compositions (Ratcliffe 1996a). In these circumstances, it is not surprising that local (minority ethnic) community groups and single-issue campaigns thrive. Even where local concerns have a national resonance, this is not necessarily apparent to, or considered significant by, the community groups concerned. This may also partly explain why urban disorder has tended to be highly localized, the broader resonance being reflected in what the media have trivialized as (mere) 'copy-cat riots'.

Conclusions and further reading

This chapter has explored very different models of community activism. The wider effects are often difficult to discern, and the unintended consequences at times actually undermine the position of minorities. But legislative changes in both the US and UK have undoubtedly strengthened the *de iure* (if not always the *de facto*) citizenship rights of minorities (see Chapter 10). As implied by the earlier discussions, it would be naïve to suggest a simple one-to-one causal relationship between ethnic mobilization and policy change. A large number of factors are involved in such change processes, not least social science as an active agent, individual and collective agency on the part of political elites, and the internal logics of a global(ized) capitalism.

These matters will be considered once again in the concluding chapter of the book, including the actual and potential efficacy of sociology and sociologists as a means of promoting change (Ratcliffe 2001b). For now, we pause to consider some of the key texts on the struggle for civil rights in the US and UK.

Here we face two contrasting problems. The US civil rights literature is vast, making the nomination of texts very much a matter of personal taste. The UK literature, on the other hand, is extremely sparse, posing a very different kind of problem. As to the US, Gunnar Myrdal's (1944) classic study provides an excellent historical backdrop to contemporary struggles. For detailed explorations of black nationalism and nationalist movements, Pinkney (1976) and Carmichael and Hamilton (1967) remain seminal texts, despite being rather dated.

In terms of mainstream civil rights, Marable (1991, and subsequent editions) is extremely useful in that it combines an attention to historical detail with a succinct, readable style. For a highly detailed profile of the life and work of Martin Luther King Jr, it would be difficult to better the seminal volume by Branch (1988). Readers requiring a more contemporary text that spans most of the concerns addressed in this chapter and the next, would do well to consult Steinberg (2000). Where this book scores in particular is in its coverage of the legacy of the US civil rights struggles.

As Britain has not experienced a civil rights movement as such, discussions about the role of collective agency in promoting change are somewhat diffuse. There is no single text that covers the material in the current chapter. This being said, Gilroy (1987) and M. Phillips and T. Phillips (1998) provide excellent accounts of the struggles for acceptance of post-war migrants: the former rather theoretical, the latter containing a wealth of illustrative material. As to the experiences of British Muslims, Lewis (1994) provides an interesting, and somewhat controversial, account – controversial in the sense of perhaps overestimating the efficacy of agency in determining their current status in British society.

10 Anti-discrimination Law, Affirmative Action and the Pursuit of 'Equal Opportunities'

Introduction: the role of law in combating exclusion

As we saw in the previous chapter, individual and collective agency has a major role in combating exclusionary processes. Collective mobilization in particular can have powerful direct and indirect effects – direct in the sense of having an immediate impact on the lives of those suffering the ill-effects of 'exclusion'; indirect in that legislative change may ensue. The big question in the latter case is whether changes in the law necessarily have the desired effect.

Most would probably suggest that the answer is a qualified 'yes'. Although outlawing certain discriminatory acts cannot, except by implication, change the way people think, it can at least remove some of the worst effects of negative thoughts. Much depends, as will be seen later in the chapter, on whether there is the political will to make the legislation work.

As to the limits of legislation, there are some much more intractable ethical and moral concerns. A core feature of the way in which individuals interact with, and then make sense of, the social world is 'discrimination', interpreted in a rather different (neutral/statistical) fashion than above. Making sense of the world typically means generating categories of 'the other'. Dimensions of otherness may be based on ethnicity, 'race', religion and culture, but are also likely to feature gender, age, disability status, class, sexual orientation, physical attractiveness, height, 'presentation of self', and so on. Judgements arise from the complex dialectical relationship between the individual, 'society', normative value systems and common sense, sedimented 'knowledge'. Where those judgements lead to exclusionary behaviour the law is seen to have a role.

But as Phillips (1999) asks: 'which equalities matter?' Whatever view one takes on the broader ethical and moral principles, in practice the law is deployed in areas where there is evidence of historically entrenched structural discrimination. In other words, it prioritizes issues such as 'race' and gender, and to a lesser extent age, disability and sexual orientation. As to those factors that lie outside the formal equalities agenda, it could be argued that they may be covered indirectly as people become more conscious of the ways in which illegitimate/inappropriate judgements are formed.

To neo-liberals and conservatives, this intrudes on the assumed sovereign rights of individuals and the workings of the 'free' market. Stretching an earlier point, they might argue that it is an intrinsic quality of human nature to discriminate (and not simply in the non-hierarchical, statistical sense). Despite protestations to the contrary (van den Berghe 1986), this was a position adopted by many of those espousing sociobiology. As Lewontin, Rose and Kamin (1979) argued, naturalizing xenophobia and altruism merely endorses biological determinism. Furthermore, even if certain forms of behaviour are encoded in one's genes, this does not make them 'right': nor does it make them socially acceptable.

Societies that have used legislation to curb exclusionary behaviour have in practice adopted markedly different approaches. At the risk of over-simplyfying rather complex matters, there are essentially two quite distinct paradigms: one that is 'means led', the other 'ends led'. These conform broadly to the 'liberal' and 'radical' models sketched out by Jewson and Mason (1989) in the context of evaluating 'equal opportunities' policies.

An exemplar of the liberal paradigm would be the UK. The focus is on the modification of policies and practices as a means of achieving equality. The argument is that, if procedures are stripped of their discriminatory potential, the desired ends will ultimately be met. In India, however, it was recognized that the only way to deal with centuries of oppression/exclusion of the un-scheduled castes, or 'untouchables', was to make a more direct intervention in the customs and practices of public institutions such as schools and universities. These groups had previously been limited to a highly marginalized existence, banished from most areas of social life and confined to segregated areas and a narrow range of menial occupations.

The new policy, within the broader remit of Sanskritization, was 'ends led' in that, for example, following reforms in the school system a certain number of university places was reserved for the unscheduled castes. This approach has much in common with the policy of 'affirmative action' adopted in the US. Once again, the central feature is a quota system, whereby jobs and college places (say) are reserved for members of those groups which have been subject, historically, to systematic discrimination.

The central focus of this chapter will be on how anti-discrimination legislation comes into being, and the factors that determine its success or failure. Particularly important here is the question of political will from central government, but there is also a variety of other factors that can limit, or indeed enhance, the transformatory potential of legislation. We will also be concerned to explore the choice of approach, in particular why very different models of intervention come to be adopted. As with the previous chapter the major exemplars will be the US and UK, and once again these will be compared and contrasted.

Affirmative action in the US: a radical model?

Once action had been deemed desirable, senior politicians in the US deployed a rather conciliatory approach to counter the obvious inequalities in material life chances between African Americans and whites, and between men and women. In the early 1940s, President Roosevelt issued Executive Orders declaring an end to discrimination in the federal civil service. He also created the Fair Employment Practices Committee (FEPC). Truman continued in this vein (in the 1950s) with the outlawing of discrimination in the federal government structure and the armed forces. Crucially, he also established a system of 'contract compliance' procedures for government contractors (that is, companies that undertook work for government). In the 1940s the keyword had had been 'non-discrimination'; in the 1950s it became 'equal opportunities'.

The policy of gentle persuasion was found to be ineffective in the extreme, especially in the South where, as was seen in the last chapter, *de facto* segregation in most areas of life continued despite the formal repeal of Jim Crow laws. It was only with the failure of these strategies to produce tangible results that first Kennedy and then LBJ, in 1961 and 1965 respectively, turned to the more radical idea of 'affirmative action' (in Executive Order 11246).

Affirmative action:

> is based on the argument that simply removing existing impediments is not sufficient for changing the relative positions of women and people of color. And it is based on the premise that to be truly effective in altering the unequal distribution of life chances, it is essential that employers take specific steps to remedy the consequences of discrimination.
>
> (Herring and Collins 1995: 164)

They further define it as:

> A government mandated or voluntary program that consists of activities specifically to identify, recruit, promote, and/or retain members of disadvantaged minority groups in order to overcome the results of past discrimination and to deter employers from engaging in discriminatory practices in the present.

The need for affirmative action therefore derives from a structural deficit reflected in the long-standing absence of a 'level playing field'. Prior to the passing of Title VII of the Civil Rights Act 1964, blacks had no legal recourse in the face of employment discrimination. Title VII resulted in the establishment of the Equal Employment Opportunity Commission (EEOC), an executive agency with the authority to investigate allegations of discrimination. Then, owing to complaints about a lack of enforcement powers, the Title was strengthened in 1972 so that 'the EEOC was now able to bring charges and bring federal court action to remedy cases of employment discrimination' (Hodge and Feagin 1995: 103).

More significant than the EEOC was the second arm of affirmative action enforcement, the Office of Federal Contract Compliance Programs (OFCCP). It 'transformed the concept of affirmative action into a specific and accountable employment practice' (Herring and Collins 1995: 166). Federal contractors were required 'to submit a written "affirmative action plan" with numerical goals and timetables for achieving these goals for hiring and promoting women, blacks and other designated groups' (ibid.: 166). This is more forthright than anything ever contemplated in the UK.

Affirmative Action was therefore the product of Presidential Executive Orders and aspects of civil rights legislation, rather than being a free standing piece of 'race' (and/or gender) legislation. The degree of intervention into the policies and practices of private companies (and institutions such as universities) provoked much anger. It was seen as a major challenge to their (assumed) sovereign authority, and an unwarranted interference in human resource matters. There was then a series of more specific complaints about the philosophical basis of the policy, and not simply from the neo-conservatives. Many argued that it has helped the wrong people, and that it has harmed the prospects of poor dispossessed whites, whilst not affecting the already privileged. Herring and Collins (op. cit.: 168) suggest three main areas of criticism:

1. Affirmative action is ineffective

Many view the program as an example of profligacy on the part of the state. Those on the political right often take this view, but so do others who simply argue that it has had no discernible impact on the mass of minority group members. Another important strand of the argument is that the wrong victims and wrong beneficiaries are targeted. Thus, for example, poor dispossessed (male) whites may be wrongly disadvantaged, and comparatively affluent middle-class blacks given a further advantage. William Julius Wilson, in a significant follow-up to his *The Declining Significance of Race* (1978), entitled *The Truly Disadvantaged* (1987), argued that the subjects of his title are left behind by the policy. They lack the resources and skills to compete effectively in the labour market. As Herring and Collins argue (1995: 169):

...policies based on preferential treatment of minorities linked to group outcomes are insufficient precisely because the relatively advantaged members of racial minority communities will be selected and will reap the benefits to the detriment of poor minorities. Moreover, those whites who are rejected due to preferential programs might be the most disadvantaged whites whose qualifications are marginal precisely because of their disadvantages.

2. Affirmative action stigmatizes minorities

The second criticism in many ways stems from the first. In a credentialized society, where rewards are normatively linked to the possession of certain qualifications, the breaking of these 'rules' is almost inevitably going to lead to a hostile reaction from the aggrieved. The argument about a level playing field and the existence of historically entrenched disadvantage is lost on those who feel cheated in the present. It was after all not they who are directly responsible for these problems. One response is to protest and then litigate: the other is to attack those who benefit from 'preferential treatment'.

It is common for those benefiting from Affirmative Action to be undermined psychologically. Colleagues are heard to whisper that person A did not win his/her post on merit: s/he was only there because of the policy. Even when no such feelings exist, it is likely that A will suspect they do. This process amplifies all of those insecurities that have been fuelled by years of virtual apartheid through Jim Crow.

But, there is a broader set of problems here:

- The policy tends to stigmatize *all* minority workers and women, simply by implying that they all need a 'hand up'.
- It can also lead to a self-fulfilling prophecy. If lower attainment targets are set for disadvantaged groups, there is less incentive for them to 'aim high'. Less will also be expected of them in the work situation, and this may lead to a reinforcement of the stigmatization process.

3. Affirmative action is reverse discrimination

In both of the cases outlined below the complainants argued that they had been the victims of reverse discrimination. The argument is that to the degree that minorities and women make economic progress, white men suffer. Moreover, as Herring and Collins (1995: 170) argue:

> ...innocent white men who have never discriminated against minorities or women might be punished unfairly while some chauvinists

and bigots might be spared. This objection to affirmative action makes the judgment (as an empirical fact) that whites lose to minorities. This empirical fact, per se, should disallow affirmative action according to these critics.

The following high-profile cases illustrate these objections to the 'radical' approach to equalities.

The case of Allan Bakke

Bakke was a 38-year-old (white) engineer who decided to undergo a radical career shift. He applied to university medical schools as a mature student. Having been rejected by the University of California at Davis (UCD) in 1973, and then again in autumn 1974, he delved into their selection procedures. This revealed that, under the University's Affirmative Action Program, 16 of the 100 first-year places were reserved for members of economically and educationally disadvantaged minority groups. Supported by a member of the University's own administration, he then employed a lawyer to file a suit against UCD on the grounds that its admissions policy had violated the equal protection clause of the Fourteenth Amendment (of the Constitution).

The Yolo County (Californian) Supreme Court decided that UCD had indeed discriminated against Bakke on grounds of his race, but did not order them to admit him. Both the University and Bakke appealed the decision. The Californian Supreme Court, in September 1976, decided in favour of Bakke, and ordered UCD to admit him. But the college was permitted to retain its admissions policy, pending a review by the US Supreme Court. This august body decided, with a majority of five to four, that the admissions program was illegal in that it contravened Title VII of the Civil Rights Act 1964. As Pinkney says (1984: 151), the 'minority declared the admissions program, if administered properly, violated neither the Civil Rights Act of 1964 nor the equal protection clause of the Fourteenth Amendment'. But the damage had been done: this was a savage blow to the Affirmative Action movement. As Pinkney points out, it also created further political rifts on ethnic lines in that a number of Jewish groups came out in support of the neo-conservative line on the Bakke case.

The case of Brian Weber

A second high profile challenge to Affirmative Action came in 1979. Brian Weber, a 32-year-old (white) employee of Kaiser Aluminum claimed that the company's policy to increase the number of minority employees violated Title VII. The policy had been instituted because, although the company denied discrimination, in the first ten years of its life less than 10 per cent of its workforce were black (in a local labour market where around 40 per cent were black). The steelworkers union devised the programme in the context of collective bargaining with the company.

The programme called for an increase in black and female representation in the better paid skilled jobs. Pinkney (1984: 163) says:

> Goals set to achieve this called for admitting blacks and women until they constituted 40 percent and 5 percent of the employees, respectively. These goals were to be accomplished by admitting workers to the training program on a fifty-fifty basis: one minority worker or woman to one white male.

Weber applied for the special training program but was turned down on the grounds that he did not have sufficient seniority. He argued that he had more than a few of the blacks who were accepted. This prompted him to file a grievance with the union. Following its rejection, and his subsequent failure to get a hearing with the EEOC, he filed a class action suit on behalf of all white workers at Kaiser (an option not available to complainants in the UK – see below). The Federal District Court upheld the claim on the grounds that 'the black workers benefiting from the program had not **themselves** been the victims of discrimination' (ibid.: 163 – emphasis added).

After much legal dispute, the US Supreme Court decided that the policy did not necessarily violate Title VII. This was seen as an important victory for minorities and women. Had the case not been won this would have dealt a well-nigh fatal blow to Affirmative Action.

As it is, the election as President of Ronald Reagan, and then George Bush Sr, signalled concerted opposition to the strategy (paralleling Thatcherite opposition to the British legislation – see below). Herring and Collins (1995) argue that Bush was particularly vigorous in opposing Affirmative Action policies. He also vetoed a new version of the Civil Rights Act on the grounds that it would have **required** employers to establish quotas. Since 1980, the retreat from 'protective legislation' and 'race-based reparations' (which continues apace with George W. Bush) has been part of what many commentators have called the end of the Second Reconstruction. The argument is that whites found new ways to keep the 'uppity Negro' in his (sic) place. Whatever view one takes on this, it is undeniably the case that Affirmative Action is in retreat. We shall return later to the question of whether it has achieved what it set out to do.

Race Relations legislation in the UK: a liberal response to exclusion?

British legislation has never sanctioned the degree of market intervention implied by Affirmative Action. Although community activism and urban unrest played a major part in promoting the need for legislation, it was largely left to a small band of highly committed parliamentary 'pioneers' to actually bring about its introduction. It took many years. As early as 1951, Reg (later Lord) Sorensen sponsored a Private Members Bill. It failed, as did a further ten attempts between 1952 and 1964 by Fenner (later Lord) Brockway.

The first piece of legislation was the Race Relations Act 1965. Many observers saw this as a mere sop to minorities and 'liberals on "race"' as its provisions were extremely narrow. Only (direct) discrimination 'in places of public resort' was covered by the legislation. In other words, a case could be brought with respect to alleged discrimination in cinemas, clubs, restaurants and cafés, but not in relation to the spheres of education, employment, housing, and so on (the issues which really concerned Britain's minorities).

Prime Minister Harold Wilson later defended his decision to go ahead with the Bill on the grounds that, with at least something on the Statute Book, he had provided a base from which other (more radical) legislation could be developed. He had a very small working majority in the House, and was acutely aware of the likely political consequences of appearing to be too liberal/'soft' on 'race'. Even though he had already demonstrated his 'toughness' on immigration (by virtue of the 1965 White Paper on Commonwealth Immigrants), it was only a matter of months since the election of Peter Griffiths in a key by-election in Smethwick (a formerly safe Labour seat lost as a result of local Tories 'playing the race card' – see Chapter 4).

Pressure to strengthen the legislation came from a number of quarters. As noted in the previous chapter, community based organizations such as CARD ensured that inequalities remained on the policy agenda. Then, a major national study undertaken by Political and Economic Planning (PEP) revealed the precise levels of disadvantage suffered by minorities (Daniel 1968). Although the result was the introduction of the Race Relations Act 1968 (RRA1968), the Labour government remained determined to pursue a hard line on 'race'. The bitter pill in effect came with the introduction of the Commonwealth Immigrants Act 1968; a measure justified on the basis that only if the influx of migrants was tightly controlled could harmonious 'race relations' be ensured (see Chapter 4).

The new RRA was in many ways the brainchild of Anthony Lester, a human rights lawyer who had been a dominant force in CARD. Although it still covered only **direct** discrimination (on grounds of colour, race or national origin) and excluded religion, its provisions were much broader than those contained in the 1965 Act (Lester 1998). It now outlawed discrimination in housing, education, the labour market, and so on.

In terms of support there were two bodies:

- The *National Committee for Commonwealth Immigrants (NCCI)* was replaced by the *Community Relations Commission (CRC)*. This was essentially tasked with the duty to promote 'racial harmony' and undertake appropriate research. It also had a more direct duty to encourage the formation of local Community Relations Councils (also, confusingly, known as CRCs). The title of these bodies gives some inkling of their role in practice, if not in theory. This was to attempt to harmonize relations between minority and majority communities.
- The *Race Relations Board (RRB)*, which had been formed at the time of the previous Act, was reconstituted but with wider responsibilities. It now had a direct duty to investigate complaints of racial discrimination (rather than simply provide advice and legal recourse).

Whereas many of the complaints brought to the RRB under the 1965 Act fell outside the remit of the legislation, this was now less likely. For a number of reasons, however, the new Act could not be regarded a success in terms of confronting discriminatory policies and practices.

- Research showed that although cases of **overt** discrimination were fewer, the incidence of **covert** acts was greater. Institutions tended to conceal discrimination rather than eliminate it.
- Investigations often took so long that complainants to the RRB were put under a great deal of pressure for protracted periods (if the Board decided that there was a case to answer). The Board was also rather conservative when judging the likelihood of victory (meaning that many 'strong' claims were never tested in court).
- Integral to the latter was the fact that the Board had too few powers. It did not even have the power to subpoena documents and witnesses. This meant, of course, that it was extremely difficult to pursue an effective case against those alleged to have committed an offence under the legislation (that is, one involving **direct** discrimination).
- One key factor limited the propensity of victims to file a complaint. Sanctions were minimal, the most likely result of a conviction being a modest fine and the serving of a 'non-discrimination notice'. Not surprisingly, minority communities remained largely unimpressed.
- The general approach was low-key and conciliatory (as is suggested by the mission/duty imposed on the CRC).
- It could be argued that a system that relies on **individual-based**

complaints is far too narrow. General processes tend to underlie, and underpin, individual behaviour.

- Finally, the definition of discrimination was too narrow. It was in practice extremely difficult, even if the Board was able to acquire the relevant documents and witnesses, to build a convincing case of direct discrimination; that a particular action(s) had knowingly been driven by a discriminatory motive as specified by the legislation.

The result was that successful convictions were few, and where companies were involved they tended not to fear the 'negative' publicity. In a society with normative value systems infused with endemic racism, it is not surprising that they would have little to fear from such public censure.

A second national study from PEP (Smith 1977) added to pressure for a rethink. The Race Relations Act 1976 (RRA1976) provided, on the surface at least, solutions to many of the earlier problems. The CRC and RRB were fused into a single body, the Commission for Racial Equality (CRE). This had a duty to provide advice to those alleging discrimination, but the cases themselves would go through the normal legal system. The legal context was strengthened in a number of ways:

- The definition of discrimination was widened to cover **indirect**, as well as **direct**, forms. This meant, for example, that the imposition of a policy or condition that had a disproportionately negative impact on minorities was deemed unlawful, unless it could be justified as necessary in the context in which it was being applied. An obvious example came to light in research conducted by Ratcliffe (1980). In recruiting shop floor workers for a foundry, one company introduced a comprehension test based on material from *The Times* newspaper. This policy was justified on health and safety grounds, in that workers needed to be in a position to understand safety signs. But the majority of applicants for these posts were recently arrived South Asian migrants with, in many cases, only a rudimentary command of English. The policy was in fact unlawful under the RRA1976 in that it would inevitably have a disproportionately adverse effect on this group, and could not be justified on the suggested grounds. On-the-job training in health and safety matters, including information on signage, would have been sufficient.
- Those pursuing a legal case now had the power to *subpoena* documents and witnesses (though it did not prevent obstruction and prevarication).
- The primary focus moved away from individual cases of discrimination. The CRE was given the power to initiate a formal investigation against an organization even in the absence of a formal

complaint. All that was needed was *prima facie* evidence of the existence of discriminatory policies and/or practices.

Through the 1980s and 1990s local CRCs gradually began to re-brand themselves as Racial Equality Councils (RECs), to indicate a greater focus on the drive for equality rather than (merely) the promotion of harmonious relations between communities. Radical writers and activists such as Anil Sivanandan (1976, 1982) had always argued that the CRCs, as well as 'incorporating' black professionals (who might otherwise have challenged the wider polity), simply performed a 'buffer function' in keeping the local peace rather than confronting racism. In this context the shift in focus sounds a promising development. But, for a variety of reasons, achievements failed to match up to the promise.

Considered (in law) civil misdemeanors rather than criminal acts, transgressions of the legislation still only attracted modest sanctions. A major corporation, such as Massey Ferguson, even when found guilty of 'racial' discrimination via word-of-mouth recruitment (CRE 1982) would merely be served a non-discrimination notice accompanied by a modest fine. They would then be informed of the CRE's intention to re-visit the plant twelve months later (to check whether the company had met the conditions of the notice).

Local RECs have always suffered from an internal contradiction. Whereas office staff are funded by the CRE, premises are provided by local authorities. The price of this shared funding relationship is an expectation of significant political representation on the part of the latter. In many Conservative-controlled areas this has (further) limited the effectiveness of bodies already hampered by funding limitations and the 'election' of 'community representatives' (often business**men**) who only too rarely actually represented the interests of the local minority populous.

This hints at the major problem: a general lack of political will (Sanders 1998). Conservative governments from 1979 to 1997 had little or no sympathy for the CRE's mission. As a result, its funding was progressively reduced, at a time when (as suggested by earlier chapters) its job was becoming more, not less, taxing. This time, a new (third) national study from the Policy Studies Institute (Brown 1984) did not result in the strengthening of legislation. Publicly, the view of ministers was that the existing legislation struck the right balance between the pursuit of equalities and the sovereign rights of private business. But there was also a strong sense that some senior ministers would not have mourned the demise of the CRE.

With the election of New Labour in May 1997 many expected, or at least hoped, that things might change. But the Conservative's policy of increasing financial austerity was retained. Had it not been for the Macpherson report in 1999 (see Chapters 8 and 9) it is highly unlikely that there would have been a strengthening of the legislation. Significantly, this came not in the form of a new Act but via an amendment to the RRA1976: the Race Relations (Amendment) Act 2000. This contained some important new provisions:

- The police were finally brought within the provisions of the legislation (they had been specifically excluded from the RRA1976).
- A new Statutory Duty in respect of racial equality was imposed on all public authorities. The latter were required to demonstrate by the end of May 2002 that they had met their obligations under the Act (CRE 2001).
- Crucially, the definition of a public authority was widened. Any private company that undertakes work for a public body (for example a local authority or health authority), by virtue of this relationship becomes a public authority itself. It remains the duty of the latter, however, to ensure that the policies of the former conform to their legal obligations.

Whilst clearly an improvement over previous legislation, this stops far short of the radical measures taken in the US. Full-blown contract compliance is difficult to pursue under current UK and European legislation (though some authorities are making pioneering moves in this direction – Orton and Ratcliffe 2003). The bottom line is that the political will (from central government) to tackle 'race' equality in a forthright manner is ultimately lacking.

Why are the US and UK approaches to combating discrimination so different?

We have seen that the approach to dealing with structural inequality varies markedly between the UK and countries like the US and India. The differences may be characterized broadly as between the 'liberal' approach focusing on means and the 'radical' model that concentrates efforts on ends. The former could be said to place the emphasis on non-discrimination (or non-exclusion) rather than anti-discrimination, the latter (at least in the US and Indian variants) on direct engagement in the market as a means of combating the legacy of age-old normative systems featuring *de iure* discrimination/exclusion. There is a strong argument that in this latter case, there is little alternative to the more interventionist approach.

Comparing and contrasting the US and UK models, there are number of key points:

- A common element of both is a general **lack of political will** at the highest level. The CRE has consistently complained of a lack of support from government, even more so as funding cuts have seriously undermined its efforts. Affirmative action has also been undermined consistently, if not from the top (for example by Presidents Reagan and Bush, both Sr and Jr) then by State legislatures. The end result is a system in at least partial retreat for three decades.

- **Class Actions**. In the US (as illustrated by the Weber case, ironically used against affirmative action in this instance), one can strengthen one's case (based on that individual's experience) by linking the substance of the complaint/allegation to the experience of others. Discrimination at an institutional level is never, by definition, a one-off, individual event: it is part of an exclusionary system. Class action suits are not permissible under UK law.

- Affirmative action effectively permits what could be termed 'positive discrimination': the UK model, in contrast, permits only 'positive action'. Hence, in the context of employment, for example, UK job advertisements may be designed so as to encourage applications from members of historically disadvantaged groups (e.g. minorities, women, and those with disabilities). This means that whereas in the US the setting of *quotas* is legal, UK legislation permits only *targets*.

- **Contract Compliance**. In the UK contract compliance, i.e. the insistence that a company's policies and practices conform to certain equalities criteria *before* they are awarded a public sector contract, has never been formally sanctioned by legislation. Lester (1998) makes a plea for its introduction and, as predicted by him, the Parekh Report (Runnymede Trust 2000), endorses this view. All the available research demonstrates that gentle encouragement simply does not work. The business case for having a 'race equality' policy can be made, as it was (very effectively) by the CRE (1998), but in practice organizations have to be **required** to do things. In this case, they need to be told that to stand a chance of winning public sector contracts they have to put their equalities house in order.

It will not have escaped the attention of the astute reader that discussions in this chapter have oscillated between 'race equality' and a more generic 'equalities' agenda. This in fact represents the final key difference between the UK and US approaches. The question of how legislation can deal effectively with intersecting arenas of exclusion, based on the social significance attached to various dimensions of difference, is extremely complex.

As seen earlier in the chapter, US affirmative action principally targets African Americans and women, two groups identified as suffering historically from both individual and institutionalized discrimination. In Britain, separate legislation deals with discrimination against minorities (of all heritages, with certain qualifications) and women. As a consequence, separate bodies are charged with responsibilities in these areas: the CRE in the arena of 'race', the Equal Opportunities Commission (EOC) in that of gender. A third body, the Disability Rights Commission (DRC) polices legislation in this area.

There are arguments for and against both approaches. Dealing simultaneously with different sources of exclusionary behaviour will help to avoid a problem that has at times blighted the UK system. Black women have sometimes found themselves being shuttled backwards and forwards between the CRE and EOC because of disputes about the precise source of alleged discriminatory treatment.

Separating cases of (say) gender and 'race' discrimination can, however, be beneficial in one very important respect. The existence of two Commissions ensures that the appropriate weight is given to forms of exclusion with very different historical roots and contemporary manifestations. From the perspective of many in the UK working to combat discrimination on grounds of 'race' and ethnicity, the dangers of moving away from the present system are clear.

The integration of the policing bodies would inevitably see their particular concerns dropping down the agenda. In justifying this view they would simply point to the experiences of local authorities in the 1980s. Under attack from Margaret Thatcher's administrations for pursuing 'loony left' policies, large metropolitan authorities were forced (via tight fiscal restraint) to cut costs in 'non-essential', in practice non-service, areas. 'Race units' and 'women's units' were merged to form unitary bodies concerned with 'equalities', or the latter function was decentralized. Whichever route was followed, the rather smaller 'race' lobby tended to lose out in the process.

The contemporary political reality, as far as the UK is concerned, is that there is growing pressure for the functions currently fulfilled by the EOC, DRC and CRE to be undertaken by a new generic body. Indeed, at the end of October 2003, the government announced plans for an Equalities and Human Rights Commission, in the process confirming the demise of the three existing commissions.

Part of the pressure is coming from the EU in the form of wider European legislation. In response, the UK government has signalled its intention to press on with plans to introduce a single equalities Act: the new commission being tasked with its policing and promotion. Bearing in mind deep reservations on the part of the 'race lobby', one suspects that this will not happen without a protracted struggle.

Engineering social change: the limits of legislation

We have spent some time looking at very different ways of tackling forms of discrimination. The big question, though, is whether they work. Probably the key issue is the political will to ensure they do: laws in themselves cannot change anything. As noted earlier, they cannot in any case change the way people think, except by a process of osmosis. They might even have the opposite effect.

In the US, massive communal pressure ultimately resulted in the adoption of a radical, interventionist approach. Focusing principally on the group that had been subjected to chattel slavery and then, following 'emancipation', a system of virtual apartheid, the policies were highly effective. They were particularly effective in the arenas of education and employment (with voting rights legislation and associated voter registration drives improving matters further). It is difficult to see how the advancement of African Americans could have been achieved without such a radical paradigm shift. The same applies in the context of the unscheduled castes of India.

Anger from neo-liberals, conservatives and those whose super-ordinate position was being threatened led to the undermining of affirmative action. But this was not before major changes had taken place (BBC2 2003a, and see Chapter 9). Some would no doubt argue that the policy has run its course: that in many ways it has achieved its goal. There is some truth in this, but there remains a massive gulf between the, admittedly expanding, black middle class and the mass of urban blacks whose routes out of poverty and urban segregation seem as limited as ever (Marcuse 1996; Massey and Denton 2000; Allen 2001).

Defence of the UK's 'softly-softly' approach might be based on the rather obvious point that our respective histories are sharply divergent. Plantation slavery was never a feature of life in Britain itself; nor was legally sanctioned segregation. This has meant that the rigid 'color line', or virtual caste line, about which W. E. B. DuBois spoke so eloquently, is not directly relevant to the British case.

Despite the consistent lack of political will (at all levels), it is clear that almost forty years of legislation has borne fruit. Advances by minorities in all the substantive areas covered by the current volume are ample testament to that (Modood et al. 1997; Mason 2000, 2003). High profile investigations of discrimination (ultimately proven) such as those involving Massey Ferguson (CRE 1982), Hackney Council (CRE 1984b) and St. George's Hospital Medical School (CRE 1988), had an immediate policy impact in employment, social housing and higher education respectively. The publishing of various Codes of Practice advocating, among other things, active 'ethnic monitoring' in employment (CRE 1984a), rented housing (CRE 1991) and owner occupied housing (CRE 1992) served a useful purpose in promoting best practice. But, as implied earlier, progress is gradual rather than dramatic. Were the government to enforce widespread contract compliance, for example, rapid progress could be made in securing greater equality in the labour market. This is, however, unlikely to happen given New Labour's ambiguous position on 'race'.

The CRE has also been forced to change its role over the past decade. Largely because of severe budget constraints it has been all but compelled to abandon formal investigations into institutional discrimination, and focus more on its promotional role. It now concentrates in particular on working with the public sector to help to change operational cultures.

Further reading

Once again, the literature in this area is vast. In terms of US debates, Pinkney (1984) provides a very readable account of the possibilities and limits of affirmative action, as do a number of essays in the Smith and Feagin reader (1995). Steinberg (2000) presents an excellent review of the impact of successive legislation and social policy measures on the position of contemporary African Americans.

In terms of UK literature, the essays by Anthony Lester and Peter Sanders in the Blackstone et al. (1998) reader represent essential reading. Very useful also is the Parekh Report (Runnymede Trust 2000). This provides a comprehensive review of the contemporary legislation in the context of the various 'sites of exclusion' discussed in Part II of the current volume. An interesting supplement to this would be the collection of essays edited by Anwar, Roach and Sondhi (2000). The product of a seminar of invited speakers held at the University of Warwick, this is a series of reflections on the role, and actual/ potential efficacy, of legislation as a means of combating discrimination and racism.

Constraints on space have inevitably limited discussion of formal investigations and the various promotional activities undertaken by the CRE. For those wishing to know rather more about these, the best source of information is the CRE's website: *www.cre.gov.uk*. The critical reader will sense the overtly conciliatory tone of many of the good practice guides on combating 'racial' discrimination. Clearly illustrated by a very recent publication on public procurement (CRE 2003) one can 'see', or at least sense, the hidden hand of government.

PART IV
CONCLUDING THOUGHTS

11 The Inclusive Society Revisited

One interpretation of the inclusive society is embodied in the idea of 'One Nation'. The current UK government has defined this as a place where:

> every colour is a good colour ... every member of every part of society is able to fulfil their potential ... racism is unacceptable and counteracted ... everyone is treated according to their needs and rights ... everyone recognises their responsibilities ... racial diversity is celebrated
>
> (Home Office 2000: 1, quoted in Runnymede Trust 2000: 40)

The Parekh Report (ibid.) was justified in adding a touch of cynicism in that the previous (pre-1997) government, ostensibly of a very different political persuasion, claimed commitment to a very similar mission. Where this vision of society may be said to fall short of the inclusive ideal is in its lack of recognition of the need to address broader social inequalities. There is, admittedly, an implicit acknowledgement of the desirability of creating a more level playing field so that the socially and materially disadvantaged can compete on more equal terms with those more fortunate. But there is little to defend the interests of those who fail to compete successfully. As argued earlier, this reflects a widespread rejection of redistributionist discourse (and, of course, the policies that might flow from it). Some would also argue that there is also an overbearing sense of communitarianism in the 'social cohesion' agenda (see Home Office 2003), in that the essence of inclusivity is not necessarily inconsistent with a willingness to tolerate, even respect, those who decide to opt out. This theme, and opposing viewpoints, will be discussed below.

Even without these qualifications the One Nation agenda is highly ambitious. The purpose of this concluding chapter is to assess the size of the task. In doing so, we need first to review the social forces that stand in the way of its fulfilment. We then need to assess the strength of opposing forces, whether these are community-based or more to do with wider political action and the deployment of legislation. It is also important to evaluate the role of social commentators, writers and activists, many based in academia or independent research units. The chapter concludes with a somewhat speculative assessment of the prospects for 'positive' social change over the coming decade.

The enemies of 'One Nation'

To talk of 'enemies' of the inclusivity project is in some senses misleading. It over-personalizes what is at core a problem of cultural value systems. As was seen in the first section of the book, deep-seated constructs of 'the other' are ultimately rooted in Britain's imperial heritage (and even in pre-colonial black-white dualisms – Césaire 1972). Western accounts of 'otherness' and the ways in which these infect contemporary relationships are now well documented, especially following the seminal work of Edward Said (1978, 1993).

The discursive content is constantly shifting due to the dialectical process outlined by Lawrence (1982a), but the very existence of negative images of 'the other' has direct material effects on those excluded from society's 'we'. In terms of social citizenship and other rights, however, it requires active agents to generate *de facto* inferior treatment. This appears as racist abuse, harassment and discrimination in the various substantive spheres addressed in Part II (and in others omitted due to constraints on space, for example health – see Nazroo 1997, 2001, 2002).

Many, if not most, exclusionary acts have rather less visible roots. 'Institutional racism' is now the generally accepted, if rather misleading, term used to describe the negative effects (at times unintentional) of organizational policies and practices (see Macpherson 1999). Intrinsic to this are rather more nebulous 'forces of regulation' (Harrison with Davis 2001) which have to do with institutional culture and ethos. We have seen compelling evidence of these less tangible forces in housing, education, employment and policing and the criminal justice system.

These processes clearly thwart the aims and aspirations of minorities. More overtly repressive are those who challenge the very essence of multiculturalism and therefore the idea of creating a One Nation culture. Most obvious amongst these, of course, are right-wing organizations such as the BNP, NF (National Front), Combat 18 and others which pursue an exclusivist, nationalist agenda. As we saw, since the devolution of powers to the Scottish and Welsh assemblies an ever-narrower form of English nationalism has flourished (in the sense of appealing to elements of the poor white, urban working class). The essence of this is a rejection of 'foreign' influences on 'English culture', a total halt to immigration (even with respect to refugees and asylum seekers) and, to the more extreme elements, a process of repatriation (despite the fact that around a half of the current 'non-white' population is UK-born).

Ironically, the appeal to certain elements of the nationalist agenda has exposed ambiguities in the New Labour agenda. Whilst formally espousing a joined-up approach to policy making, it has retained a 'Janus-faced' character in relation to issues of 'race'. As was seen in Chapter 4, the Party in government has consistently attempted to present itself as tough on immigration but fair towards settled migrants. Central to this is a constant 'bidding war' with the Tory opposition, but it does beg the question as to the message this transmits to migrants and their families already settled in Britain.

A less visible threat to the One Nation project comes from discord amongst various minority communities and, although their prevalence should not be exaggerated, separatist tendencies on the part of some groups. In the former category are reported tensions between those of West African and Caribbean origin, principally in London where both groups are fairly populous and often live in close proximity to one another. Elsewhere there is some evidence of the replication of sub-continental religious conflict between various South Asian groups. In the 1990s, for example, Birmingham REC was extremely concerned about the emergence of skirmishes between gangs of Sikh and Muslim youth in various parts of the city. It is important not to exaggerate the significance of these tensions, however, not least because of the likelihood that they will add fuel to the arguments of the (white) nationalists.

The evidence of, and reasons behind, separatism (spatial and otherwise), are more difficult to discern. There is clearly no separatist movement along the lines (say) of the Nation of Islam in the US (though the organization does have a modest UK presence). Levels of residential segregation between whites and minority groups are, on the whole, relatively low in Britain and levels of intermarriage are increasing. As noted earlier, contemporary debates about separatism tend to focus on concerns about the implications of communities living 'parallel lives'. But it is important to remember that this relates almost exclusively to urban working-class Muslims in a small number of locations (principally in West Yorkshire and the former textile towns of Lancashire).

Furthermore, there is little evidence to support the claims of Ouseley (2001) and others that there is an increasing tendency towards self-segregation. In so far as there is, it is more likely to be a reflection of constrained options rather than a desire for a separatist future. Were those constraints to be removed, levels of segregation would undoubtedly fall, though the utopian ideal (for some) of creating a One Nation Britain with thoroughly mixed communities in terms of ethnicity, culture, religion and class is beyond the grasp of even the most determined social engineer. This said, there is undoubted merit in the current idea of attempting to build more heterogeneous 'sustainable communities'.

Promoting a 'One Nation' Britain

The Parekh Report sees a cohesive society as one with both a 'community of communities' and a 'community of citizens' (Runnymede Trust 2000: 56, para. 4.36). In other words, there will be relatively distinct, but equally valued, communities (if ever more complex with successive generations) but also a common unified sense of citizenship and nationhood, with equal rights (*de facto* as well as *de iure*). Bearing in mind the problematic notion of "community" (cf. chapter 1), the question is – How do we get there from where we are now?

Some of the potential answers are to be found in the earlier chapters. There has to be a major role for community activism and mobilization in challenging and negating the nationalist forces that aim to undermine inclusivity. In doing so they need to receive unambiguous support from both local and central government as well as the CRE and local RECs. As in the US civil rights movement, people from all communities (and not just minorities) have an important role to play, in that the ultimate goal has to be a consensual vision of what it means to be British in the twenty-first century.

An obvious response would be to question its viability given the presence of much fertile ground for the purveyors of racism and nationalism. The answer has to be a focus on angry, dispossessed whites on the poorest estates, i.e. those now labelled 'socially excluded'. To its credit the current government has responded positively in its neighbourhood renewal programme. New Deal for Communities is a case in point. Here the intention is that policy should be substantially resident-led, a radical move away from the conventional top-down model.

The problem is that the approach has not been sufficiently well thought through. An element of capacity building has to precede such an initiative. Otherwise the old division between the professional and lay person creates an unbridgeable gulf in the quest for appropriate policy solutions (for local people). In addition, the reliance on private capital in funding partnerships (with the public sector) means an almost inevitable clash between the profit motive and the desire to meet social goals. There are also largely unresolved issues such as the relative weight to be given to the often competing claims of different segments of, and interests groups within, the local population.

The bottom line is that the poorest members of these communities are apt to harbour deep cynicism towards 'yet another' government initiative. They in turn are labelled as 'hard to reach'. But clearly they also have the right to be 'included'. (This credibility gap also means that many of those whose interests are addressed in the 'race' legislation need some persuasion that there is the political will to make it work (especially in the case of a government that too often panders to the immigration lobby).)

In defence of the current policy agenda one might argue that it has the potential at least to make inroads into material inequalities across all communities. Despite a notional commitment to the One Nation idea, the Conservative Party (in power and in opposition) has always opposed any legislation that interferes with the workings of the market. It has also continually worked to expand the private sector in a way that has reduced the scope for the public sector to promote equalities. Only with the introduction of the recent Human Rights Act and, in particular, the Race Relations (Amendment) Act 2000 has the agenda been re-centred.

As noted earlier, these policies did not emerge out of the ether. Pressure from minority groups, the voluntary sector, local activists and writers/researchers provided the momentum for change. It was concerted community pressure (spearheaded by his parents) that eventually brought about the public inquiry into the murder of Stephen Lawrence. Sir William Macpherson's findings then made it extremely difficult for the government to ignore the demand for a strengthening of existing legislation. This illustrates that, as in the US, there is a powerful synergy between civil rights, empowerment, mobilization and legislative change. What is less clear is the role of the social scientist in promoting change.

There is one key question that lies at the heart of this book. It concerns the age-old debate concerning the sociologist as advocate (Steinberg 2000: xv). What role (if any) do (or 'should') sociologists play in promoting, even working towards, a more inclusive society? Those who take on the advocacy role tend to take it for granted that they represent 'the good guys': that their work contributes to the reduction of oppression and inequality. But adopting the moral high ground is not enough. Is there not a possibility that their work may be regarded either as irrelevant, or worse, as simply adding to the panoply of oppressive forces limiting the life chances of many minority citizens, and others who lie beyond the world of the 'included'?

There is no space here to devote to a full discussion of these issues, but then the current author has already written about them at length elsewhere (Ratcliffe 2001b). The essence of the debate is that 'we' have been seen at times as part of the problem rather than part of the solution. Adopting a Poulantzian position, Bourne with Sivanandan (1980) focused on both the structural position of academia (and that of a key research unit in particular), and the nature, and identity, of those seen as controlling the agenda. An essential component of the transformative process, they argued, was a greater input from black researchers.

Since the essay was published there has been a marked increase in the number of black researchers and academics in the UK, both male and female. But simply being 'black' is not enough, as was clear from Ken Pryce's (1979) research in Bristol. In reinforcing racist stereotypes about 'West Indians' in St Paul's he, unwittingly one assumes, effectively endorsed the heavy-handed policing policy adopted by the local force. His identity as a Jamaican was taken as a further endorsement of the veracity of his account.

In Chapter 6, there was evidence of academic research, in this case on educational inequalities, impacting in negative ways on certain minority communities. By endorsing, and then perpetuating, the notion of underachievement in respect of young black males, the futures of many were (and still are) blighted. Theories, in this case endorsed by two government inquiries, have material effects in that they become incorporated into the commonplace of policy and practice.

Focusing mainly on the US, Yehudi Webster (1992) also implicates academe in the racialization process. He says that 'social scientists are perhaps unwittingly part of the racialization of social consciousness' and that they provide 'multifarious definitions of "reality"'which constitute 'a further relapse into ambiguity' (ibid.: 4). He would no doubt, therefore, be concerned that social scientists are becoming more involved than ever in national censuses in the US and UK. As we saw in Chapter 3, there is a sense in which these exercises influence both the way that individuals come to define themselves and the nature of contemporary discourse about the appropriate way to slice social reality. But there is another way of looking at this.

Social science research has contributed to the pressure on governments to legislate against racism and discriminatory processes (see Chapter 10). Censuses then provide an extremely useful way of accruing evidence on material inequalities (and changes over time therein). Without good quality (that is, reliable and valid) national data on putative 'ethnic groups' there is no sound way of assessing the impact of legislation.

It is appropriate at this point to return to a theme raised in the opening paragraph of the volume. Alain Touraine (2000) asked whether we can (learn to) live together, given increasing diversity accompanied by a stubborn adherence to the idea of attributing significance to ascribed social difference. Part of his proposed solution was a form of reflexivity applied to the personal experience of schooling. This appears to be a variation on a potentially important theme currently being pursued in Britain: the idea of citizenship training. This was picked up more recently by Ouseley (2001) if in a more localized context. A key element in the solution to what he saw as Bradford's 'parallel lives' dilemma was an inclusive interpretation of a Bradfordian identity. One obvious benefit of this focal point is that it conveys a greater sense of immediacy. Students can relate more readily to Bradford as a representation of multiculturalism than they can to say Britain or the UK.

Imagining the inclusive society

Its proponents have a long way to go to convince the general populous that an inclusive approach benefits all in the long term. Too often responding to the needs and aspirations of minorities is attacked as mere 'political correctness'. Nowhere is this more apparent than in the so-called white highlands. Countless examples could be produced: here we have space to consider only one.

A recent *Daily Express* article entitled 'Centuries-old village service scrapped . . . for not being ethnic' (Broster 2003) reported on a political row in the sleepy Cheshire village of Bollington. The 'service' referred to in the headline involved the handover of the mayoral 'chains of office to a successor in a civic celebration at a Christian place of worship' (ibid.: 5). The Deputy Mayor felt that the venue should be changed on the grounds that '(W)e do have some people from ethnic backgrounds (sic) and the current policy is to be completely inclusive'. What she might have added is that this is clearly a civic celebration and not a Christian one. The Conservative opposition saw this as an assault on tradition, especially unwarranted given that minorities were said to constitute only two per cent of the town's population of just under seven thousand.

Although of minor significance in itself, this represents the essence of the conflict between those 'traditionalists' who wish to retain a single national culture based on a fusion of (Christian) church and state, and those who, however reluctantly, have come to accept that twenty-first century Britain is rather different (say) than that pertaining a century earlier. As we saw in Chapter 1, the Parekh Report (Runnymede Trust 2000: 42) sees the appropriate route for a cohesive, and more 'equal', Britain as a fusion of 'liberal' and 'plural' models of society.

The problem with the first of these is that it entails an unrealistic distinction between public and private spheres. As Ratcliffe (2000) argues, one cannot (say) confine Islam to the private domain: it necessarily embraces all aspects of a person's life. The plural model envisions a dynamic multi-ethnic society with cohesion coming from interdependence combined with commonalities in certain aspects of the private domain. Where the liberal model is useful is in stressing the need for a common national culture: a common sense of nationhood and citizenship.

To a greater extent than was the case with previous governments, New Labour seems to be embracing core elements of this vision. The focus on self-determination and empowerment at the neighbourhood level is a positive development, if rather weakened by the absence of prior capacity building. Much will also depend on whether residents' voices are inclusive and exhaustive, so that neighbourhood change reflects (as far as is possible given competing aims and aspirations) the wishes of those whose views have rarely been heard in the past (the genuinely 'excluded').

The ongoing problem, as noted earlier, is the perpetuation by government of confused, and mixed, messages. A key exemplar of this is the plan for citizenship classes (for would-be British citizens) which, if successfully completed, would lead to a citizenship ceremony. As usual much of the devil would be in the detail, such as the content of the syllabi, the degree of compulsion, the level of 'competency' required and the form of the ceremony itself (especially bearing in mind the US model – with its stress on swearing allegiance to the flag). Set in the context of a government that appears at times to veer towards assimilationism and even hostility to 'the other' (in the shape of Muslims and asylum seekers), one might fear the worst. One might add that the English, as 'migrants', have rarely submitted or been required to submit, to lessons about the history and culture of their 'hosts'.

To sum up: the vision of an inclusive society presented here is one that has at its core a number of key features:

- A 'One Nation' culture: a common-sense of nationhood accompanied by a respect for, and acceptance of, difference and diversity.
- A universal condemnation of racism and 'racial' discrimination accompanied by the political will to ensure their eradication. The rejection of discrimination also incorporates negative treatment on the grounds of, for example, religion, class, gender, disability and sexual orientation.
- A commitment to the creation of a society that recognizes the need for a greater overall degree of material equality. Although governments may recognize the potential benefits in terms of social integration it is, of course, difficult for them to embrace the necessary policies. This is because the latter would, in practice, demand sacrifices on the part of those currently in superordinate positions.
- A *qualified* acceptance of the right of individuals to opt out of the social and spatial integrationism embodied, for example, in the drive for sustainable (socially mixed) communities. The element of conditionality is necessary in that a rigid separatism (whether based, say, on ethnicity, religion or class) almost inevitably leads to suspicion and hostility of 'the other' (however defined). It therefore presents a potential threat to overall social cohesiveness.

The sort of society envisioned here is far from becoming a reality in the UK: nor is there evidence to suggest it exists elsewhere in the contemporary world. We have seen throughout this book that there are major countervailing forces committed to the task of ensuring that it does not become a reality. These forces, as has been shown, are at one and the same time structural, systemic, institutional and cultural. For a variety of reasons, attempts to negate them cannot be left solely to the state (however benign) via legislation and social policy. It requires a collective marshalling of (positive) agential forces. This implies concerted 'bottom-up' pressure from neighbourhood and community, and maybe also from those social scientists who see their role as more than mere commentators on the human condition.

Bibliography

Alibhai-Brown, Y. (2000) *Who Do We Think We Are? Imagining the New Britain*. Harmondsworth: Penguin Books.

Allen, S. and Wolkowitz, C. (1987) *Homeworking: Myths and Realities*. Basingstoke: Macmillan.

Allen, W.R. (1994) 'The dilemma persists: race, class and inequality in American life', in P. Ratcliffe (ed.) *'Race', Ethnicity and Nation: International Perspectives on Social Conflict*. London: UCL Press.

Allen, W.R. (2001) 'Whatever tomorrow brings: African-American families and Government social policy', in P. Ratcliffe (ed.) *The Politics of Social Science Research: 'Race', Ethnicity and Social Change*. Basingstoke: Palgrave Macmillan.

Anderson, B. (1993) *Imagined Communities: Reflections on the Origin and Spread of Nationalism*. London: Verso.

Anwar, M. (1979) *The Myth of Return: Pakistanis in Britain*. London: Heinemann.

Anwar, M., Roach, P. and Sondhi, R. (2000) *From Legislation to Integration?* Basingstoke: Palgrave Macmillan.

Archer, M.S. (1995) *Realist Social Theory: The Morphogenetic Approach*. Cambridge: Cambridge University Press.

Askonas, P. and Stewart, A. (eds) (2000) *Social Inclusion: Possibilities and Tensions*. Basingstoke: Macmillan.

Back, L. (1996) *New Ethnicities and Urban Culture*. London: UCL Press.

Ballard, R. and Ballard, C. (1977) 'The Sikhs: the development of South Asian settlements in Britain', in J.L. Watson (ed.) *Between Two Cultures: Migrants and Minorities in Britain*. Oxford: Blackwell.

Banton, M. (1972) *Racial Minorities*. London: Fontana/Collins.

Barratt, G.A. (1999) 'Overcoming the obstacles? Access the bank finance for African-Caribbean enterprise', *Journal of Ethnic and Migration Studies*, 25(2): 303–22.

Barth, F. (ed.) (1969) *Ethnic Groups and Boundaries: The Social Organisation of Culture Difference*. London: Allen and Unwin.

Baumann, G. (1996) *Contesting Culture: Discourses of Identity in Multi-ethnic London*. Cambridge: Cambridge University Press.

Becker, H. (1970a) 'Problems of inference and proof in participant observation', in W.J. Filstead (ed.) *Qualitative Methodology: Firsthand Involvement with the Social World*. Chicago: Markham, pp. 189–201.

Becker, H. (1970b) 'Whose side are we on?', in W.J. Filstead (ed.) *Qualitative*

Methodology: Firsthand Involvement with the Social World. Chicago: Markham, pp. 15–26.

Benyon, J. (ed.) (1984) *Scarman and After.* Oxford: Pergamon.

Benyon, J. and Bourne, C. (eds) (1986) *The Police: Powers, Procedures and Proprieties.* Oxford: Pergamon.

Benyon, J. and Solomos, J. (eds) (1987) *The Roots of Urban Unrest.* Oxford: Pergamon.

Berger, J. and Mohr, J. (1975) *A Seventh Man.* Harmondsworth: Pelican.

van den Berghe, P. (1967) *Race and Racism.* New York: Wiley.

van den Berghe, P. (1986) 'Ethnicity and the sociobiology debate', in J. Rex and D. Mason (eds) *Theories of Race and Ethnic Relations.* Cambridge: Cambridge University Press.

Berthoud, R. (1998) *The Incomes of Ethnic Minorities.* ISER Report 98–1. Colchester: Institute for Social and Economic Research, University of Essex.

Bhachu, P. (1985) *Twice Migrants: East African Sikh Settlers in Britain.* London: Tavistock.

Blackstone, T., Parekh, B. and Sanders, P. (eds) (1998) *Race Relations in Britain: A Developing Agenda.* London: Routledge.

Blair, M. (2002) 'Effective School Leadership: the multi-ethnic context', *British Journal of Sociology of Education* 23(2): 179–91.

Blauner, R. (1972) *Racial Oppression in America.* New York: Harper and Row.

Boal, F.W. (ed.) (2000) *Ethnicity and Housing: Accommodating Differences.* Aldershot: Ashgate.

Bourne, J., Bridges, L. and Searle, C. (1994) *Outcast England: How Schools Exclude Black Children.* London: Institute of Race Relations.

Bourne, J. with Sivanandan, A. (1980) 'Cheerleaders and ombudsmen: the sociology of race relations in Britain', *Race and Class*, XXI(4): 331–52.

Bradby, H. (1999) 'Negotiating marriage: Young Punjabi women's assessment of their individual and family interests', in R. Barot, H. Bradley and S. Fenton (eds) *Ethnicity, Gender and Social Change.* Basingstoke: Macmillan.

Bradford Commission (1996) *The Bradford Commission Report.* London: The Stationery Office.

Branch, T. (1988) *Parting the Waters: America in the King years 1954–63.* New York: Simon and Schuster.

British Broadcasting Corporation 2 (BBC2) (2003a) *America Beyond the Colour Line?* Documentary series introduced by Henry Louis 'Skip' Gates. London: BBC.

British Broadcasting Corporation 2 (BBC2) (2003b) *Double Prejudice.* Television documentary screened on 6 August. London: BBC.

Brooks, D. (1975) *Race and Labour in London Transport.* Oxford: IRR/Oxford University Press.

Broster, P. (2003) 'Centuries-old village service scrapped ... for not being ethnic', *Daily Express*, 16 October: p. 5.

Brown, C. (1984) *Black and White Britain*. London: Heinemann/Policy Studies Institute.

Brown, C. and Gay, P. (1985) *Racial Discrimination: 17 Years after the Act*. London: Policy Studies Institute.

Brown, P. (2002) 'Family-run Asian shops disappear', *The Guardian*, 5 January, p. 9.

Bulmer, M. (1986) 'Race and Ethnicity', in R. G. Burgess (ed.) *Key Variables in Social Investigation*. London: Routledge and Kegan Paul.

Burnley Task Force (2001) *Burnley Task Force Report*. Burnley: Burnley Task Force.

Byrne, D. (1999) *Social Exclusion*. Buckingham: Open University Press.

Cabinet Office (2003) *Ethnic Minorities and the Labour Market: Final Report*. London: Cabinet Office Strategy Unit.

Cantle, T. (2001) *Community Cohesion: A Report of the Independent Review Team*. London: Home Office.

Carby, H. (1982a) 'White women listen! Black feminism and the boundaries of sisterhood', in Centre for Contemporary Cultural Studies (ed.) *The Empire Strikes Back*. London: Hutchinson/Routledge.

Carby, H. (1982b) 'Schooling in Babylon', in Centre for Contemporary Cultural Studies (ed.) *The Empire Strikes Back*. London: Hutchinson/Routledge.

Carmichael, S. and Hamilton, C.V. (1967) *Black Power: The Politics of Liberation in America*. New York: Vintage Books.

Carter, B. (2000) *Realism and Racism: Concepts of Race in Sociological Research*. London: Routledge.

Carter, B., Harris, C. and Joshi, S. (1987) 'The 1951–55 Conservative government and the racialisation of black immigration', *Immigrants and Minorities*, 6(3): 335–47.

Cashmore, E.E. and McLaughlin, E. (eds) (1991) *Out of Order? Policing Black People*. London: Routledge.

Cashmore, E.E. and Troyna, B. (eds) (1982) *Black Youth in Crisis*. London: Allen and Unwin.

Castles, S. (2000) *Ethnicity and Globalisation*. London: Sage.

Castles, S. and Kosack, G. (1973) *Immigrant Workers and Class Structure in Western Europe*. London: IRR/Oxford University Press.

Castles, S. and Miller, M.J. (1998) *The Age of Migration: International Population Movements in the Modern World*. Basingstoke: Macmillan.

Cebulla, A. (1999) 'A geography of insurance exclusion: perceptions of unemployment risk and actuarial risk assessment', *Area*, 31(2): 111–21.

Centre for Research in Ethnic Relations (1995) *Annual Report 1994–5*. Coventry: ESRC/Centre for Research in Ethnic Relations.

Césaire, A. (1972) *Discourse on Colonialism*, New York: Monthly Review Press.

Coard, B. (1971) *How the West Indian Child is Made Educationally Sub-Normal in the British School System*. London: New Beacon Books.

Cohen, R. (1994) *Frontiers of Identity: The British and the Others*. Harlow: Longman.

Cohen, R. (1997) *Global Diasporas*. London: UCL Press.

Coleman, D. and Salt, J. (1996) *Demographic Characteristics of the Ethnic Minority Populations. [Ethnicity in the 1991 Census, Volume 1.]* London: HMSO.

Commission for Racial Equality (1982) *Massey Ferguson Perkins Ltd.: Report of a Formal Investigation.* London: CRE.

Commission for Racial Equality (1984a) *Code of Practice: For the Elimination of Racial Discrimination and the Promotion of Equality of Opportunity in Employment.* London: CRE.

Commission for Racial Equality (1984b) *Race and Council Housing in Hackney.* London: CRE.

Commission for Racial Equality (1988) *Medical School Admissions: Report of a Formal Investigation into St. George's Hospital Medical School.* London: CRE.

Commission for Racial Equality (1991) *Code of Practice in Rented Housing: For the Elimination of Racial Discrimination and the Promotion of Equal Opportunities.* London: CRE.

Commission for Racial Equality (1992) *Code of Practice in Non-Rented (Owner-Occupied) Housing: For the Elimination of Racial Discrimination and the Promotion of Equal Opportunities.* London: CRE.

Commission for Racial Equality (2001) *The General Duty to Promote Racial Equality: Guidance for Public Authorities on their Obligations under the Race Relations (Amendment) Act 2000.* London: CRE.

Commission for Racial Equality (2003) *Race Equality and Public Procurement: A Guide for Public Authorities and Contractors.* London: CRE.

Cooke, L., Halford, S. and Leonard, P. (2003) *Racism in the Medical Profession: The Experience of UK Graduates.* London: British Medical Association.

Cox, O.C. (1970) *Caste, Class and Race.* New York: Monthly Review Press.

Cross, M. with Brar, H. and McLeod, M. (1991) *Racial Equality and the Local State: An Evaluation of Race Policy in the London Borough of Brent.* Monographs in Ethnic Relations No. 1, Coventry: ESRC/Centre for Research in Ethnic Relations.

Cross, M., Wrench, J. and Barnett, S. (1990) *Ethnic Minorities and the Careers Service.* Employment Department Research Paper Series No. 73. London.

Dadzie, S. (1990) 'Searching for the invisible woman: slavery and resistance in Jamaica', *Race and Class*, 32(2): 22–37.

Dahya, B. (1974) 'The nature of Pakistani ethnicity in industrial cities in Britain', in A. Cohen (ed.) *Urban Ethnicity.* London: Tavistock.

Dale, A. and Marsh, C. (eds) (1993) *The 1991 Census User's Guide.* London: HMSO.

Daniel, W.W. (1968) *Racial Discrimination in England.* Harmondsworth: Penguin.

Danziger, N. (1997) *Danziger's Britain: A Journey to the Edge.* London: Flamingo.

Davidovic, M. (2001) 'Social Change and Sociological Research on the "Nation" Issue in Yugoslavia', in P. Ratcliffe (ed.) *The Politics of Social Science Research: 'Race', Ethnicity and Social Change.* Basingstoke: Palgrave Macmillan.

Davis, A., Gardner, B. and Gardner, M. (1941) *Deep South: A Social Anthropological Study of Caste and Class.* Chicago: Chicago University Press.

Denham, L. (2001) *Building Cohesive Communities: A Report of the Ministerial Group on Public Order and Community Cohesion*. London: Home Office.

DfEE (2000) *Race Research for the Future: Ethnicity in Education, Training and the Labour Market. RTP01*. London: DfEE.

DETR (2001) *A Review of the Evidence Base for Regeneration Policy and Practice*. London: DETR.

Dex, S. (1978/9) 'Job search methods and ethnic discrimination', *New Community*, 7(1): 1–22.

Doherty, P. and Poole, M. (2000) 'Living apart in Belfast: residential segregation in a context of ethnic conflict', in F.W. Boal (ed.) *Ethnicity and Housing: Accommodating Differences*. Aldershot: Ashgate.

Duffield, M. (1988) *Black Radicalism and the Politics of De-industrialisation*. Aldershot: Avebury.

Ellison, M. (1974) *The Black Experience: American Blacks since 1965*. London: Batsford.

Eriksen, T.H. (1993) *Ethnicity and Nationalism: Anthropological Perspectives*. London: Pluto.

Eyesenck, H. (1971) *Race, Intelligence and Education*. London: Temple Smith.

Fekete, L. (2001) 'The emergence of xeno-racism' and 'The Terrorism Act 2000: an interview with Gareth Peirce', *Race and Class*, 43(2), October–December.

Fenton, S. (1999) *Ethnicity: Racism, Class, and Culture*. Basingstoke: Palgrave Macmillan.

Fenton, S. (2003) *Ethnicity*. Cambridge: Polity Press.

Fieldhouse, E.A., Kalra, V.S. and Alam, S. (2002) 'How new is the New Deal? A qualitative study of the New Deal for Young People on minority ethnic groups in Oldham', *Local Economy*, 17(1): 50–64.

Foner, N. (1977) 'The Jamaicans: Cultural and social change among migrants in Britain', in J.L. Watson (ed.) *Between Two Cultures: Migrants and Minorities in Britain*. Oxford: Blackwell.

Fryer, P. (1984) *Staying Power*. London: Pluto.

Fryer, P. (1988) *Black People in the British Empire: An Introduction*. London: Pluto.

Gifford, Lord et al. (1986) *The Broadwater Farm Enquiry*. London: Karia.

Gill, D., Mayor, B. and Blair, M. (eds) (1992) *Racism and Education: Structures and Strategies*. London: Sage.

Gillborn, D. (1990) *'Race', Ethnicity and Education*. London: Unwin Hyman.

Gillborn, D. (1995) *Racism and Antiracism in Real Schools*. Buckingham: Open University Press.

Gillborn, D. and Gipps, C. (1996) *Recent Research on the Achievements of Ethnic Minority Pupils*. London: HMSO.

Gillborn, D. and Youdell, D. (2000) *Rationing Education*. Buckingham: Open University Press.

Gilroy, P. (1987) *There Ain't No Black in the Union Jack*. London: Hutchinson.

Guibernau, M. and Rex, J. (eds) (1997) *The Ethnicity Reader*. Cambridge: Polity Press.

Gutzmore, C. (1983) 'Capital, "black youth", and crime', *Race and Class* XXV(2), Autumn: 13–30.

Hall, S., Critcher, C., Jefferson, T., Clarke, J. and Roberts, B. (1978) *Policing the Crisis: Mugging, the State, and Law and Order*. Basingstoke: Macmillan.

Harrison, M. with Davis, C. (2001) *Housing, Social Policy and Difference: Disability, Ethnicity, Gender and Housing*. Bristol: The Policy Press.

Herring, C. and Collins, S.M. (1995) 'Retreat from Equal Opportunity? The case of affirmative action', in M.P. Smith and J.R. Feagin (eds) *The Bubbling Cauldron: Race, Ethnicity and the Urban Crisis*. Minneapolis: University of Minnesota Press.

Herrnstein, J. and Murray, C. (1994) *The Bell Curve: Intelligence and Class Structure in American Life*. New York: The Free Press.

Hesli, V. and Kessel, B. (2001) 'The State and social science research in Russia', in P. Ratcliffe (ed.) *The Politics of Social Science Research: 'Race', Ethnicity and Social Change*. Basingstoke: Palgrave Macmillan.

Hiro, D. (1971) *Black British, White British*. Harmondsworth: Penguin.

Hodge, M. and Feagin, J.R. (1995) 'African American entrepreneurship and racial discrimination: A Southern Metropolitan case', in M.P. Smith and J.R. Feagin (eds) *The Bubbling Cauldron: Race, Ethnicity and the Urban Crisis*. Minneapolis: University of Minnesota Press.

Hoel, B. (1982) 'Contemporary clothing "sweatshops", Asian female labour and collective organisation', in J. West (ed.) *Work, Women and the Labour Market*. London: Routledge and Kegan Paul.

Home Office (2003) *Building a Picture of Community Cohesion: A Guide for Local Authorities and their Partners*. London: Home Office Community Cohesion Unit.

Hood, R. (1992) *Race and Sentencing*. Oxford: The Clarendon Press.

Iganski, P. and Paine, G. (1996) 'Declining racial disadvantage in the British labour market', *Ethnic and Racial Studies*, 19(1): 113–34.

Ignatieff, M. (1994) *Blood and Belonging: journeys into the new nationalism*. London: Vintage.

Inglis, C. (1994) 'Race and ethnic relations in Australia: theory, methods and substance', in P. Ratcliffe (ed.) *'Race', Ethnicity and Nation: International Perspectives on Social Conflict*. London: UCL Press.

Inglis, C. (2001) 'Independence, incorporation and policy research: an Australian case study', in P. Ratcliffe (ed.) *The Politics of Social Science Research: 'Race', Ethnicity and Social Change*. Basingstoke: Palgrave Macmillan.

IRR (Institute of Race Relations) (1981/2) 'Rebellion and repression', *Race and Class*, XXII(2/3): Autumn/Winter.

Jenkins, R. (1986a) 'Social anthropological models of inter-ethnic relations', in J.

Rex and D. Mason (eds) *Theories of Race and Ethnic Relations*. Cambridge: Cambridge University Press.

Jenkins, R. (1986b) *Racism and Recruitment*. Cambridge: Cambridge University Press.

Jenkins, R. (1987) 'Doing research into discrimination: Problems of method, interpretation and ethics', in G. Clare Wenger (ed.) *The Research Relationship*. London: Allen and Unwin.

Jenkins, R. and Solomos, J. (eds) (1989) *Racism and Equal Opportunity Policies in the 1980s*. Cambridge: Cambridge University Press.

Jenson, A. (1969) 'How much can we boost IQ and scholastic achievement?', *Harvard Educational Review*, 39(1): 1–123.

Jewson, N. and Mason, D. (1989) 'Monitoring equal opportunities policies: principles and practice', in R. Jenkins and J. Solomos (eds) *Racism and Equal Opportunity Policies in the 1980s*. Cambridge: Cambridge University Press.

Jones, T. (1993) *Britain's Ethnic Minorities*. London: Policy Studies Institute.

Kalra, V. (2000) *From Textile Mills to Taxi Ranks: Experiences of Migration, Labour and Social Change*. Aldershot: Ashgate.

Kalra, V.S. (2003) 'Police lore and community disorder: diversity in the criminal justice system', in D. Mason (ed.) *Explaining Ethnic Differences: Changing patterns of disadvantage in Britain*. Bristol: The Policy Press.

Karn, V. (ed.) (1997) *Employment, Education and Housing among the Ethnic Minority Population of Britain*. Ethnic Minorities in the 1991 Census, Volume 4. London: HMSO.

Keith, M. (1993) *Race, Riots and Policing: Lore and Disorder in a Multi-racist Society*. London: UCL Press.

Killian, L.M. (1968) *The Impossible Revolution: Black Power and the American Dream*. New York: Random House.

Kitano, H.H.L. (1985) *Race Relations*. New Jersey: Prentice-Hall.

Kuhn, T. (1970) *The Structure of Scientific Revolutions, 2nd edn*. Chicago: Chicago University Press.

Kuper, L. (1974) *Race, Class and Power: Ideology and Revolutionary Change in Plural Societies*. London: Duckworth.

Kuper, L. and Smith, M.G. (eds) (1969) *Pluralism in Africa*. Berkeley: University of California Press.

Lawrence, D. (1974) *Black Migrants, White Natives*. Cambridge: Cambridge University Press.

Lawrence, E. (1982a) 'Just plain common sense: the roots of racism', in Centre for Contemporary Cultural Studies (ed.) *The Empire Strikes Back*. London: Hutchinson/Routledge.

Lawrence, E. (1982b) 'In the abundance of water the fool is thirsty: sociology and black "pathology"', in Centre for Contemporary Cultural Studies (ed.) *The Empire Strikes Back*. London: Hutchinson/Routledge.

Layton-Henry, Z. (1992) *The Politics of Immigration: Immigration, 'Race' and 'Race' Relations in Post-war Britain*. Oxford: Blackwell.

Lee, G. and Wrench, J. (1981) *In Search of a Skill*. London: CRE.

Lester, A. (1998) 'From legislation to integration: Twenty years of the Race Relations Act', in T. Blackstone, B. Parekh and P. Sanders (eds) *Race Relations in Britain: A Developing Agenda*. London: Routledge.

Levitas, R. (1996) 'The concept of social exclusion and the new Durkheimian hegemony', *Critical Social Policy*, 46(16): 5–20.

Levitas, R. (1999) *The Inclusive Society: Social Exclusion and New Labour*. Basingstoke: Macmillan.

Lewis, P. (1994) *Islamic Britain: Religion, Politics and Identity among British Muslims*. London: I.B. Tauris.

Lewontin, R., Rose, S. and Kamin, L. (1982) 'Bourgeois ideology and the origins of biological determinism', *Race and Class*, XXIV(1).

Lister, R. (ed.) (1996) *Charles Murray and the Underclass: The Developing Debate*. London: The Institute of Economic Affairs.

Mac an Ghaill, M. (1988) *Young, Gifted and Black: Student-Teacher Relations in the Schooling of Black Youth*. Milton Keynes: Open University Press.

Mac an Ghaill, M. (1992) 'Coming of age in 1980s England: reconceptualising black students' schooling experiences', in D. Gill, B. Mayor and M. Blair (eds) *Racism and Education: Structures and Strategies*. London: Sage.

Macdonald, I., Bhavnani, T., Khan, L. and John, G. (1986) *Murder in the Playground: The Report of the Macdonald Inquiry into Racism and Racial Violence in Manchester Schools*. London: Longsight Press.

Macpherson, W. (1999) *The Stephen Lawrence Inquiry: The Report of an Inquiry by Sir William Macpherson of Cluny*. London: The Stationery Office.

Malik, K. (1996a) *The Meaning of Race*. London: Macmillan.

Malik, K. (1996b) 'Universalism and difference: race and the postmodernists', *Race and Class*, 37(3): 1–17.

Mann, S. (2002) *Chinese Food Catering in Scotland: Ethnic Business, Work and Gender*. Unpublished Ph.D. Thesis, Department of Sociology, University of Warwick.

Marable, M. (1991) *Race, Reform and Rebellion*. Basingstoke: Macmillan.

Marcuse, P. (1996) 'Space and race in the post-Fordist city: the outcast ghetto and advanced homelessness in the United States today', in E. Mingione (ed.) *Urban Poverty and the Underclass: A Reader*. Oxford: Blackwell.

Marshall, T.H. (1950) *Citizenship and Social Class and Other Essays*. Cambridge: Cambridge University Press.

Mason, D. (1990) 'A rose by any other name ...? Categorisation, identity and social science', *New Community*, 17(1): 123–33.

Mason, D. (2000) *Race and Ethnicity in Modern Britain*. Oxford: Oxford University Press.

Mason, D. (ed.) (2003) *Explaining Ethnic Differences: Changing Patterns of Disadvantage in Britain*. Bristol: The Policy Press.

Massey, D.S. and Denton, N.A. (1988) 'The dimensions of residential segregation', *Social Forces*, 67: 281–315.

Massey, D.S. and Denton, N.A. (2000) 'The Future of the Ghetto', in S. Steinberg (ed.) *Race and Ethnicity in the United States*. Malden, MA and Oxford: Blackwell.

Maunier, R. (1949) *The Sociology of Colonies: An Introduction to the Study of Race Conflict*. London: Routledge and Kegan Paul (2 vols).

May, R. and Cohen, R. (1974) 'The interaction between race and colonialism: The Liverpool race riots of 1919', *Race and Class*, 16(2).

Memmi, A. (1974) *The Colonizer and Colonized*. London: Souvenir Press.

Miles, R. (1982) *Racism and Migrant Labour*. London: Routledge and Kegan Paul.

Miles, R. (1993) *Racism after 'Race Relations'*. London: Routledge.

Miles, R. and Brown, M. (2003) *Racism*. London: Routledge.

Miles, R. and Phizacklea, A. (1984) *White Man's Country: Racism in British Politics*. London: Pluto.

Mirza, H. (1992) *Young, Female and Black*. London: Routledge.

Modood, T. et al. (1997) *Ethnic Minorities in Britain: Diversity and Disadvantage*, The Fourth National Survey of Ethnic Minorities. London: Policy Studies Institute.

Montagu, A. (ed.) (1964) *The Concept of Race*. London, Macmillan.

Montagu, A. (1974) *Man's Most Dangerous Myth: The Fallacy of Race*. New York: Oxford University Press.

Montagu, A. (ed.) (1999) *Race and IQ*. New York: Oxford University Press.

Morokvasic, M. (1983) 'Women in Migration', in A. Phizacklea (ed.) *One Way Ticket*. London: Routledge and Kegan Paul.

Morris, L. (2002) 'Britain's asylum and immigration regime: the shifting contours of rights', *Journal of Ethnic and Migration Studies*, 28(3), July.

Murray, C. (1996) 'The emerging British underclass' and 'Underclass: The crisis deepens', in R. Lister (ed.) *Charles Murray and the Underclass: The Developing Debate*. London: The Institute of Economic Affairs.

Myrdal, G. (1944) *An American Dilemma*. New York: Harper & Row.

Nazroo, J. (1997) *The Health of Britain's Ethnic Minorities: Findings from a National Survey*. London: Policy Studies Institute.

Nazroo, J. (2001) *Ethnicity, Class and Health*. London: Policy Studies Institute.

Nazroo, J. (2002) 'The racialisation of ethnic inequalities in health', in D. Dorling and L. Simpson (eds) *Statistics in Society*. London: Arnold.

Oldham Independent Review Panel (2001) *Oldham Independent Review Report*. (www.oldhamir.gov.uk/OIR%20report.pdf)

Oliver, M.L. and Shapiro, T.M. (1997) *Black Wealth/White Wealth: A New Perspective on Racial Equality*. New York and London: Routledge.

Omi, M. and Winant, H. (1994) *Racial Formation in the US*. London: Routledge.

Orton, M. and Ratcliffe, P. (2003) *Working for an Inclusive Britain: An Evaluation of the West Midlands Forum Pilot Project*. Sandwell: WMF in association with the CRE and Employers' Organisation.

Ouseley, H. (2001) *Community Pride not Prejudice: Making Diversity Work in Bradford.* Bradford: Bradford Vision.

Owen, D. (1997) 'Labour force participation rates, self-employment and un-employment', in V. Karn (ed.) *Employment, Education and Housing among the Ethnic Minority Population of Britain.* Ethnic Minorities in the 1991 Census, Volume 4. London: HMSO.

Owen, D. and Green, A. (2000) 'Estimating Commuting Patterns for Minority Ethnic Groups in England and Wales', *Journal of Ethnic and Migration Studies,* 26(4): 581–608.

Owen, D., Green, A., Pitcher, J. and Maguire, M. (2000) *Minority Ethnic Participation and Achievements in Education, Training and the Labour Market.* London: Department for Education and Employment.

Parekh, B. (2000) *Beyond Multiculturalism: Cultural Diversity and Political Theory.* Basingstoke: Palgrave Macmillan.

Park, R.E. (1950) *Race and Culture.* New York: The Free Press.

Parmar, P. (1982) 'Gender, race and class: Asian women in resistance', in Centre for Contemporary Cultural Studies (ed.) *The Empire Strikes Back.* London: Hutchinson/Routledge.

Patterson, O. (1967) *The Sociology of Slavery: An Analysis of the Origins, Development and Structure of Negro Slave Society in Jamaica.* London: McGibbon & Kee.

Patterson, S. (1965) *Dark Strangers: A Study of West Indians in London.* Harmonds-worth: Penguin.

Peach, C. (1968) *West Indian Migration to Britain.* Oxford: Oxford University Press.

Peach, C. and Rossiter, D. (1996) 'Level and nature of spatial concentration and segregation of minority ethnic populations in Great Britain, 1991', in P. Ratcliffe (ed.) *Social Geography and Ethnicity in Britain: Geographical Concentration, Spatial Segregation and Internal Migration,* Ethnicity in the 1991 Census, Volume 3: 111–34. London: HMSO.

Phillips, A. (1999) *Which Equalities Matter?* Cambridge: Polity Press.

Phillips, D., Law, I. and Turney, L. (2003) 'Widening participation in UK universities: the challenges of achieving race equality', paper presented at UCLA 21st Century Project – Special International Conference, Rockerfeller Foundation, Bellagio, Italy, March.

Phillips, D. and Ratcliffe, P. (2002) *Movement to Opportunity? South Asian Relocation in Northern Cities.* Economic and Social Research Council (ESRC) End of Award Report (Ref.: R000238038).

Phillips, M. and Phillips, T. (1998) *Windrush: The Irresistible Rise of Multi-racial Britain.* London: Harper/Collins.

Phizacklea, A. and Miles, R. (1990) *Labour and Racism.* London: Routledge and Kegan Paul.

Phizacklea, A. and Wolkowitz, C. (1995) *Homeworking Women: Gender, Class and Racism at Work.* London: Sage.

Pilkington, A. (2003) *Racial Disadvantage and Ethnic Diversity in Britain*. Basingstoke: Palgrave Macmillan.

Pinkney, A. (1975) *Black Americans*. Englewood Cliffs, N.J.: Prentice-Hall.

Pinkney, A. (1976) *Red, Black and Green: Black Nationalism in the United States*. Cambridge: Cambridge University Press.

Pinkney, A. (1984) *The Myth of Black Progress*. Cambridge: Cambridge University Press.

Piore, M.J. (1979) *Birds of Passage: Migrant Labor and Industrial Societies*. Cambridge: Cambridge University Press.

Power, A. (1997) *Estates on the Edge: The Social Consequences of Mass Housing in Northern Europe*. Basingstoke: Macmillan.

Pryce, K. (1979) *Endless Pressure: A Study of West Indian Life-styles in Bristol*. Harmondsworth: Penguin.

Ram, M. (1992) 'Coping with racism: Asian employers in the inner city', *Work, Employment and Society*, 6(4): 601–18.

Ratcliffe, P. (1980) *Race Relations at Work: An Investigation into the Extent and Sources of Inequality in the Treatment of Ethnic and Racial Minorities*. Leamington Spa: CRE/Warwick District Community Relations Council.

Ratcliffe, P. (1981) *Racism and Reaction: A Profile of Handsworth*. London: Routledge and Kegan Paul.

Ratcliffe, P. (1992) 'Renewal, regeneration and "race": Issues in urban policy', *New Community*, 18(3): 387–400.

Ratcliffe, P. (ed.) (1994) *'Race', Ethnicity and Nation: International Perspectives on Social Conflict*. London: UCL Press.

Ratcliffe, P. (ed.) (1996a) *Social Geography and Ethnicity in Britain: Geographical Concentration, Spatial Segregation and Internal Migration*, Ethnicity in the 1991 Census, Volume 3: 1–22. London: HMSO.

Ratcliffe, P. (1996b) *'Race' and Housing in Bradford: Addressing the Needs of the South Asian, African and Caribbean Communities*. Bradford: Bradford Housing Forum.

Ratcliffe, P. (1999a) ' "Race", Housing and Social Exclusion', *Housing Studies*, 13(6): 1–22.

Ratcliffe, P. (1999b) ' "Race", Education and the Discourse of "Exclusion": a critical research note', *Race, Ethnicity and Education*, 2(1): 149–55.

Ratcliffe, P. (2000) 'Is the assertion of minority identity compatible with the idea of a socially inclusive society?', in P. Askonas and A. Stewart (eds) *Social Inclusion: Possibilities and Tensions*. Basingstoke: Macmillan.

Ratcliffe, P. (2001a) ' "Ethnic Group" and the Population Census in Great Britain: mission impossible?' Paper presented to joint INED/CERI conference, Paris, 18 December.

Ratcliffe, P. (ed.) (2001b) *The Politics of Social Science Research: 'Race', Ethnicity and Social Change*. Basingstoke: Palgrave Macmillan.

Ratcliffe, P. et al. (2001) *Breaking Down the Barriers: Improving Asian Access to Social Rented Housing*. Coventry: Chartered Institute of Housing.

Ratcliffe, P. (2005, forthcoming) *Accommodating Difference*. London: Routledge.

Rattansi, A. and Westwood, S. (1994) *Racism, Modernity and Identity on the Western Front*. Cambridge: Polity Press.

Rees, P. and Phillips, D. (1996) 'Geographical spread: the national picture', in P. Ratcliffe (ed.) *Social Geography and Ethnicity in Britain: Geographical Concentration, Spatial Segregation and Internal Migration*, Ethnicity in the 1991 Census, Volume 3: 23–109. London: HMSO.

Rex, J. (1983) *Race Relations in Sociological Theory*. London: Routledge and Kegan Paul.

Rex, J. and Mason, D. (eds) (1986) *Theories of Race and Ethnic Relations*. Cambridge: Cambridge University Press.

Rex, J. and Moore, R. (1967) *Race, Community and Conflict: A Study of Sparkbrook*. Institute of Race Relations/Oxford University Press.

Rex, J. and Tomlinson, S. (1979) *Colonial Immigrants in a British City: A Class Analysis*. London: Routledge and Kegan Paul.

Richmond, A. (1961) *The Colour Problem*. Harmondsworth: Penguin.

Rowe, M. (1998) *The Racialisation of Disorder in Twentieth Century Britain*. Aldershot: Ashgate.

Runnymede Trust (1997) *Islamophobia*. London: Runnymede Trust.

Runnymede Trust (2000) *The Future of Multi-Ethnic Britain: The Parekh Report*. London: Profile Books.

Said, E. (1978) *Orientalism: Western Concepts of the Orient*. Harmondsworth: Penguin.

Said, E. (1993) *Culture and Imperialism*. London: Vintage Books.

Saifullah Khan, V. (1977) 'The Pakistanis: Mirpuri villagers at home and in Bradford', in J.L. Watson (ed.) *Between Two Cultures: Migrants and Minorities in Britain*. Oxford: Blackwell.

Saifullah Khan, V. (1979) 'Work and network: South-Asian women in South London', in S. Wallman (ed.) *Ethnicity at Work*. Basingstoke: Macmillan.

Samad, Y. (1992) 'Book burning and race relations: Political mobilisation of Bradford Muslims', *New Community*, 18(4): 507–19.

Sanders, P. (1998) 'Tackling racial discrimination', in T. Blackstone, B. Parekh and P. Sanders (eds) *Race Relations in Britain: A Developing Agenda*. London: Routledge.

Sardar, Z. and Davies, M.W. (2002) *Why Do People Hate America?*, Cambridge: Icon Books.

Sarre, P., Phillips, D. and Skellington, R. (1989) *Ethnic Minority Housing: Explanations and Policies*. Aldershot: Gower.

Scarman (Lord) (1982) *The Scarman Report*. Harmondsworth: Penguin.

Shiner, M. and Modood, T. (2002) 'Help or Hindrance? Higher Education and the Route to Ethnic Equality', *British Journal of Sociology of Education*, 23(2): 209–32.

Sibley, D. (1995) *Geographies of Exclusion: Society and Difference in the West*. London: Routledge.

Silberman, C. (1964) *Crisis in Black and White*. New York: Vintage Books.

Simpson, S. (1997) 'Demography and ethnicity: case studies from Bradford', *New Community*, 23(1): 89–107.

Sivanandan, A. (1976) 'Race, Class and the State', *Race and Class*, Spring: 347–68.

Sivanandan, A. (1982) *A Different Hunger*. London: Pluto.

Small, S. (1994) *Racialized Barriers: The Black Experience in the United States and England in the 1980s*. London: Routledge.

Smith, D.J. and Tomlinson, S. (1989) *The School Effect: A Study of Multi-Racial Comprehensives*. London: Policy Studies Institute.

Smith, M.P. and Feagin, J.R. (eds) (1995) *The Bubbling Cauldron: Race, Ethnicity and the Urban Crisis*. Minneapolis: University of Minnesota Press.

Smith, S. (1989) *The Politics of 'Race' and Residence: Citizenship, Segregation and White Supremacy in Britain*. Cambridge: Polity Press.

Solomos, J. (1987) *Riots, Urban Protest and Social Policy*. Policy Papers in Ethnic Relations, No. 7, Coventry: ESRC/Centre for Research in Ethnic Relations.

Solomos, J. (2003) *Race and Racism in Britain (3rd edn)*. Basingstoke: Palgrave Macmillan.

Somerville, P. and Steele, A. (eds) (2002) *'Race', Housing and Social Exclusion*. London: Jessica Kingsley.

Steinberg, S. (ed.) (2000) *Race and Ethnicity in the United States*. Malden, MA and Oxford: Blackwell.

Swann Report (1985) *Education for All: Report of the Committee of Inquiry into the Education of Children from Minority Ethnic Groups*. London: HMSO.

Taeuber, K.E. and Taeuber, A. (1964) *Negroes in Cities: Residential Segregation and Neighbourhood Change*. Chicago: Aldine Publishing Co.

Taguieff, P.A. (1985) 'L'Identité française au mirour du racisme differentialiste', *Espaces 89, L'Identité française*. Paris: Editions Tierce.

Thomas, J.M. (1998) 'Ethnic variation in commuting propensity and unemployment spells: Some UK evidence', *Journal of Urban Economics*, 43: 385–400.

Touraine, A. (2000) *Can We Live Together? Equality and Difference*. Stanford, CA: Stanford University Press.

Troyna, B. (1988) 'Paradigm regained: a critique of "cultural deficit" perspectives in contemporary educational research', *Comparative Education*, 24(3).

Troyna, B. and Ball, W. (1985) *Views from the Chalk Face: School Responses to an LEA's Multicultural Education Policy*, Policy Papers in Ethnic Relations, No. 1, ESRC/Centre for Research in Ethnic Relations.

Troyna, B. and Carrington, B. (1990) *Education, Racism and Reform*. London: Routledge.

Troyna, B. and Hatcher, R. (1992) *Racism in Children's Lives*. London: Routledge.

Wainwright, M. (2000) 'Approval for first Muslim secondary state school', *The Guardian*, 7 October.

Wallace, T. and Joshua, H. (1983) *To Ride the Storm*. London: Heinemann.

Ward, R. and Jenkins, R. (eds) (1984) *Ethnic Communities in Business*. Cambridge: Cambridge University Press.

Watson, J.L. (ed.) (1977) *Between Two Cultures: Migrants and Minorities in Britain*. Oxford: Blackwell.

Webster, Y.O. (1992) *The Racialization of America*. New York: St. Martin's Press.

West Midlands County Council (1986) *A Different Reality: An Account of Black People's Experiences and their Grievances before and after the Handsworth Rebellions of September 1985*. WMCC.

White, L. (2002) 'This ghetto is the home of a racial minority in Oldham: Its residents are white English people', *The Sunday Times Magazine*, 13 January, 46–54.

Wilson, A. (1979) *Finding a Voice*. London: Virago.

Wilson, W.J. (1978) *The Declining Significance of Race: Blacks and Changing American Institutions*. Chicago, Ill.: Chicago University Press.

Wilson, W.J. (1987) *The Truly Disadvantaged*. Chicago, Ill.: Chicago University Press.

WING (Women, Immigration and Nationality Group) (1985) *Worlds Apart*. London: Pluto.

Wolpe, H. (1988) *Race, Class and the Apartheid State*. Paris: UNESCO.

Ziatdinov, V. and Grigoriev, S. (1994) 'Between west and east: Tartars in the former USSR', in P. Ratcliffe (ed.) *'Race', Ethnicity and Nation: International Perspectives on Social Conflict*. London: UCL Press.

Index